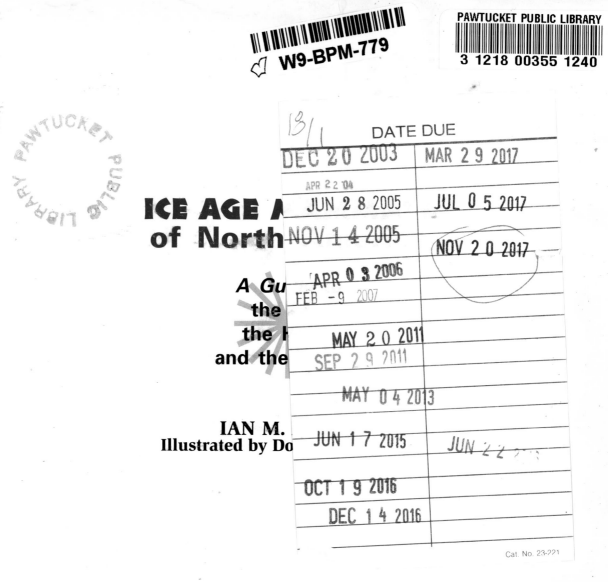

ICE AGE MAMMALS
of North America

A Guide to
the
the
and the

IAN M. LANGE
Illustrated by Dorothy Sigler Norton

MOUNTAIN PRESS PUBLISHING COMPANY
Missoula, Montana — 2002

Library of Congress Cataloging-in-Publication Data

Lange, Ian M.
  Ice Age mammals of North America : a guide to the big, the hairy, and
the bizarre / Ian Lange ; illustrated by Dorothy S. Norton.
     p. cm.
Includes bibliographical references and index.
  ISBN 0-87842-403-2 (acid-free : alk. paper)
  1. Mammals, Fossil—North America. 2. Glacial epoch—North America.
I. Title.
  QE881 .L25 2002
  569'.097—dc21

                                        2002004607

PRINTED IN HONG KONG BY MANTEC PRODUCTION COMPANY

Mountain Press Publishing Company
P. O. Box 2399 • Missoula, MT 59806
(406) 728-1900

To my loving wife, Jo-Ann

CONTENTS

Preface   *vii*

1 Dinosaurs and Woolly Mammoths   *1*

2 A Cast of Continents   *9*

3 The Pleistocene Epoch   *21*

4 Why the Ice Ages?   *49*

5 The Pleistocene Animals   *65*

   Xenarthrans or Edentates—Order Xenarthra—
     Sloths and Armadillos   *69*

   Carnivores—Order Carnivora   *92*

   Rodents—Order Rodentia   *117*

   Odd-Toed Ungulates—Order Perissodactyla—
     Horses, Rhinos, and Tapirs   *121*

   Even-Toed Ungulates—Order Artiodactyla—
     Deer, Bison, and Camels   *137*

   Elephants and Their Relatives—Order Proboscidea   *163*

6 Extinctions: Why Are the Big Guys Gone?   *181*

Appendix I   Selected Sites to Visit:
   Museums, Fossil Sites, and Web Sites   *199*

Glossary   *211*

Bibliography   *213*

Index   *219*

PREFACE

You might wonder how I, an economic geologist who studies the characteristics and genesis of ore deposits, became interested in Pleistocene animals. It all started on October 19, 1953, when *Life* magazine published part four of the series "The World We Live In: The Age of Mammals." This edition included a piece about extinct Pleistocene animals and featured color paintings of many gargantuan beasts, which I imagined were contemplating eating one another. A later issue of *Life* showed a photograph of a baby woolly mammoth that had been frozen and preserved in the permafrost and finally unearthed in gold diggings near Fairbanks, Alaska. As a youth, I found those articles captivating, and I have been fascinated with the great Ice Age animals and their times ever since. This book, then, is a culmination of my interest in mammals that lived during the ice ages in North America. The largest animals of Pleistocene time are gone, but many of the different animal species that lived with those big fellows are still with us. This book describes both living and extinct mammals that lived during Pleistocene time, so you can compare the humongous Ice Age species with their much smaller surviving relatives.

I find these strange animals especially interesting because, at the end of their earthly reign, they coexisted with modern humans—us! While I don't lose sleep over their extinction, I am sad about their demise. I hope we can prevent future extinctions of other wonderful and not-so-wonderful animals that are only trying to go about their daily lives as we do.

Many individuals lent their expertise to this project. In particular, Dr. Christopher L. Hill at the Museum of the Rockies in Bozeman, Montana, and Dr. John M. Harris, chief curator at the George C. Page Museum in Los Angeles, critically reviewed the book and offered many helpful suggestions, corrections, and useful information. Illustrator Dorothy Norton shared her knowledge of animals and biology and offered many suggestions for improving the manuscript. I take full responsibility for any remaining errors.

I used many sources in writing this book. They are cited at the end of each chapter and referenced in full in the bibliography.

I am grateful to the following individuals for information, photographs, and illustrations: Dr. Larry Agenbroad at Northern Arizona University and the Mammoth Site of Hot Springs, South Dakota; Dr. R. George Corner at The University of Nebraska State Museum; Mary E. T. Flint at the Idaho Museum of Natural History; Dr. John Harris and Cathy McNassor at the George C. Page Museum; Dr. James I. Mead at Northern Arizona University; Suzanne J. Miller at CRM Services in Idaho Falls, Idaho; Joe Muller at the Mammoth Site of Hot Springs, South Dakota; Dorothy S. Norton and O. Richard Norton at Science Graphics; and Patricia J. Wynne at *American Scientist.* Thank you for your help!

Finally, I offer words of praise to Kathleen Ort, my editor at Mountain Press, who spent countless hours helping to improve the early, rough drafts of the manuscript. She offered many fine suggestions and asked many critical questions in subsequent drafts that helped me focus on important aspects.

DINOSAURS AND WOOLLY MAMMOTHS

Dinosaurs! It is hard to think of other creatures that excite the imagination more. But what of the other huge animals that lived on the earth—and much more recently? Our ancestors ran with and from not dinosaurs but a host of mammals that became huge before and during the ice ages and then suddenly went extinct only about 10,000 years ago. Those Ice Age mammals were every bit as dangerous and bizarre as, and some were probably more intelligent than, the giant reptiles that vanished mysteriously from the earth 65 million years ago.

Humans coinhabited the earth with such remarkable animals as elephant-like woolly mammoths, woolly rhinoceros, giant Irish elk, lions bigger than Indian tigers, knife-fanged scimitar and saber-toothed cats, 600-pound (270-kilogram) armadillos, and beavers that weighed 400 pounds (180 kilograms). In addition to giant mammals, birds that dwarfed the ostrich were also about. The time was the Pleistocene epoch, which began almost 2 million years ago and ended approximately 10,000 years ago.

The Pleistocene animals and early humans witnessed the waxing and waning of continent-sized ice sheets that at their maximum extent covered approximately 30 percent of the earth's entire land surface. In comparison, glaciers cover only about 10 percent of the earth's surface today. The amazingly large amount of water derived by evaporation from the sea, and locked in these glaciers, lowered sea level by as much as 280 feet (85 meters).

Imagine the earth then! Glaciers over central Canada and Scandinavia were as much as 10,000 feet (3,050 meters) thick. Virtually all of Canada was buried beneath glaciers, and the ice sheet reached as far south in the United States as present-day Olympia, Washington; Chicago, Illinois; Kansas; and Long Island, New York. Glacially produced scratches on rock surfaces prove that glaciers rode over the top of 6,288 foot (1,916 meter) Mount Washington in New Hampshire. In Europe, an ice cap developed on Scandinavia and reached south across the North Sea to cover much of what is now Germany, Poland, western Russia, and all but the southern part of England. The

In search of its next meal, a scimitar cat (Homotherium serum) *eyes a pair of peccaries.* —Collection of Larry Martin

lowered sea level changed England and Ireland from islands to an extension of Europe; animals and people inhabited the now-submerged English Channel.

In North America, stumps of drowned trees and terrestrial peat deposits found along the Atlantic Coast from New England to the Carolinas attest to the lowered sea level. In places, the coastal plain of North America's east coast extended as much as 190 miles (300 kilometers) east of the present shoreline, and

animals inhabited it. Teeth of mammoths and mastodons have been dredged from the ocean bottom that far off the present coastline. People also probably lived on the wide coastal plain, especially along the coastline, where food was abundant. More importantly, the lower sea level allowed for the great overland migration of animals and humans between Siberia and Alaska.

"The Pleistocene," wrote the famous Yale University geologist Richard F. Flint in 1957, "has witnessed changes in physical aspects of

The largest glacier in Alaska, the Malaspina Glacier is several thousand feet thick in places. Its appearance is reminiscent of the way Ice Age continental glaciers would have looked along their southern margins. —Ian Lange photo

the earth and in the distribution of animals and plants on the earth's surface such as not recorded in any earlier span of time of comparable length."

Certainly there have been other times of dramatic and profound change on the earth, but the recency of the Pleistocene epoch has left largely intact the sculptured landforms, sedimentary deposits, and fossil plant and animal remains for scientists in many fields to inspect and analyze. The last of the Ice Age giants vanished only about 10,000 years ago. Their very recent extinction left a wealth of animal tissue, collection sites, and available data.

For decades, scientists and others have pondered and proposed explanations for the apparently sudden demise of the dinosaurs, including death following a giant meteorite impact or huge volcanic eruptions. The Pleistocene beasts may have vanished from the earth much faster than the dinosaurs did, perhaps over a few thousand years. So what killed the Ice Age animals so rapidly? Did humans hunt the animals to extinction? Did climatic warming kill them off? Did a combination of these factors, or other causes, do them in? This book explores these and many other questions.

Until the early part of the eighteenth century, some people believed these giants might still be thriving somewhere in the world. For example, amateur paleontologist Benjamin Franklin took special interest in the significant discovery of elephant fossils at Big Bone Lick, in what is now Kentucky. And Meriwether Lewis collected a suite of fossils for Thomas Jefferson at the Big Bone Lick site before setting out with William Clark and the Corps of Discovery. Fascinated with woolly mammoths and giant ground sloths, Jefferson instructed co-commanders Lewis and Clark to keep an eye peeled for those animals as the explorers trekked west across North America starting in 1804.

On February 24, 1803, before Lewis and Clark departed, Jefferson wrote the following to French naturalist Bernard de Lacépède (1756–1825):

The narrow-mouthed ground sloth (Megalonyx leptostomus), *an ancestor of Jefferson's ground sloth* (Megalonyx jeffersonii) —Courtesy of The University of Nebraska State Museum

It happens that we are now actually sending off a small party to explore the Missouri [River] to its source, and whatever other river, heading nearest with that, runs into the Western ocean; to enlarge our knowledge of the continent, by adding information of that interesting line of communication across it, and to give us a general view of its population, natural history, productions, soil and climate. It is not improbable that this voyage of discovery will procure us information of the Mammoth, and of the *Megatherium* [giant ground sloth], mentioned by you on page 6. For you have possibly seen in our Philosophical transactions, that before we had seen the account of that animal by Mr. Cuvier [French naturalist who lived from 1769 to 1832] we had found some remains of an enormous animal incognitium, whom, from the disproportionate length of his claw, we had denominated *Megalonyx*, and which is probably the same animal; and that there are symptoms of its late and present existence. The route we are exploring will perhaps bring us further evidence of it, and may be accomplished in two summers.

While none of these animals was alive while Jefferson wrote the above, some argue that mastodons may have survived until recent times in Mexico. Some of the Mayan temples, such as Chichén Itzá, built about 1,500 years ago, bear decorations of animals with elephant-like trunks. We do know for sure, however, that dwarf mammoths lived on Wrangell Island, off the coast of Siberia, until about 4,000 years ago.

Human fascination with Pleistocene animals goes back to the dawn of recorded history. Fossil bones of the large Pleistocene animals are intertwined with history, legends, and the gods. Some of the most prized possessions of the Greeks, Romans, and the Tlascalan Indians of what is now Mexico were the tusks and leg bones of extinct elephants and other proboscideans. These remains spawned legends of giants among these peoples. Modern vertebrate paleontology also had its beginnings with the study of the remains of extinct species of elephants. The discovery of the remains of some of these animals has even brought a measure of prosperity to some northern peoples. Siberians alone may have collected and sold more than 50,000 mammoth tusks into the ivory trade.

As unlikely as it is, someday we may even be able to bring selected beasts back from the dead using genetic engineering, as imaginatively visualized in the *Jurassic Park* movies. The first to be resurrected, because of the amount of available preserved matter in the frozen tundra, may be a woolly mammoth calf born to a modern elephant (See the sidebar "DNA and Dung," in Chapter 5 on page 90).

Chapters that follow in this book expand on many of the thoughts introduced here. We'll begin with descriptions of the Pleistocene world and the geologic time leading up to it, then look at possible causes for the ice ages. The heart of the book focuses on the animals that ranged over North America during Pleistocene time: their characteristics, origins, time of extinction, and interactions with early humans. This book also includes some of the hardy animals that made the transition from the Ice Age into the present. We then consider the various theories of extinction, including possible human influences. The book concludes with a list of museums and web sites where you can learn more about and view the remains and reconstructions of these beasts in all their glory.

ABOUT SCIENTIFIC NAMES

Before we begin, let's take a look at how scientists classify living organisms. Scientists, and perhaps most humans, love to organize and classify things. We have classification schemes for buttons, motor vehicles, dirt, snakes, birds—you name it. The Greek scholar and teacher Aristotle (384 to 322 B.C.) developed one of the earliest known classifications of organisms. Pliny the Elder, the Roman scholar lost during the A.D. 79 eruption of Mount Vesuvius, devised another early classification scheme for plants and animals. However, the classification system in common use today for both plants and animals was developed by the Swedish naturalist Carl von Linné, or Linnaeus, who lived from 1707 to 1778. Linnaeus devised the system whereby plants and animals have both generic, or genus, and specific, or species, names. For example, the American black bear is *Ursus americanus,* the grizzly or Alaskan brown bear is *Ursus arctos,* and the polar bear is *Ursus maritimus.* In these examples, *Ursus* is the genus and *Ursus americanus, Ursus arctos,* and *Ursus maritimus* are the species.

Taxonomists classify living and extinct organisms in increasingly smaller groups starting with kingdom (animal, plant, or protist), and proceeding through phylum, class, order, family, genus, and species. Families are groups of related genera named by choosing one of the included genera as a type family and then adding "idae" to the root. The cat family, then, is the family Felidae. And so it goes with the succeedingly larger groupings of the classification. Within a family, some genera are more closely related than others and are referred to as subfamily and tribe. A genus is a collection of different species that have significant common attributes. For example the lion, tiger, puma, and leopard all are members of the genus *Panthera.* A species is an assemblage of individuals that have a common form and are measurably different from other assemblages. The members of a species can produce viable offspring that in turn can produce viable offspring.

An example that should be familiar to all of us is:

Kingdom—Animalia

Phylum—Chordata

Subphylum—Vertebrata

Class—Mammalia

Order—Primates

Family—Hominidae

Genus—*Homo*

Species—*Homo sapiens*

A new classification system called cladistics organizes animals and plants by how closely they are related to one another evolutionarily. Cladistics, then, is based upon evolutionary characteristics that show relatedness between organisms. This classification system contrasts sharply with the Linnaean classification system, which arranges organisms according to similar physical characteristics. Scientists developed and universally used the Linnaean system before they understood that all organisms had evolved from other, more primitive organisms.

An example of how the systems differ can be seen in the Class Reptilia. Under the Linnaean system it contained all egg-laying, land-dwelling vertebrate animals except birds and mammals. In the cladistic system turtles, lizards, snakes, crocodiles, dinosaurs, pterosaurs, *and birds* constitute the new Reptilia group. Birds are included because they and, for example, dinosaurs have a common ancestor.

References: Colbert and Morales, 1991; Flint, 1971; Jackson, 1978; MacFadden, 1992; Moore et al., 1952

GEOLOGIC TIME SCALE *

Era	Period	Epoch	Age in millions of years**
CENOZOIC	Quaternary	Holocene	0.01
		Pleistocene	1.8–1.9
	Tertiary	Pliocene	5.3
		Miocene	23.8
		Oligocene	36.6
		Eocene	57.8
		Paleocene	65.4
MESOZOIC	Cretaceous		144
	Jurassic		199
	Triassic		251.6
PALEOZOIC	Permian		290
	Pennsylvanian		320
	Mississippian		362
	Devonian		418
	Silurian		439
	Ordovician		491
	Cambrian		543
PRECAMBRIAN			3800?

* Adapted from Erwin and Wing, 2000
** millions of years represent the base of each time unit.

A CAST OF CONTINENTS

Throughout most of the history of the earth, continents have joined and separated, creating large supercontinents and small micro-continents. The breakup and recombination of landmasses is critical in the evolution of life. Small landmasses surrounded by wide expanses of water isolate nonflying and nonswimming life-forms. Isolated plants and animals evolve along different paths than do organisms that are able to mix on a larger landmass. Modern-day examples of evolutionary isolation include the Galápagos and Hawaiian Islands in the

A reconstruction of the single supercontinent Pangaea at about 250 million years ago. Pangaea consisted of two parts: Gondwanaland in the south and Laurasia in the north. —Modified after Dietz and Holden, 1970

250 Million Years Ago

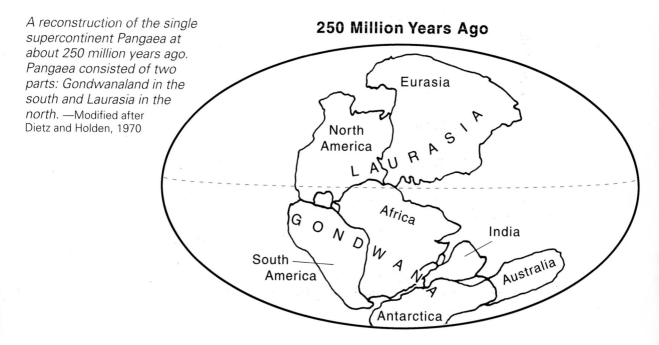

Pacific Ocean. When landmasses join together, as North and South America did about 3 million years ago, formerly isolated plants and animals can interact. On one large supercontinent, climate notwithstanding, animal species can move around and colonize large parts of it. As flora and fauna distribute widely, species tend to homogenize, and the arrival of newcomers produces competition that may trigger extinctions of earlier inhabitants. Over geologic time, the moving continents greatly influenced the evolution of plant and animal life and set the stage for migration and extinction of animals during the Ice Age.

For more than 350 million years, starting about 535 million years ago, South America, Africa, Antarctica, Australia, and India were part of a huge landmass in the Southern Hemisphere known as Gondwana. About 500 million years

ago, Gondwanaland and Laurasia—which contained North America, Europe, and Asia— started to merge and became part of the ultimate supercontinent, Pangaea, meaning "all lands." Pangaea ultimately extended geographically from the South Pole to the North Pole. All the continental pieces of Pangaea were connected by approximately 300 million years ago, when Europe finally sutured to Asia.

The supercontinent Pangaea remained intact for about 100 million years. As you might expect, formerly isolated plant and animal species spread widely throughout Pangaea. Pieces of the supercontinent began to break apart starting about 200 million to 180 million years ago. Most of the breakup happened during the Jurassic and Cretaceous periods, about 200 million to 65 million years ago. The final separation of Europe from

180 Million Years Ago

The early stages of the breakup of Pangaea at the end of Triassic time, approximately 180 million years ago. Note the development of the east-west-trending Tethys Sea as Laurasia moves northward and splits away from the fragmenting Gondwanaland. India will soon become an island moving north toward Asia. At 135 million years ago, Africa, Antarctica, Australia, and South America are still attached. —Modified from Dietz and Holden, 1970

EVIDENCE FOR PANGAEA

In 1912 German meteorologist Alfred Wegener (1880–1930), a doctor of astronomy, son of an evangelical minister, and world-record holder (in 1906) for ballooning, presented a lecture to the German Geological Association entitled "Die Entstehung der Kontinente und Ozeane" ("The Origin of the Continents and Oceans"). A monograph with the same title followed in 1915. In the monograph, Wegener proposed that long ago a supercontinent containing all the bits and pieces of presently existing land formed, and then began to break apart in early Mesozoic time. He named the supercontinent Pangaea, which is Greek for "all earth."

Wegener visualized continents plowing through the oceanic crust and pushing up mountains along their margins. The Andes along the west coast of South America are but one example. Wegener called the southern part of the supercontinent Gondwanaland, a name coined by Austrian geologist Eduard Suess in the latter part of the nineteenth century. Suess had already theorized that the continents of the Southern Hemisphere had once formed a giant landmass, which he named Gondwanaland after a geological province in east-central India.

The idea that continents had moved was not entirely new. In 1596, Dutch cartographer Abraham Ortelius suggested in his work *Thesaurus Geographicus* that South America and Africa were once joined and later separated. In 1620, Francis Bacon observed that the shapes of the two continents fit together. And in 1858, Antonio Snider-Pellegrini also proposed that the two continents had split apart. He attributed the separation to the great biblical flood.

Wegener's monograph generated little response until 1924, when it was translated into English. The publication sparked a great and heated debate that lasted into the 1960s, well after Wegener's death. Wegener presented several important pieces of evidence, but because his theory lacked a convincing mechanism to move the continents, scientists did not readily accept it. He proposed that tidal forces, driven by the gravitational pull of the Sun and the Moon on Earth, did the deed.

So what was the evidence Wegener presented in 1915? First and foremost was the fit of the continents. Who hasn't looked at the coastlines of eastern South America and western Africa and noted that they look like pieces of a puzzle? The fit is even better if you examine the edge of the continental shelves of Africa and South America at a depth of about 2,900 feet (900 meters). Other evidence included the similar rock types and mountain trends found opposite each other on portions of the northern and southern coasts of Africa and South America. Stratigraphers and sedimentologists of Wegener's time also observed evidence of continental-style glaciation in rocks of the same age in what are now southeastern South America, southern Africa, India, and southern Australia. Because glaciers can form only on land, the directions of ice movement onto these continents recorded in the rocks required an ice cap sitting over the interior of a formerly large continent, or Gondwanaland.

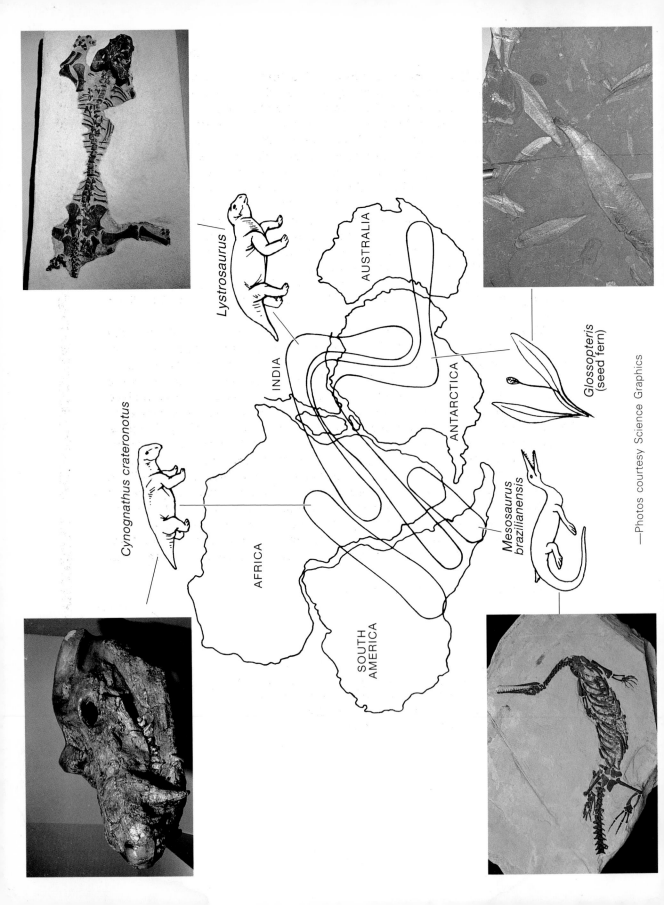

Lystrosaurus

Cynognathus crateronotus

AUSTRALIA

INDIA

ANTARCTICA

AFRICA

SOUTH AMERICA

Glossopteris (seed fern)

Mesosaurus brazilianensis

—Photos courtesy Science Graphics

Finally, definitive fossil evidence also linked some of the present continents together as Gondwanaland in late Paleozoic and early Mesozoic time. The remains of the Permian freshwater reptile *Mesosaurus brazilianensis* have been found in Argentina and in southern Africa. Fossils of the 9-foot-long (3-meter-long) *Cynognathus crateronotus,* an early Triassic land reptile, exist in Argentina and in South Africa. *Lystrosaurus,* another Triassic land-dwelling reptile, appears to have inhabited South Africa, Madagascar, southern India, southern South America, and Antarctica. And remains of *Glossopteris* ferns appear in Permian and Triassic rocks in the southern parts of all these landmasses, and of Australia as well. Because these were land or freshwater inhabitants, the respective landmasses must have been connected when they lived, during late Paleozoic to early Mesozoic time, about 285 million to 200 million years ago. All the major pieces of Pangaea were assembled by approximately 300 million years ago, but the supercontinent started to rift apart early in Jurassic time, about 200 million years ago.

Wegener's study of late Paleozoic rocks, 300 million years old, and the coal, salt, potash, desert sands, and glacial deposits in them allowed him to develop a coherent picture of climates that produced those materials during that time period. The problem he faced was the present location of some of the rocks. For example, glacial deposits called tillites seemed out of place in their present equatorial setting. To explain these situations Wegener envisioned polar wandering. We now know that Earth's pole of rotation does not move, at least not by very much. Instead, the 60-mile-thick (100-kilometer) rigid lithospheric plates bearing the continents and ocean floor move.

Most earth scientists did not accept the idea of continental drift until the mid-1960s, when an alternate theory called plate tectonics was proposed and then endorsed. Now most geologists embrace the concept of a former supercontinent that subsequently rifted apart. We now also know that slow movement of hot, upwelling or convecting mantle material, not tidal forces or a great flood, drives the surface plates that carry continents and ocean floor.

References: Hallam, 1975; Oreskes, 1999

Left: *The discoveries of fossils of the same species across broad swaths of different landmasses are among the evidence that the continents of Africa, South America, Antarctica, and Australia and the subcontinent of India were once part of Gondwanaland, the southern part of the supercontinent of Pangaea*

Greenland took place in early Tertiary time, approximately 57 million years ago.

By about 180 million years ago, Laurasia had broken away from Gondwanaland to the south, opening the east-west Tethys Sea. By 170 million years ago, southern Africa had split away from Antarctica, and about 135 million years ago, South America started to separate from Africa along a north-trending rift system. As South America moved westward and Africa eastward, the South Atlantic Ocean was born. By about 120 million years ago, the mass of South America, Antarctica, and Australia completely separated from Africa as the ancestral Atlantic Ocean widened.

By approximately 65 million years ago, the configuration of continents and oceans began to resemble what we see on our modern maps, with the exception of the North Atlantic Ocean—you still could not sail between Greenland and Norway. North America entirely separated from Europe about 57 million years ago. That rifting broke the last land link between Norway and Greenland. Since then, the Atlantic Ocean has grown wider at about 1.75 inches (4 centimeters) per year, or about the rate of growth of a human fingernail. In the Southern Hemisphere, South America, Antarctica, and Australia finally began to break apart 60 million to 55 million years ago. South America remained an island continent, like present-day Australia and Antarctica, until 3.5 million to 2.5 million years ago, when the Panamanian land bridge rose and linked South America to North America. The Panamanian land bridge opened the door for land plants and animals to move between South and North America.

65 Million Years Ago

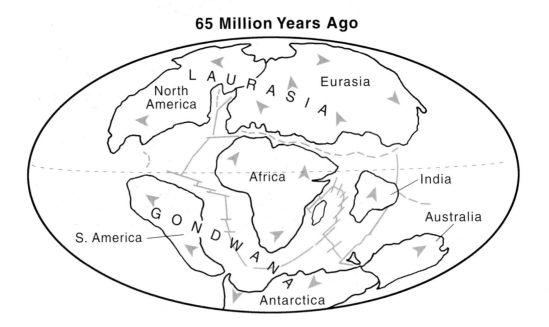

The world's landmasses approximately 65 million years ago. North America is still attached to Europe with Greenland sandwiched between. South America, Australia, and Antarctica are still a threesome while India continues its trek northward towards Asia, and South America rifts away from Africa. —Modified from Dietz and Holden, 1970

The ice ages that began 2 million or 3 million years ago further changed the migration paths of animals. As ice sheets grew, sea level dropped, and other land bridges formed. Several times in the last few million years a land bridge temporarily connected North America to Asia, by way of Alaska, across the present Bering Strait. Some animal immigrants came to North America from Asia across this northern route, called Beringia. Beringia emerged as sea level fell at least 164 feet (50 meters) from the present level during the ice ages.

With the Panamanian and Beringian land bridges in place, animals headed south if they could to avoid the increasingly cold climate; others that could not escape either adapted or went extinct.

The land connections allowed for the homogenization of Western Hemispheric, Eurasiatic, and African animals. The result was that many of the animal families and genera inhabited these areas simultaneously, but species went extinct at different times in different regions.

Why did the mammoths cross the land bridge?

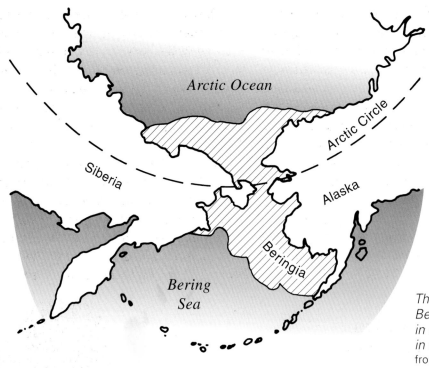

The Pleistocene land bridge Beringia connected Alaska in North America to Siberia in eastern Asia. —Modified from Hopkins, 1967

During Pleistocene time, then, local evolution and migrations from South America and Eurasia brought changes in North American mammal faunas. However, a far greater number of species emigrated from Asia to North America and then to South America than emigrated from North America to either Asia or South America.

Cold-adapted animals apparently predominated during the southward migration from Beringia—and for good reason. They were better adapted to the rigors of crossing the high-latitude land bridge. The result was that while Europe had such warm-climate animals as hippopotamuses, North America did not. Neither did the woolly rhinoceros colonize North America; it was certainly adapted to cold weather but for some reason did not make the trip.

Compared with that of Eurasia, North American mammal fauna was more uniformly distributed during Pleistocene time. This apparently was due to the geography: the north-south orientation of North American mountain ranges allowed animals to migrate south and north as ice distributions and plant life changed during the alternating cold and warm climatic conditions. Unfortunately for some of the Eurasian animals, the east-west orientation of mountain ranges, such as the Alps and Pyrenees, blocked the animals' southward escape from hostile glacial environments. Many great beasts, including the mastodon, became extinct much earlier in Eurasia than in North America.

Animals common to both North America and Eurasia in earliest Pleistocene time include proboscideans—mammoths and their relatives the mastodons. Mastodons soon became extinct in the Old World but lasted until about the end of Pleistocene time in North America. One-toed horses of the genus *Equus* evolved in North America from the three-toed *Pliohippus* of late Tertiary time, about 5 million years ago. Horses arrived in Africa by late Pliocene time and were roaming Eurasia before early Pleistocene time. *Equus* became extinct in North America more than 10,000 years ago. The Spanish reintroduced the horse to North and South America during their conquest.

The Great American Animal Interchange—a term coined in 1976 by noted paleontologist S. David Webb—followed establishment of the land bridge reconnecting North and South America. The original hoofed animals, or ungulates, colonized North America from Asia, and many also eventually spread south into Central and South America. New World models such as llamas, camels, and pronghorn evidently developed later in North America. Animals that eventually reached South America include llamas, peccaries, and camels. The camel subsequently became extinct in the New World but not in the Old. Late in Pleistocene time, bison (Bovidae family) and deer

The Great American Animal Interchange

About 8 million years ago animals from South America started arriving in North America by either island-hopping—swimming from island to island—or rafting on floating vegetation. The Panamanian land bridge between South and North America was established between 3.5 million and 2.5 million years ago, allowing animals to travel on land to and from North America.

The 10-foot-tall (3-meter) Titanis, a flightless, fast-running, predaceous bird from South America

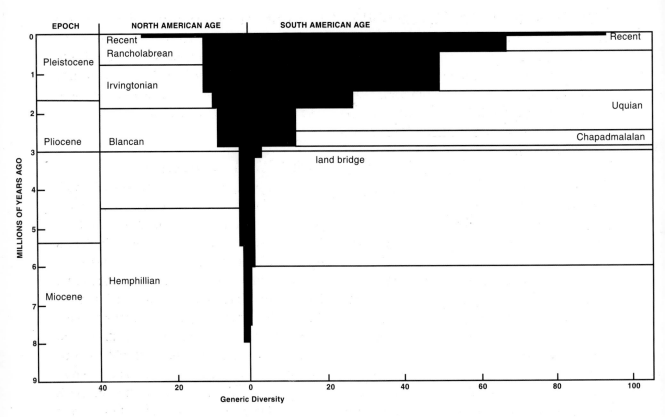

The generic diversity of land mammals in North America and South America over the last 9 million years. Note the striking increase in diversity starting about 3 million years ago and coinciding with the connection of North and South America. South America witnessed a much greater increase in genera than did North America. —Modified from Marshall, 1988

(Cervidae family) reached North America from Asia.

Because of South America's isolation before reconnecting with North America, animals on the southern island continent had few counterparts elsewhere and few competitors. The largest South American carnivore prior to the arrival of North American animals was not a mammal but a 10-foot-tall (3 meters), rapid-running flightless bird of the genus *Titanis*.

Titanis was one of the last of twelve genera and twenty-five species of terror birds, so named because of their size, speed, and appetite for meat. They inhabited the Americas and Europe and lived from Oligocene time through most of Pleistocene time. This creature could probably run more than 40 miles (70 kilometers) per hour. It laid two basketball-sized eggs. Remains of the bird have been found in northern Florida. It went extinct perhaps because of competition for prey from the faster and more intelligent North American mammals, such as members of the dog (Canidae) and cat (Felidae) families. These newcomers also probably ate the birds' eggs or the birds themselves.

SOUTH AMERICAN EMIGRANTS

South American emigrants apparently came north in waves. The first travelers arrived during late Miocene time, about 8 million years ago, well before the South American–North American land bridge emerged from the sea. Animals that made the float trip included large, plant-eating ground sloths of the families Megalonychidae (*Pliometanastes protistus)* and Mylodontidae (the bear-sized *Thinobadistes*). Without the use of boats, they probably made the journey by island-hopping through the West Indies or on rafts of edible vegetation.

The first land migrants arrived about 3.5 million to 2.5 million years ago, during what scientists call Blancan Land Mammal Time. Their remains have been found in Florida, Texas, and California. They include the big bird *Titanis,* two armadillos (*Dasypus* and *Kraglievichia* of the family Dasypodidae), two ground sloths (*Paramylodon* and *Nothrotheriops*), a porcupine (*Erethizon* of the family Erethizontidae), a giant armadillo-like glyptodont (*Glyptotherium* of the family Glyptodontidae), and a large aquatic rodent called a capybara (*Neochoerus* of the family Hydrochoeridae).

Sedimentary deposits across the southern United States and Central America dated at 1.9 million years and younger contain the remains of different immigrants. They include a ground sloth (*Eremotherium rusconii*), a giant anteater *(Myrmecophaga),* and a giant armadillo *(Pampatherium).* The remains of an opossum (*Didelphis* of the family Didelphidae) have been uncovered in younger deposits in Florida and another ground sloth (*Meizonyx*) in El Salvador. Late Pleistocene arrivals to Central America, during what scientists call the Rancholabrean Land Mammal Age, include

toxodonts, rhinoceros-sized animals of the Toxodontidae family. Since the end of Pleistocene time about 10,000 years ago, South American emigrants to North America include marmosets, tamarins, New World monkeys, tree sloths, anteaters, and spiny rats.

THE NORTH AMERICAN INVADERS

While a significant number of genera left South America for the north, ten times as many genera and families went the other direction. The first North American arrivals in South America also date to about 8 million years ago and also must have island hopped and rafted. They include raccoons and other relatives of the family Procyonidae. Researchers have found remains of these omnivores, the size of their modern descendants, in 8-million-year-old Argentinean rocks. Subsequent raccoon species eventually reached the size of black bears. Remains of rats and mice, of the family Cricetidae, exist in somewhat younger rocks of early Pliocene age, or about 5 million to 4 million years old. Argentina and, to a lesser extent, Bolivia contain most of these Miocene through Pleistocene animal remains because their climates favored fossil preservation. The wet climates of tropical forests rarely allow preservation of animal parts, so little is known of the migrations during interglacial times in South America's wetter climes.

In late Pliocene time, about 3 million years ago, the first land migrants to reach South America over the newly established Panamanian land bridge included sixteen genera representing nine families. Among these new immigrants were skunks of the family Mustelidae and peccaries of the family Tayassuidae, as well as the horse *Hippidion* (family Equidae). Following them in early Pleistocene time were dogs, wolves, and foxes (family Canidae), cats, including saber-toothed cats, jaguars, and smaller species (family Felidae), bears (family Ursidae), camels and llamas (family Camelidae), deer (family Cervidae), horses (family Equidae), tapirs (family Tapiridae), and mastodons (family Gomphotheriidae), rabbits (family Leporidae), and squirrels (family Sciuridae). Ancestors of modern kangaroo rats (family Heteromyidae), pocket gophers (family Geomyidae), and shrews (family Soricidae) also came at this time.

All the nonflying animals that made the trip north and south were either adapted for or could tolerate savannas and grasslands but not deserts. Researchers theorize that the more hospitable savanna and grassland environments existed along most of or the entire length of the land route. The apparent pulses of animal migrations appear to correlate well with marine regressions—drops in sea level that coincided with the times of major glacial advances. These glacial periods would not only have produced wider land bridges and coastal plains because of lower sea level, but also a major savanna corridor south from the terminus of the North American ice sheets through the presently humid subtropical and tropical climates of Central America and northern South America.

The result of the Great American Animal Interchange is that eighty-five genera, or 50 percent, of today's South American land mammals came from North American ancestral families, whereas twenty-nine genera, or 21 percent, of North American land mammals have South American ancestors. The disparity in percentages reflects how well the North American invaders overwhelmed their South American counterparts.

References: Butler et al., 1984; Coates et al., 1992; Dalziel, 1995; Dietz and Holden, 1970; Hopkins, 1967; Marshall, 1988, 1994; Marshall et al., 1982; Menon, 1995; Nilsson, 1983; Oreskes, 1999; Webb, 1978, 1985; White and McKenzie, 1989; Windley, 1984

THE PLEISTOCENE EPOCH

3

The geologically recent past when massive, continent-sized glaciers, giant mammals, and early humans coexisted is called the Pleistocene epoch. English scientist Charles Lyell (1797–1875), one of the founding fathers of geology, introduced the term in his three-volume series *Principles of Geology*, published between 1830 and 1833. The name comes from the Greek words *pleistos* meaning "most" and *kainos* meaning "recent." Lyell initially did not know that the giant animals, ice sheets, and early humans coexisted, but by 1859 he supported the connections. British geologist Edward Forbes in 1846 redefined the Pleistocene epoch as the time equivalent to the ice ages. The Pleistocene epoch is the second youngest time period within the Cenozoic era, which began approximately 65 million years ago with the extinction of the dinosaurs. The Pleistocene epoch started sometime between 2.48 million to 1.65 million years ago, depending on whether you accept a geologic, climatic, or biologic definition. It ended about 10,000 years before the present.

Lyell distinguished the geologic times based on marine fossils and sedimentary layers he observed in France and Italy. Rocks in Europe that Lyell classified as Pleistocene contained the fossil remains of at least 70 percent of living mollusk species, invertebrate animals including snails, clams, and squids. Other European geologists, including Forbes, found that glacial debris deposited on land correlated well in time with the marine Pleistocene strata, and so the Pleistocene epoch became synonymous with the ice ages.

The Pleistocene epoch was truly a bizarre time when we consider both the animals that lived then and the dramatic shifts in climate. These climate changes affected the landscapes and the lives of animals and early peoples. This chapter describes just some of the attributes of the Ice Age and provides a context for the descriptions of the animals that lived then. Let's look at what scientists have learned about ice ages and the Pleistocene epoch.

The major continental glaciations of Pleistocene time, while unusual, were not unique in the earth's history. Glacial geologists have discovered evidence for four major times of continental glaciation during the last 2.6 billion years. The first glacial episode occurred sometime between about 2.6 to 2.1 billion years ago and affected the landmasses that presently make up North America, South Africa, India, Australia, and Scandinavia. The second, most widespread, and longest-lasting glaciation affected all continents between approximately 900 million and 700 million years ago. The third major episode of continental glaciation lasted between about 440 million and 255 million years ago on the parts of Gondwanaland situated over the South Pole at that time. As the supercontinent moved over the South Pole, glaciation shifted from what is now western Africa and Saudi Arabia to the area where South America, South Africa, India, Antarctica, and Australia were joined.

The fourth major ice age—and the focus of this book—started during late Pliocene time and continued until the end of Pleistocene time, about 10,000 years ago. Climatic cycles became more extreme—temperatures became considerably cooler and then warmer than climates of today's world. Analyses of plant and tree pollen within early Pliocene sediments in currently temperate climates show that the climate during the Pliocene epoch, which preceded the Pleistocene epoch, was milder than it is today. For example, England was subtropical. However, late Pliocene and Pleistocene time brought major and rapid climatic fluctuations, eventually culminating in the ice ages. Major changes in flora and fauna accompanied these climatic changes. For example, the remains of hippopotamuses found in Great Britain in deposits from an interglacial time demonstrate the climate was warmer than it is today.

There have been at least seventeen complete glacial-interglacial cycles since the start of Pleistocene time. Of these, the seven complete glacial-interglacial cycles during the past 620,000 years lasted between 88,000 years and 118,000 years each, averaging about 100,000 years long. Of the last five complete cycles, dating back 529,000 years, the warmer interglacial episodes lasted 28,000 years to 49,000 years, or 22 percent to 42 percent of each cycle. Based on the past climatic record, it seems reasonable to predict that another glacial episode will follow the present warm Holocene time.

Discovery of the Ice Ages

So, who "discovered" the Pleistocene ice ages? When and how was this momentous discovery made? The credit for at least popularizing the concept of the ice ages goes to a Swiss zoologist, Jean Louis Rodolphe Agassiz (1807–1873). At a meeting of the prestigious Swiss Society of Natural Sciences in 1837, Agassiz stated that a continent-sized ice sheet had spread southward from the North Pole to the Alps, resulting in a catastrophic climate change. This pronouncement startled the scientific world and sparked one of the most intense and longest-running scientific disputes of the nineteenth century.

Certainly one reason the debate raged was that Agassiz's theory went against the strict biblical interpretations of the time. Biblical scholars believed, for example, that the huge boulders, which geologists now call glacial erratics, lying all over northern Europe were deposited during the great flood of Noah's time, certainly not dropped by glaciers. Many Europeans still believed that fossils were the remains of animals that had died in the flood, and all creatures still living were descendants of the contingent from Noah's ark.

Large boulders or erratics deposited by a receding glacier near Tioga Pass, Sierra Nevada, California. Such erratics were once believed to have been deposited by the biblical flood. The boulders rest on a large granite mass that has been polished by the glacier's movements. —Courtesy of Science Graphics

Imagine the reaction of people upon reading, or hearing, the following passage by Agassiz:

> [T]he development of these huge ice sheets must have led to the destruction of all organic life at the earth's surface. Europe, previously covered with tropical vegetation and inhabited by herds of great elephants, enormous hippopotami, and gigantic carnivores, suddenly became buried under a vast expanse of ice covering plains, lakes, seas and plateaus alike. The silence of death followed . . . springs dried up, streams ceased to flow, and sun rays rising over that frozen shore . . . were met by the whistling of the northern winds and the rumbling of the crevasses as they opened across the surface of that huge ocean of ice.

Earlier workers in the Alps had surmised that mountain glaciers had once been more extensive but only a few scientists, such as Johann Bernhardi (1774–1850) of Germany, thought glaciers had been extensive in Germany. Bernhardi postulated late in the eighteenth century that an ice sheet had formed over Scandinavia and spread south to cover northern Germany. Agassiz, after his visits to the Alps to inspect active glaciers, also became convinced that ice sheets had covered northern Europe. Later, he went to the United States to teach at Harvard University, and he discovered signs of recent glaciation in Massachusetts and other parts of North America. Agassiz substantiated his case with evidence that included rock surfaces glacially polished to mirror finishes and glacially scratched grooves on rock surfaces that show the direction of former ice movement.

Agassiz noted ridges of unsorted and unstratified rock, silt, and sand, called glacial moraines, that the glaciers had dumped at their southern margins. He also examined glacial deposits called drift that veneered the lowlands where the glaciers had once been.

Grooves are visible in bedrock that has been scratched and polished by debris pushed along beneath an advancing glacier. Swiss zoologist Jean Louis Rodolphe Agassiz first pointed to similar markings as evidence of continental glaciation. —Ian Lange photo

The drift contained erratics—large, glacially transported boulders of rock types that do not match those at their present resting places, indicating that they were transported from distant sources. Some erratics may rest hundreds of miles from their source.

Swiss geologist and physicist Horace Bénédict de Saussure (1740–1799) originally recognized in 1787 that the erratics came from someplace else. He noted that the composition of the boulders on the slopes of the Jura Mountains, along the French-Swiss border, was such that they could only have come from the Alps about 50 miles (80 kilometers) away. Saussure, however, believed that the great biblical flood had deposited the boulders. A few years later the famous Scottish geologist James Hutton (1726–1797) reasoned that the erratics littering the Scottish countryside were ice-rafted to their locations, that is, transported on floating ice and deposited as the ice melted. The concept of ice-rafting was not new in Hutton's day. Whalers had observed iceberg-rafted boulders during their polar wanderings. Later, during his voyage on the *Beagle* in the 1830s, Charles Darwin noted erratics miles from their sources in parts of Tierra del Fuego. Darwin also thought the ice had rafted the boulders while water submerged the countryside. The theories of ice-rafted boulders and the water-borne origin of drift lingered until English geologists T. F. Jamieson and Archibald Geikie reasoned in their now-classic papers about Scottish glacial deposits that glaciers directly deposited the rock debris, littering the countryside with what scientists call glacial drift.

Over the years, researchers found more and more evidence of continental glaciation. Scientific thought finally embraced Agassiz's theories, and the great debate over the existence of ice ages ended.

Glacial Time

Until recently, geologists thought four major glacial episodes, each separated by warm, interglacial times, swept North America during the Pleistocene epoch. Scientists called the glacial advances, from youngest to oldest, the Wisconsinan, Illinoian, Kansan, and Nebraskan. They named the interglacial periods, from youngest to oldest, Sangamonian, Yarmouthian, and Aftonian. Scientists also accepted that the North American chronology probably correlated with the European glacial-interglacial timescale. Researchers now know that the correlations between glacial and interglacial times at different locations are more complex. However, the terms for these four glacial and three interglacial episodes remain in common use.

By convention of active researchers, scientists divide the Pleistocene epoch into late, middle, and early times. In North America, paleontologists divide Pliocene and Pleistocene time into land mammal ages. The Blancan Land Mammal Age, named for the Mount Blanco site in Texas, started about 3.5 million years ago in the late Pliocene epoch with the arrival of deer, voles, and gophers to North America. Geologists commonly consider the beginning of the Irvingtonian Land Mammal Age to coincide with the "official start" of the Pleistocene epoch—although they do not yet agree on the exact number of years before present. The arrival of the first true elephants, southern mammoth (*Mammuthus meridionalis*), heralded the beginning of the Irvingtonian Land Mammal Age about 1.9 million years ago. This age also marks the appearance of saber-toothed cats, jaguars, wolverines, scimitar cats, hares, and biologically advanced voles. The Irvingtonian Land Mammal Age includes at least the

Duration of Glacial and Interglacial Episodes in Thousands of Years

EPOCH	AGE OF WHOLE CYCLE	AGE OF GLACIAL CYCLE PORTION	AGE OF INTERGLACIAL CYCLE PORTION	NORTH AMERICAN DIVISIONS	EUROPEAN DIVISIONS	LAND MAMMAL AGES
Holocene			Present to 10			
Late Pleistocene	10 to 128	10 to 71		Wisconsinan	Weichsel or Wurm	Rancholabrean *
	129 to 245	129 to 187	72 to 128	Sangamonian	Eem	bison
			188 to 245	Illinoian	Saale or Riss	?
	245 to 338	245 to 301		Yarmouthian (?)		
			302 to 337	Kansan (?)		
				Aftonian (?)		
Middle Pleistocene	338 to 426	338 to 390		Nebraskan (?)		
			391 to 425			Irvingtonian
	426 to 529	426 to 477				mammoth
			478 to 506			
	529 to 620	529 to 571				
			572 to 618			1.9 Ma
	750 to 775 Ka—Matuyama-Brunhes magnetic reversal boundary					
Early Pleistocene	1.65 Ma—Upper boundary of Olduvai magnetic reversal Pleistocene-Pliocene Epoch boundary or					Blancan
	2.48 Ma—Gauss-Matuyama magnetic reversal boundary Pleistocene-Pliocene boundary					deer, voles, gophers
Pliocene	5.0 to 5.5 Ma					
Miocene						

*estimates for the start of the Rancholabrean vary from 300,000 to 100,000 years ago

Time scale of the Pleistocene epoch, showing the time and duration of glacial and interglacial periods in thousands of years and the corresponding land mammal ages. North American and European divisions are based upon works of early researchers into Pleistocene history. —Modified from Morrison, 1991, and from Kurten and Anderson, 1980

Nebraskan glacial stage in North America. The Irvingtonian age takes its name from the fossil site at Irvington, near San Francisco, California.

The arrival of the genus *Bison*, which includes bison, onto the American stage from Eurasia between 300,000 and 150,000 years ago marked the start of the Rancholabrean Land Mammal Age. Woolly mammoths also entered the North American scene during the Rancholabrean Land Mammal Age, though arriving much later than bison. The Rancholabrean age contains most of the Illinoian glacial, Sangamonian interglacial, and all of Wisconsinan glacial time. The Rancholabrean age is based upon the fantastic mammal finds in the Rancho La Brea tar pits in Los Angeles, California.

Of Ice and Oxygen

The picture of Pleistocene glaciation has become even more complex with recent work on sedimentary layers derived from drill cores from the floors of all major oceans and ice cores from the Greenland ice cap. Research demonstrates that there were at least seventeen major glacial-interglacial cycles and possibly many more during the last 1.65 million years.

What were the glacial and interglacial periods like? Detailed studies of glacial deposits, marine sediments, and cores from the Greenland and Antarctica ice caps tell of pulses of major glacial expansion and minor glacial retreats. The changes apparently happened suddenly—within decades or less.

Deep-sea sediments provide some of the best information about glacial and interglacial events. Sediments commonly contain the remains of plants and animals that live near the water's surface, providing a record of changes in those communities. Scientists study the tiny shells of calcareous foraminifera and coccoliths and siliceous radiolaria for clues of climate changes. Ratios of the isotopes oxygen 18 and oxygen 16 in the animal shells reveal corresponding temperature shifts as well. The oxygen 16 isotope is lighter than the oxygen 18 isotope because each atom of oxygen 16 contains two fewer neutrons. Seawater molecules containing the lighter oxygen 16 consequently evaporate more easily than seawater enriched in the heavier oxygen 18. Rain and snow derived from the evaporated seawater enrich the ice caps in oxygen 16 and leave the seawater enriched in oxygen 18. Animal shells and cores from the seafloor record the oxygen-isotope shifts and reflect the climatic changes—the more enriched the shells and cores are in oxygen 18, the cooler the temperatures of water in which these organisms lived. Conversely, deep cores of ice from Greenland and Antarctica show enrichment trends in heavier isotopes as the temperatures warmed, continental glaciers melted, and sea level rose.

By examining oxygen-isotope values recorded in fossil foraminifera in marine sediments, scientists know that the average annual world temperature during the greatest advance of the glaciers was only 7 to 9 degrees Fahrenheit (4 to 5 degrees Celsius) cooler than today. Temperatures in the tropics were only slightly cooler than today, but temperatures in the Northern Hemisphere north of latitude 30 degrees—that of present-day southern California or South Carolina—were significantly cooler. Average temperatures in July and August were as much as 18 to 28 degrees Fahrenheit (10 to 15 degrees Celsius) cooler than today in regions immediately south of the ice sheets.

Standing water over pools of asphalt lured many thirsty animals to their deaths. Here a Harlan's ground sloth (Paramylodon harlani) *is attacked by a young California saber-toothed cat* (Smilodon californicus). *Three California condors* (Breagyps clarki) *wait, while giant* Teratornis merriami *soars overhead. Imperial mammoths* (Mammuthus imperator) *and a dire wolf* (Canis dirus) *look on.*

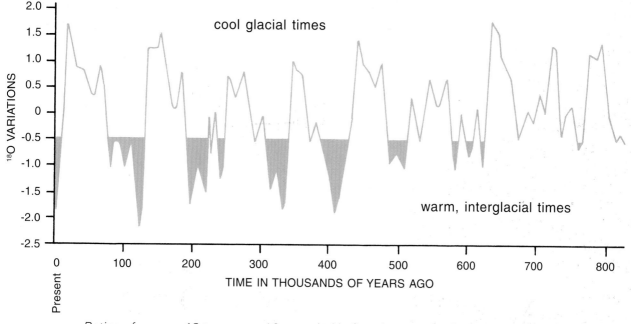

Ratios of oxygen 18 to oxygen 16 recorded in five deep-sea sediment cores over the past 800,000 years. Ratios from times of greatest glacial advances form the peaks above the 0 value. The dark negative peaks represent ratios from interglacial times, which all are below today's ratio value of -0.5. —Modified from Morrison, 1991, with data from Imbrie et al., 1984

As the glaciers melted during the interglacial times, which were as warm as or warmer than today's world, the voluminous meltwater raised the level of the seas. In east-central Virginia, a Pleistocene Atlantic Ocean shoreline at an elevation of 90 to 100 feet (30-plus meters) above present sea level is a clue that the world must have been warmer then than now.

Lakes and Floods

Climates differed from those of today even in areas that glaciation did not directly affect. For example, the Great Basin of Nevada, Utah, and parts of Oregon, Arizona, and California apparently were cooler and much wetter during Pleistocene time than they are today. The result was that many of today's arid valleys contained huge lakes during the Ice Age.

Most of the 141 closed basins—those having no external river drainage—in the Great Basin contained lakes. Death Valley, California, contained a lake 90 miles (140 kilometers) long with a maximum depth of 600 feet (more than 200 meters). The largest lake by far was Lake Bonneville, centered in Utah. At greater than 20,000 square miles (52,000 square kilometers), it extended into Nevada and Idaho and was as much as 1,115 feet (340 meters) deep.

Strandlines, or wave-cut beach terraces, tell us that the site of present-day Salt Lake

Lakes that existed in the Great Basin during the Pleistocene epoch. Dotted lines mark the overflow channels from some lakes during their maximum filling. Most of these lakes no longer exist, but shorelines from old beaches record their former depths. —Modified from Flint, 1957 and Strahler, 1971

City was under more than 950 feet (290 meters) of water during Pleistocene time. Lake Bonneville grew so large that it completely filled the huge closed basin and drained north from Idaho into the Snake River, its waters eventually reaching the Pacific Ocean. Today, all that remains of Lake Bonneville are Great Salt, Provo, and Sevier Lakes, and the Bonneville Salt Flats.

The second largest lake, Lahontan, occupied north-central Nevada. Less than half the size of Lake Bonneville, Lake Lahontan was 620 feet (190 meters) deeper than its modern successor, Pyramid Lake. Walker and Winnemucca Lakes are other remnants of Lake Lahontan. Numerous strandlines around the valley margins record the fluctuating water levels of these Pleistocene lakes. Fossil sites

Strandlines on a hillside mark the former shorelines of a Pleistocene lake in Nevada. —Ian Lange photo

show that while the lakes existed, living and extinct species of animals, and later people, inhabited the shores during Pleistocene time.

Other interesting phenomena related to glaciation exist elsewhere in the Northern Hemisphere. The deep, rich soils of the wheat-growing Palouse region of eastern Washington and northeastern Oregon are dust, called loess, blown south by the strong winds that swept off the ice margin in north-central Washington. And in other places across the northern United States, winds blew fine-grained sediment away from the glacier margins and deposited it as sand dunes. Close to the edges of the continental ice sheet other exciting things happened. Enormous ice-dammed lakes existed. The most famous was Glacial Lake Missoula in western Montana.

GLACIAL LAKE MISSOULA

Glacial Lake Missoula formed when a lobe of the Canadian ice sheet plugged the Clark Fork River canyon near what is now Clark Fork, Idaho, along the Idaho-Montana border. This 3,000-square-mile (7,770-square-kilometer) lake in western Montana contained 600 cubic miles (2,500 cubic kilometers) of water, or half the volume of Lake Michigan. Water depth reached 3,670 feet (1,265 meters) at the ice dam and 950 feet (328 meters) at Missoula, Montana. The story of its discovery and what happened as it eroded or floated its ice dam and discharged catastrophic floods west across Idaho and eastern Washington into the Columbia River was one of the greatest and longest lasting geological debates of the twentieth century. While few geologists disputed the existence of glacially dammed Lake Missoula, several prominent glacial geologists in the early twentieth century were not convinced that floods released when Glacial Lake Missoula drained created the Channeled Scablands of central Washington. The debate about the origin of the strange topography raged from the 1920s into the 1950s, until the theory was conclusively proved.

What a spectacle the emptying of the lake must have been as the lake waters rushed more than 500 miles (800 kilometers) to the Pacific Ocean. Estimates place the maximum volume of water flowing past the site of the ice dam at up to 27 million cubic yards (21 million cubic meters) per second, or ten times the combined flow of all the world's present rivers. At that rate, the lake emptied in just over four days. But it didn't happen just once. The lake may have filled and then catastrophically emptied several dozen times between about 16,000 and 12,000 years ago.

As the water drained west out of Montana, it not only eroded the lake bottom sediment in many places but also created some of the largest ripple marks in the world. The floodwaters roared westward across what is now Lake Pend Oreille in Idaho into the Spokane Valley of Washington. The water then headed west, southwest, and south toward the Columbia River, scouring a giant drainage system of anastomosing, or networking, channels similar to a braided stream. The water surged at speeds of up to 45 miles (70 kilometers) per hour. It ripped soil, vegetation, and blocks of rock weighing tons from the flat-lying and fractured 15-million-year-old Columbia River basalt lava flows. It left behind the Channeled Scablands southwest of Spokane, Washington. The power and volume of the rushing water even moved boulders *up* the Willamette Valley south of Portland, Oregon.

Was glacially dammed Lake Missoula a unique Pleistocene phenomenon? Evidently not. Other glacially dammed lakes existed, and as many as fifty-three such lakes still periodically form and drain in Alaska. Twelve-mile-long (19 kilometer) Lake George in the Copper River drainage basin is the most famous. Until 1967, Knik Glacier impounded the lake almost yearly. As the glacier retreated from the drainage outlet in summer, the lake drained. Betting on the day and time of the Lake George Breakout was as popular for gamblers in Alaska as the Kentucky Derby and the Super Bowl are in the Lower 48.

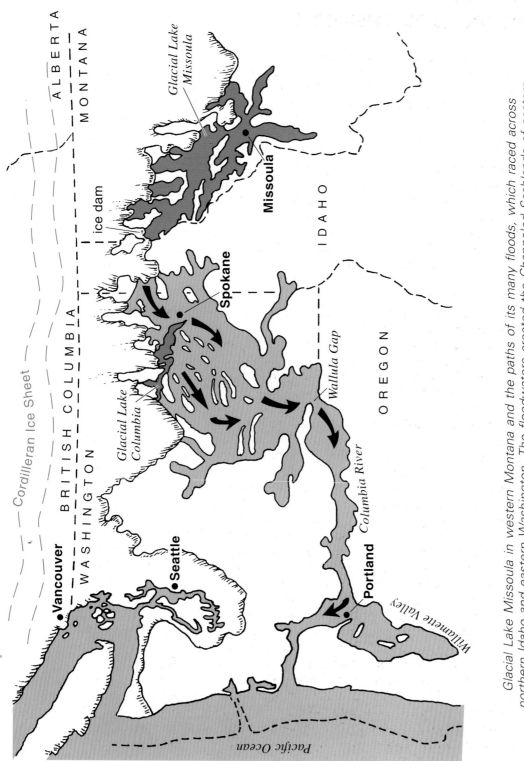

Glacial Lake Missoula in western Montana and the paths of its many floods, which raced across northern Idaho and eastern Washington. The floodwaters created the Channeled Scablands of eastern Washington and eventually reached the Columbia River at Wallula Gap. —Modified after Alt, 2001

Glacial Deposits and Landforms

Along the margins of the great ice sheets, the generally southward-flowing glaciers deposited rocks and sand that they plucked and eroded from the bedrock beneath the ice. The glaciers dumped their debris in large, elongate, and typically crescent-shaped piles called moraines.

The longer the terminus of the glacier stayed in the same place, the more eroded material the ever-flowing glacier brought, and the larger its moraines grew. Some of North America's prominent landforms, including Long Island in New York, part of Cape Cod, and the islands of Nantucket and Martha's Vineyard in Massachusetts, are glacial moraines.

During the summer melt season, sand- and silt-laden streams carried and subsequently redeposited large volumes of glacial debris, creating large sand and gravel deposits in the northern states. As workers have mined these deposits, they have uncovered many fine specimens of such extinct Pleistocene animals as mammoths and mastodons. Why do we find animal remains, especially herbivores, in these deposits? First, herbivores are more common than carnivores, so we should expect to find

In North Cascade National Park in Washington State, a small moraine has formed at the end of this glacier. Fossils are sometimes found in Ice Age moraines, where the animals' remains might have been rapidly buried and preserved by outwash or glacial till. —Ian Lange photo

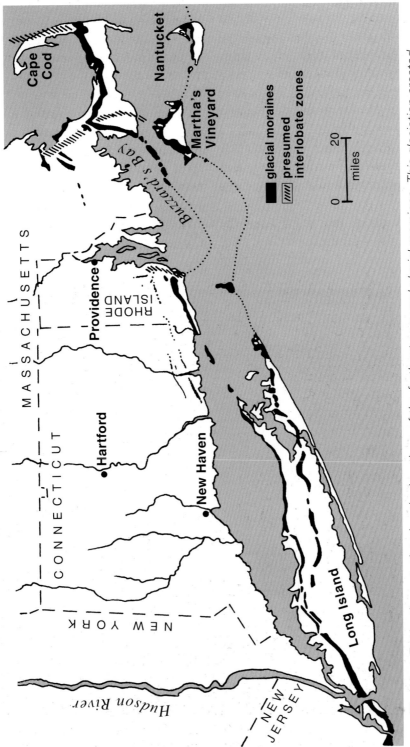

The New England coast, showing the locations of the farthest seaward glacial moraines. This glaciation created the vacation islands of Nantucket and Martha's Vineyard. —Modified from Flint, 1971, and Nilsson, 1983

glacial moraines
presumed interlobate zones

0   20
miles

more fossilized remains of herbivores than of carnivores. Also, as the glaciers retreated, the grasses and small plants that the animals favored quickly established themselves along the margins of retreating glaciers, before forests could get a toehold. So, herbivores might have congregated to feed near freshly deglaciated ground. Finally, should an animal die along a glacial margin, glacial debris would quickly bury, and thus preserve, the animal's remains before local carnivores could scavenge the animal.

Behind the glacial moraines, once the glaciers melted, lay a landscape littered with debris that glaciers had eroded and then dumped. Geologists call such glacial deposits till, drift, or ground moraine.

The melting ice sheets commonly left behind a hummocky countryside with lots of ponds, swamps, erratic boulders, and disrupted drainage patterns. The tens of thousands of lakes in the upper midwestern and northeastern United States and much of Canada are products of the ice ages, as are the "haystack" rocks—enormous erratics of basalt—that cover north-central Washington State.

While glaciers buried some areas in glacial drift, they severely eroded other areas. Glaciers ground over bedrock, plucking rocks that then embedded in the base of the ice

Gravel and other materials cover the Mount Hayes glacier in Alaska. Melting glaciers at the end of the Pleistocene epoch deposited such debris, known as glacial till or ground moraine, offering geological clues as to their size and movements. —Ian Lange photo

sheet. As the ice moved, those embedded rocks subsequently scraped grooves in and polished the underlying rock. The generally southward-flowing glaciers significantly deepened many north-south trending valleys, including Lake Michigan and the Finger Lakes of New York.

Elsewhere, the huge glaciers altered preglacial drainage patterns, forcing rivers south of the ice margins into new and sometimes permanent channels. The entire Great Lakes system experienced various changes in drainage direction. Glaciers modified the drainages of almost every river in Canada and those in the United States north of the southern limit of the ice. In New England, the glaciers affected such rivers as the Kennebec and Penobscot in Maine, the Merrimack in New Hampshire and Massachusetts, and most of the small streams in New Hampshire and Vermont. Farther west, the ice sheets shifted the upper reaches of the Mississippi River, the Missouri River in Montana and South Dakota, and the Columbia River in Washington. Together with the Yellowstone and Little Missouri Rivers, in Montana the Missouri River apparently flowed north into Canada and then east into Hudson Bay prior to glaciation. Now the three rivers are tributaries of the Mississippi River, which empties into the Gulf of Mexico. Not all rivers changed course during glacial times, though. Today the Connecticut River and the Hudson River in New York probably follow drainage patterns similar to those of preglacial times.

Crustal Depression and Rebound

We know about the surface erosion the glaciers caused and deposits the glaciers left behind, but what, if anything, did the great mass of ice do to the earth's crust beneath the ice? Researchers estimate that the largest ice sheet of the Pleistocene world was centered over northern North America and inundated approximately 6,176,000 square miles (16,000,000 square kilometers). It formed by the coalescence of the Laurentide glacier that developed over Labrador and the Ungava region of northern Quebec, the Keewatin ice cap centered northwest of Hudson Bay, and the Cordilleran ice sheet that originated in the Rocky Mountains of western Canada. This enormous ice sheet probably also connected to the nearly 900,000 square miles (2,300,000 square kilometers) of ice on Greenland. Northern Europe had an ice cap covering 2,586,200 square miles (6,700,000 square kilometers). By comparison, Antarctica presently has 5,326,800 square miles (13,800,000 square kilometers) of ice that is more than 13,000 feet (3,950 meters) thick in places.

Geologists have learned that the tremendous weight of the ice actually depressed the crust. Since the glaciers melted, the crust has rebounded, often in lurches, triggering earthquakes in New England, southcentral Canada, and northern Europe. This upwarping following deglaciation demonstrates that the earth's crust is elastic.

How do the dynamics of crustal depression and subsequent rebound work? The crust is stronger than the underlying mantle because it is cooler and therefore more rigid. The weight of the ice pushes the crust beneath it into the mantle, and the mantle material flows away. After the glacier melts, the crust rebounds, and the mantle material flows back beneath it. A time lag between the ice's melting and total crustal rebound allows scientists to measure amounts and rates of crustal rebound. An ice sheet 3 miles (4.8 kilometers)

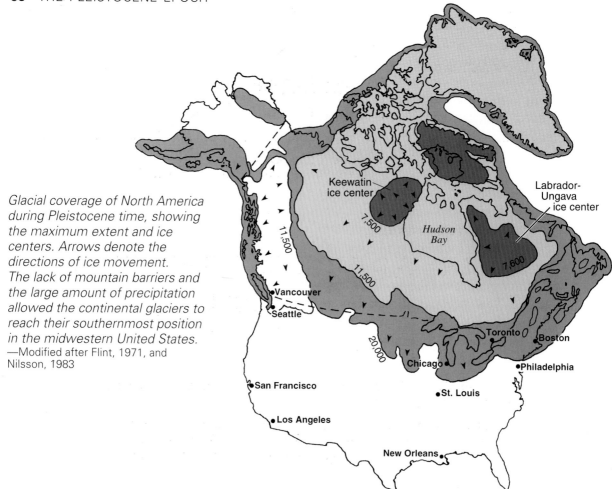

Glacial coverage of North America during Pleistocene time, showing the maximum extent and ice centers. Arrows denote the directions of ice movement.
The lack of mountain barriers and the large amount of precipitation allowed the continental glaciers to reach their southernmost position in the midwestern United States.
—Modified after Flint, 1971, and Nilsson, 1983

thick should cause the elastic crust beneath it to subside up to 1 mile (1.6 kilometers) to accommodate the ice mass.

Glaciers and the Earth's Elastic Crust

Yale professor Richard Foster Flint (1902–1976), considered to be the "dean" of North American glacial geology, studied crustal rebound associated with deglaciation. Flint found that the amount of crustal rebound correlated directly with the

thickness of ice formerly over an area: the thicker the ice was, the greater the rebound.

In Fennoscandia (Finland and Scandinavia), measurements of emerged former shorelines (strandlines) prove the region has been rising for the last 10,000 years. Estimates based on uplifted marine deposits and strandlines indicate that Fennoscandia has already rebounded at least 1,610 feet (520 meters) and that rebound will cease with approximately another 690 feet (210 meters). These uplift

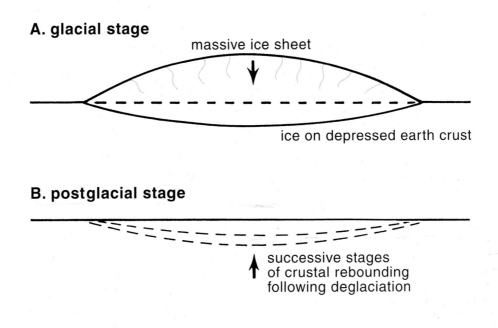

A. glacial stage

massive ice sheet

ice on depressed earth crust

B. postglacial stage

successive stages
of crustal rebounding
following deglaciation

A. *A massive, continent-sized ice sheet depresses the crust beneath it (illustration not to scale).*

B. *Following deglaciation, the elastic nature of the crust allows the depressed surface to rebound in stages until it nearly reaches its original elevation. Rebound is most rapid just following deglaciation.*

values led European geophysicist Erkki Niskanen to estimate that the ice sheet over Fennoscandia reached a maximum thickness of 8,200 feet (2,650 meters).

Northeastern North America also experienced domelike uplift during the last 10,000 years, but the huge size of the affected area and the paucity of strandlines provide less complete data than exist for Fennoscandia.

What were the implications of crustal rebound for Pleistocene animals? In many places, lakes existed in the depressed regions before complete deglaciation and significant glacial rebound. Animals probably favored habitat near the edges of these lakes, where food and fresh water were readily available. Conversely, rising sea level that immediately followed the retreat of the glaciers would have submerged some deglaciated coastal areas, making them unavailable to land animals. Those coastal areas rose above sea level once the rate of crustal rebound exceeded the rate of sea level rise.

PLEISTOCENE ANIMAL COMMUNITIES

Generally, the farther back in time earth scientists probe, the less information they can find about the rocks and the types and habitats of the plants and animals that lived then. Geological processes such as floods, changing sea level, volcanic eruptions, rock weathering, erosion, and sediment deposition rapidly remove or obscure traces of ancient plants and animals. Fortunately, these processes sometimes, though rarely, preserve plant and animal remains. (See the sidebar "Preservation: An Unlikely Fate" in Chapter 5 on page 170 for methods of preservation; see the sidebar "Special Fossil Sites" in Chapter 5 on page 76 for classic examples of preservation.) Researchers learn more about Pleistocene animal communities as different types of earth scientists probe into the geological record.

Scientists usually place the beginning of the Pleistocene epoch at the end of the Blancan and beginning of the Irvingtonian Land Mammal Age, or approximately 1.8 million years ago. The accompanying table lists some of the significant animals, or "key players," that came and went within the Blancan, Irvingtonian, and Rancholabrean Land Mammal Ages. Some of the animals, such as Jefferson's ground sloths and Columbian mammoths, ranged far and wide across North America; other beasts had much more restricted ranges. But we base our knowledge of the ranges of different animals mainly on where remains have been found. As more remains are found, our understanding of an animal's Ice Age range increases. Tomorrow, for example, someone might find the fossilized bones of a woolly mammoth in Mexico, which would tell us that this big fellow lived over a much larger and more southerly area than formerly thought.

During Pleistocene time, and especially during glacial episodes, the vegetation growing in any particular area of North America was probably different from that growing there today. Studies of pollen, seeds, and spores from plants and trees show that grasslands, steppes, tundra, deserts, and expanses of glacial outwash expanded at the expense of forested regions. Grasslands and steppes can sustain much higher densities of herbivores, and therefore carnivores, than forests or tundra can. And thick ice sheets buried almost all of Canada and large parts of the northern United States during glacial maxima. Ice-free areas in northern North American included Beringia (northeast Siberia eastward into central Alaska), Yukon, and the Northwest Territories. The north-south ice-free corridor opened periodically and allowed both plants and animals to migrate either north or south.

So what were the Pleistocene animal communities like? Clearly, the hardier animals could inhabit the more northerly regions and the more heat-tolerant creatures stayed south of the glacial margins. Perhaps one can imagine the communities formerly living on the grasslands, steppes, and, in some cases, tundra by visiting some of these areas today. For example, the north slope of the Brooks Range in Alaska is home to some 300,000 caribou, and the big east African game parks such as the Serengeti have huge herds of grazing animals with predators ever near. Alternatively, one can read about the animals that Lewis and Clark encountered two hundred years ago—the vast

The animal community of the mammoth steppe included animals still extant today, such as the gray wolf (Canis lupus), *seen here menacing a steppe bison calf (Bison priscus). In the* background humans encounter a group of woolly mammoths (Mammuthus primigenius).

Late Pliocene and Pleistocene Land Mammal Age Communities in North America*

Appearances of Some Important Animal Genera and Species

RANCHOLABREAN LAND MAMMAL AGE
(between 300,000 and 150,000 to 10,000 years ago) [†]

Bison *(Bison)* appearance marks beginning of the Rancholabrean LMA
Woolly mammoth *(M. primigenius)*—approximately 100,000 years ago
Caribou *(Rangifer)*
Mountain Goats *(Oreamnos)*
Sheep *(Ovis)*
Moose *(Alces)*
Musk oxen *(Symbos)*
Dire wolves *(Canis dirus)*
Humans *(Homo)*

IRVINGTONIAN LAND MAMMAL AGE
(1.9 million to about 300,000 to 150,000 years ago) [‡]

***Mammuthus meridionalis* appearance marks beginning of the Irvingtonian LMA**
Comumbian mammoth *(Mammuthus columbi)*—late Irvingtonian
Hares *(Lepus)*
Jaguar *(Panthera)*
Shrub oxen *(Euceratherium)*—or late Blancan
Some muskrat species *(Ondatra)*
Some kangaroo rat species *(Dipodomys)*
Saber-toothed cats *(Smilodon)*—or late Blancan

Blancan taxa absent in the Irvingtonian LMA include:
Hyenas *(Chasmaporthetes)*
Some dog species *(Borophagus)*
Gazelle-horses *(Nannippus)*
Some rabbit species *(Hypolagus)*
Approximately 50% of animal species living in late
    Irvingtonian are still alive

BLANCAN LAND MAMMAL AGE
(3.5 to 1.9 million years ago)

The Pliocene epoch begins 5 million years ago, coincident with the start of the Blancan LMA

Mastodon *(Mammut)*
Deer *(Odocoileus)*
Voles *(Pliophenacomys)*
Some gopher species *(Geomys)*
Some ground sloth species *(Paramylodon)*
Glyptodonts *(Glyptotherium)*
Pronghorns *(Tetrameryx)*
Florida cave bears *(Tremarctos floridanus)*

Sources: Kurten and Anderson, 1980; Salvage and Russell, 1983; Woodburne and Swisher, 1995.

* Beginning and most ending dates for land mamamal ages are not exactly known

† Of the 133 genera of land mammals recognized in the Rancholabrean LMA, 34 were new appearances, 10 of which, mainly bats and rodents, came from South America, with 16 being Asian immigrants. Eighty-four of the 311 species, and 39 of the 133 genera (29%) are extinct.

‡ Of the 119 genera of land mammals recognized in the Irvingtonian LMA, 41 were new appearances, 20 of which came from South or Central America. At least 32 genera came from Asia. Nineteen percent of the genera were extinct by the Rancholabrean LMA. Thirty-six percent of Blancan genera were extinct by the Irvingtonian LMA.

herds of bison, estimated to have numbered 70 million, and elk grazing the grasslands of the western states. The view then might have resembled that during Pleistocene time but without sloths, mammoths, saber-toothed cats, and many other Ice Age species that are no longer with us.

The steppes of central Alaska, presently forested, supported herds of caribou, with grizzlies and wolves running after them. Also ranging over the grasslands were small herds of yaks and musk oxen and extinct species of bison. There were solitary American mastodons, flat-headed peccaries, groups of woolly mammoths, and Jefferson's ground sloths. American lions, saber-toothed cats, and giant short-faced bears hunted these animals.

Farther west, animals inhabited the huge area of Beringia, about twice the size of Texas. Scientists disagree over how nourishing the vegetation growing there was and, so, how many animals could have flourished there. Drill cores into the now-submerged portion of Beringia reveal fossil pollen and spores of highly nutritious sagebrush and grasses, plus the less beneficial shrub birch, sedges, and sphagnum moss. One camp of scientists thinks that at least central and southern Beringia was a highly productive region of dry grassland or steppe, whereas the northern part was a water-logged tundra. The other camp thinks that less nutritious tundra plants covered most of Beringia, leaving it incapable of supporting vast herds of animals.

About 16,000 years ago in what is now the continental United States, lakes, marshes, bogs, and parklike spruce and poplar forests covered the very recently deglaciated areas of what is now northern Minnesota and Wisconsin. Farther south, grasslands covered the landscape. Various studies, including FAUNMAP, provide much of this information. FAUNMAP is a huge electronic database of information collected by the Illinois State Museum. FAUNMAP amassed data from more than 2,920 sites in the lower forty-eight states spanning 40,000 years. The region encompasses the eastern Dakotas east to the Appalachian Mountains and south to northern Tennessee, Arkansas, and southern Missouri. You can view the FAUNMAP website and learn about what went on during late Pleistocene time.

The extinct animals that lived in the region FAUNMAP covers included horses, tapirs, woolly and Jefferson's or Columbian mammoths, Jefferson's and Harlan's ground sloths, both the woodland and modern musk oxen, flat-headed and long-nosed peccaries, saber-toothed and scimitar cats, and dire wolves. Along the southern part of the region beautiful armadillos and giant jaguars roamed.

The northern Great Plains grasslands supported herds of pronghorns, horses such as the giant horse, bison including giant bison, elk milling around with groups of Columbian and Jefferson's mammoths, and Jefferson's and Shasta ground sloths. These creatures tried to avoid becoming dinner for the ever-present American lions, saber-toothed cats, giant short-faced bears, and gray and dire wolves. Shrub and musk oxen also roamed parts of what is now the northern tier of states as far west as Montana.

A variety of animals inhabited the southwestern states. In particular, studies reveal that the Colorado Plateau, a high region cut by the Colorado River encompassing northeastern Arizona, northwestern New Mexico, southwestern Colorado, and eastern Utah, was covered with grassland and sagebrush uplands with birch, spruce, and shrubs growing along creeks. Animals having a wonderful life in this upland region included Columbian mammoths, American mastodons, Shasta and Harlan's ground sloths, musk and shrub oxen, Yesterday's and giant Nebraska camels, horses, Merriam's tapirs, bison, giant short-faced bears, American lions, and saber-toothed cats, plus the presently living and—by modern standards—less exotic inhabitants.

The woodlands and meadows of the northeastern United States contained mastodons, ground sloths, bison, bears, wolves, and probably saber-toothed cats and American lions.

The southeastern states were home to bears, including the Florida cave bear, cats, wolves, lions, mastodons, giant armadillos, glyptodonts, and Jefferson's and Harlan's ground sloths. Horses ranged the grasslands.

Wandering the open country of the south-central United States and northern Mexico were several species of horses; Harlan's, Jefferson's, and *Eremotherium* ground sloths; camels and llamas; Jefferson's mammoths; giant armadillos; dire wolves; giant short-faced bears; and American lions and saber-toothed cats.

References: FAUNMAP; Kurten and Anderson, 1980; Nelson, 1990; Voorhies, 1994

Global Climate Patterns

Since the discovery of the ice ages, scientists have sought to understand what the earth was like then. In the 1970s, a consortium of scientists from many institutions undertook just such a study. The purposes of the project, known as CLIMAP, were to estimate global climate change over the past million years and to reconstruct the surface of the earth at particular times in the past. The initial effort simulated global climate during an average August 21,000 years ago, when Wisconsinan continental glaciers were close to their maximum extent.

To simulate the August climate, the scientists needed to know the geography of the continents, the extent and configuration of glacial ice, the reflectivity of solar radiation from land and ice surfaces, and sea-surface temperature patterns. Researchers based the land configurations on a globally prominent wave-cut beach strandline 265 feet (85 meters) below present sea level. The old shoreline exists along generally tectonically stable continental coasts such as the east coasts of South America and Australia.

The scientists derived the extent of permanent sea ice by analyzing cores of Pleistocene sediment at the bottom of the northern and southern oceans. Sediment deposited during interglacial times contains the siliceous microscopic organisms diatoms and radiolaria. During glacial times, sea ice inhibited growth of diatoms and radiolaria. Knowing the extent of the sea ice, researchers could then calculate measurements of solar reflectivity and global sea-surface temperatures.

CLIMAP scientists measured the temperature of the sea's surface by analyzing ocean-bottom cores that contained coccoliths, foraminifera, and radiolaria, all microscopic animals that live on the ocean's surface. The oxygen isotopic ratio in these animals' shells and skeletons provide information about the relative surface temperature of the oceans. Carbon-14 age dating of organic material in the cores revealed detailed age relationships between the various ocean core sites. Construction of a temperature contour map of the oceans followed the compilation of data from 247 collection sites

Results of this and other land-based studies show that grasslands, deserts, steppes, and glacial outwash regions expanded during Pleistocene time at the expense of forested regions. These dramatic changes in habitats, particularly increased grassland and steppe environments, greatly benefitted grazing animals with the rich food value of the plants growing there. Glaciation and permanent pack ice in the Northern Hemisphere were the most striking features of the world 21,000 years ago. Glacial ice covered most of northern North America and significant portions of northwestern Eurasia. Pack and shelf ice covered large areas of the North Atlantic Ocean between North America and Europe. Perhaps surprisingly, the entire northernmost parts of the Northern Hemisphere were not under glacial ice—large areas of central Alaska and Siberia were ice-free, as those areas lacked sufficient precipitation to sustain ice sheets.

Permanent sea ice insulated the North Atlantic Ocean and greatly reduced heat loss there. Masses of dense, cold water that today form at the surface, sink to the bottom, and flow south were diminished. The warm, relatively saline Gulf Stream, which originates in the Gulf of Mexico, shifted its course southward across the North Atlantic Ocean east to Spain, rather than continuing northeast toward Norway. The result was a rapid decrease in temperature northward, or a steep thermal gradient, near the northern boundary of the

current. Therefore central and northern Europe were much cooler than they are today.

In the northern Pacific Ocean, there was only a small southward shift and steepening of the temperature gradient. Land exposed by the lower sea level blocked Arctic Ocean water from flowing south into the Bering Sea. That resulted in less cooling in that region compared with the same latitude in the North Atlantic Ocean.

In the Southern Hemisphere, sea ice covered a larger area than it does today, but land-based glaciers in the Southern Hemisphere covered only slightly more area than they do today. There was also a shift to the north of cold Antarctic weather.

Middle-latitude oceans of 21,000 years ago showed only slight differences in temperature and circulation when compared with those of today. But differences did exist. For example, cool-water-loving radiolaria, now found off the coast of Washington, Oregon, and northern California, lived as much as 600 miles (1,000 kilometers) farther south. The southward penetration of cold water accompanying the south-flowing current along the west coast extended the range of these microscopic animals.

Except in a few places, such as the subtropical parts of the eastern North Pacific and eastern North Atlantic, low latitude or equatorial oceans were cooler than they are today. The increased upwelling of cool, nutrient-laden bottom water off the west coasts of both Africa and South America resulted in surface water temperatures as much as 11 degrees Fahrenheit (6 degrees Celsius) cooler than found there today. CLIMAP researchers theorized that a change in water temperature of this magnitude would have had a major effect on the geographical distribution of phytoplankton, with the more cold-tolerant species expanding

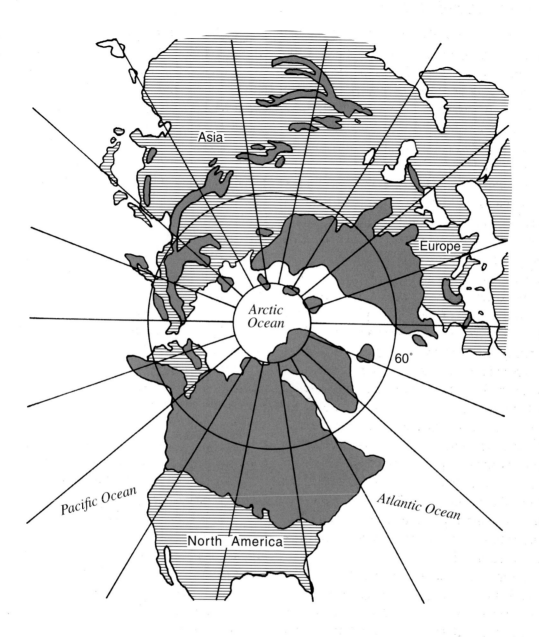

Map of the maximum extent of glacial coverage in the Northern Hemisphere during Pleistocene time. Note the lack of continental glaciation in the very cold lowlands of eastern Siberia and central Alaska and the northeast-trending maximum extent of glaciation from western Europe into Russia. These distributions of ice were a function of precipitation necessary to sustain glaciers. —Modified from Antevs, 1929, and Judson et al., 1987

their ranges and those less tolerant of cold water contracting theirs. Those changes in the distribution of phytoplankton would have directly affected the many animals that depend on this basal part of the food chain. In the western Pacific Ocean, Gulf of Mexico, and Caribbean Sea, surface water temperatures were probably less than 3.6 degrees Fahrenheit (2 degrees Celsius) cooler than today. Overall, the average worldwide temperature of surface water has been estimated at about 4.7 degrees Fahrenheit (2.6 degrees Celsius) less than it is today.

On land during the glacial maximum, the average annual temperature in Greenland was as much as 29 degrees Fahrenheit (16 degrees Celsius) cooler and the tropics were 7 degrees Fahrenheit (4 degrees Celsius) cooler than they are today. Mountain snow lines, the lower limit of snow melt at the end of summer melt season, decreased by 2,950 feet (900 meters) compared with today.

The worldwide drop in sea level exposed more coastal land in North America, particularly along the east coast, to animals and humans. The lowered sea level also connected land that seawater now separates, allowing greater distribution of animals and plants. However, the continental glaciers greatly restricted habitable environments in northern temperate and polar regions for both animals and humans.

The world of 21,000 years ago, then, was vastly different and in places unrecognizable compared to today's world. The cooler climate extended both mountain and ice-sheet glaciation. Grasslands spread at the expense of forested habitats, and sea level dropped to expose more coastland. All these changes, of course, affected the distribution of humans and other animals during the Ice Age.

References: Agassiz, 1837; Alt, 2001; Alt and Hyndman, 1995; Antevs, 1929; Baker, 1995; Bernhardi, 1832; Bretz, 1923; Bretz et al., 1956; Broecker, 1999; Chambers, 1971; CLIMAP, 1976, 1981; Flint, 1957; Forbes, 1846; Gates, 1976; Geikie, 1863; Imbrie and Imbrie, 1979; Jamieson, 1865; Kurten and Anderson, 1980; McDonald and Buscacca, 1988; Morrison, 1991; Nilsson, 1983; Niskanen, 1939; O'Connor and Baker, 1992; Pardee, 1910, 1922; Saussure, 1787; Stanley, 1986; Strahler, 1971; Venetz, 1829; Waitt, 1987

4

WHY THE ICE AGES?

What causes ice ages? This is the most profound yet the most basic question in our understanding of the evolution and extinction of species in the Pleistocene epoch. Scientists have painted a vivid picture of what the world was like during the last great Ice Age, but what caused the series of major glacial advances and retreats during Pleistocene time? The basic mechanism is simple: for glaciers to form, more snow must accumulate during the winter months than melts during the summer. If glaciers gain more snow in the cold months than they lose in the warm months, they thicken, expand, and advance. If the reverse situation prevails, the glaciers thin, retreat, and eventually disappear. However, the causes underlying this basic mechanism are far more complex.

To pinpoint the causes of the ice ages, researchers must consider interactions between many variables. These include both short-term and long-term variations in solar radiation, variations in Earth's orbit around the Sun, configurations and elevations of the continental landmasses relative to latitude and oceans, compositional changes in Earth's atmosphere, and even volcanic activity. And the list goes on from there.

It is almost impossible to get reliable long-range weather forecasts today, let alone look back thousands or millions of years to explain climatic cooling and warming then. Still, researchers have proposed many theories to explain these astounding times. Of these, no single hypothesis has gained the general acceptance of most scientists. The theories for what causes ice ages fall into two broad categories: those that are external to Earth and those that are Earth-related.

External Causes for Ice Ages

The main theories for external causes of the ice ages include variation in solar output, the Milankovitch or orbital forcing theory, and changes in amounts of interplanetary dust.

VARIATIONS IN SOLAR RADIATION

One intuitively reasonable idea for what causes ice ages concerns variations in the amount of radiation our sun produces. We know that 11-year sunspot cycles cause short-term variations in solar radiation. During these times, solar storms erupt on the Sun's surface. These storms, which last for days to weeks, cause visible dark spots 500 to 50,000 miles (800 km to 80,000 km) across on the Sun's surface and disrupt radio transmission on Earth. The storms cool the Sun's surface and consequently allow slightly less heat to reach Earth's surface. But does the Sun go through periods of high or low solar output that last tens of thousands of years or more? We do not know. Large variations in solar output are probably not necessary to spawn an ice age, though. A decline in average annual world temperature of perhaps only 5 to 9 degrees Fahrenheit (3 to 5 degrees Celsius) from today's average temperature would initiate another major ice age.

THE MILANKOVITCH CYCLES

We know the Pleistocene epoch was not unique in its ice ages. The geologic record shows major advances of glaciers in both the northern and southern hemispheres since the Cambrian period, 570 million years ago. Within these ice ages appear to be episodes of glacial advance and retreat over roughly 40,000-year cycles. Several factors acting simultaneously seem to influence the waxing and waning of

The upper end of a glacier in the Alaska Range. The glacier originates in a cirque, a high-walled basin, and flows into the valley below. —Ian Lange photo

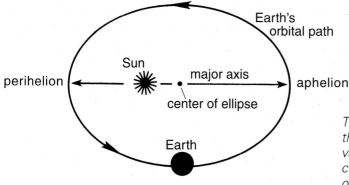

perihelion ← | → aphelion

Sun — major axis

center of ellipse

Earth's orbital path

Earth

The shape of Earth's orbital path around the Sun today is an ellipse. However, it varies in approximately 100,000-year cycles from almost a circle to an ellipse of greater eccentricity than occurs today.

glacial ice. In 1875, Scottish geologist James Croll postulated that variations in Earth's orbital motion around the Sun along with variations in Earth's axial tilt were responsible for variation in the total amount of solar energy reaching Earth's surface. Beginning in 1930, Milutin Milankovitch, a Serbian astronomer and geophysicist, expanded upon Croll's earlier hypotheses. Milankovitch's hypothesis considered three variable quasi-cyclic components acting together over thousands of years that provided cyclic changes in the heat energy budget of Earth. These involved secular changes in the eccentricity of Earth's orbit, the tilt of Earth's axis, and a wobbling of Earth's axis, called precession. One additional quasi-cyclic component that acts with the others is the gyration of the major axis of Earth's orbit.

Changes in Earth's Orbital Eccentricity

Earth's orbit around the Sun is an ellipse. Since the Sun is not in the center of the ellipse, Earth's distance from the Sun varies over the course of each year, moving closest to the Sun in January and farthest from it in July. Astronomers generally describe the ellipticity or eccentricity of an orbit as a number

without units that varies between an eccentricity of 0, which describes a circle, to an eccentricity of 1, which describes a straight line. The current eccentricity of Earth's orbit, 0.017, is very close to a circle. The difference between Earth's closest point to the Sun, its perihelion, and its farthest distance from the Sun, its aphelion, amounts to only about 3,000,000 miles—which is only 3 percent of Earth's total orbital distance. Thus, Earth's current annual variation in distance from the Sun is not large enough to affect the climate on Earth. But other planets that orbit in nearly the same plane as Earth's orbit exert gravitational forces upon Earth that change Earth's orbit from a circle with an eccentricity of 0 to an ellipse of 0.067 eccentricity. The largest eccentricity is four times the current value, which amounts to an annual change in distance from the Sun of more than 12,000,000 miles. Such a change would certainly affect the climate of Earth. In the great landmasses of the Northern Hemisphere, where glaciers are most likely to form, the climate changes would be most severe—hotter at perihelion and colder at aphelion. Researchers think these changes in orbital eccentricity and, thus, Earth's climate, occur over a 100,000-year period.

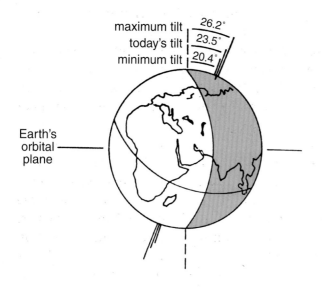

maximum tilt 26.2°
today's tilt 23.5°
minimum tilt 20.4°

Earth's orbital plane

The axis of rotation of Earth is presently tilted at approximately 23.5 degrees in relation to the plane in which Earth revolves around the Sun.

The Variable Tilt of Earth's Axis

The second variation involves the tilt of Earth's axis. Presently, Earth's rotational axis tilts 23.45 degrees with respect to a vertical line drawn perpendicular to its orbital plane (the plane of the Solar System). This angle has varied cyclically from 20.4 degrees to 26.2 degrees. Today, Earth's axis tilts at an angle almost exactly at the midpoint between the two extremes, and that tilt is decreasing at the rate of 0.01 degree per century. This effect is cyclic over a period of about 41,000 years. A greater axial tilt brings increasingly more severe winters and summers, while a lesser tilt tends to produce less pronounced seasons. If the angle diminished to zero, short-term seasonal variations would essentially vanish.

Variations in Earth's orbital eccentricity and variations in the tilt of Earth's axis operate simultaneously and can produce extremely hot summers or very cold winters in both the Northern and Southern Hemispheres, with the greatest effect in the Northern Hemisphere, where landmasses more easily accumulate snow. For example, if Earth's orbital eccentricity

reached a maximum that brought Earth more than 6 million miles closer to the Sun during the Northern Hemisphere's summer and, at the same time, Earth's axis is tilted its maximum of 26.2 degrees toward the Sun, the Northern Hemisphere would experience very hot summers while the Southern Hemisphere would experience very harsh, cold winters. The situation would inevitably reverse itself in time, producing hot southern summers and very cold northern winters.

Precession of Earth's Axis

Another cyclic effect known since ancient times is the wobbling, or precession, of Earth's axis. Gravitational perturbations by the Sun and the Moon on the equatorial bulge of Earth cause Earth's axis to slowly wobble in a clockwise direction. Earth's axis retains its 23.5-degree inclination with respect to its orbit as it gyrates. If Earth were not rotating, the effect would be to pull Earth's equator into the plane of its orbit around the Sun. In other words, the Earth's axis would straighten perpendicular to its orbital plane. This does not happen, however, because the rotating Earth acts as a spinning gyroscope, resisting the tidal forces of the Sun and Moon. Instead, those forces create a slow, clockwise gyration of the rotation axis. This is much like the slow wobble, or precession, of a spinning top superimposed over its spinning motion. Unlike a top that slowly gives way to Earth's pull of gravity, spinning more slowly as it wobbles more widely, Earth retains its spin, and its axis simply gyrates, retaining the 23.5-degree inclination of its axis. It scribes one complete gyration in 26,000 years.

During this 26,000-year wobble, Earth's axis points to different stars along the way, giving each a turn as Earth's north star. Polaris is today's north star, situated less than a degree from the true north celestial pole. Almost five thousands years ago when the Egyptian pyramids were being built, a star called Thuban, the brightest star in the constellation Draco, was Earth's north star. Two thousand years ago, when Greek civilization was at its summit, Thuban had wandered from the pole position. There was no bright star to mark the pole in the sky. Some 12,000 years from now, the bright star Vega will take the honors, coming within 5 degrees of the true north celestial pole.

Precession also slowly changes the positions of the stars with respect to the seasons. Today we are used to seeing the constellation Orion rising in the early evening around the winter solstice. About 13,000 years from now, with Vega near the pole, the rising of Orion will mark the first day of summer. This is because the positions of the equinox and solstice precess along Earth's orbit at the same time Earth's polar axis is precessing. This is referred to as the precession of the equinoxes. Today, winter in the Northern Hemisphere occurs when Earth is at perihelion. This tends to moderate Northern Hemisphere winters. But 13,000 years from now, winter will occur

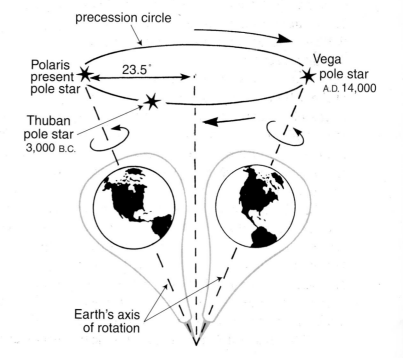

Because the axis of Earth's rotation wobbles like that of a spinning top as the top slows, the axis points to different places in the heavens over a cycle of about 26,000 years. For the ancient Egyptians, Thuban was the north star. The star we currently call the north star, Polaris, will eventually be replaced, and Vega will take a turn at indicating the north celestial pole.

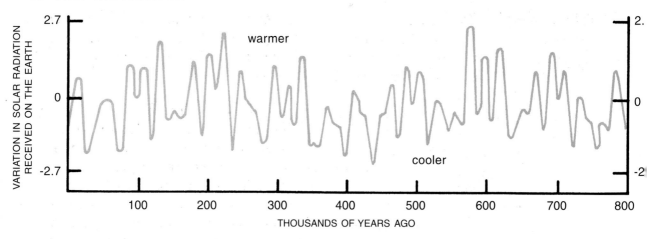

VARIATION IN SOLAR RADIATION RECEIVED ON THE EARTH

THOUSANDS OF YEARS AGO

The variations through time of Earth's orbital motions result in the eccentricity-precession-tilt or the Milankovitch curve. The curve shows the variation in how much of the Sun's heat reaches Earth. Higher values correspond to warmer times; lower values correspond to cooler periods. —Modified from Skinner and Porter, 1995

in the Northern Hemisphere when Earth is at aphelion. This will make winters in the Northern Hemisphere much colder, possibly cold enough to favor increased snowfall and the growth of glaciers.

The 26,000-year precession cycle is somewhat counteracted by another effect working in the opposite direction. Gravitational perturbations by other planets on Earth's orbit not only change its eccentricity over a 100,000-year cycle but also slowly rotate the major axis of Earth's elliptical orbit. The major axis skews eastward, opposite the precession direction. The interaction of the precession of the equinoxes westward and the eastward skewing of the major axis of Earth's elliptical orbit effectively shortens the absolute precession cycle from 26,000 years to two dominant cycles: one every 19,000 years and another every 23,000 years.

In summary, these cycles all occur simultaneously, all superimposed and interacting in

complex ways. Milankovitch developed mathematical solutions that demonstrated the effects of these cycles on Earth's changing climate over millions of years. All these variable factors with their different quasi-cyclic periods change the amount of solar radiation Earth receives by as much as 10 percent over a period of perhaps 40,000 years. The Milankovitch cycles, as they are now called, have a greater climatological effect in the Northern Hemisphere where most of Earth's landmass is located. Here, given the right combinations of cycles, glaciers can build up over thousands of years. The geologic record seems to imply that major periods of cooling occur approximately every 250 million years. Within this enormous span of time glacial cycles seem to appear about every 40,000 years.

Even though orbital variations appear to be of fundamental importance, recent work shows that glacial advances vary more than predicted by orbital forces alone.

INTERPLANETARY DUST

Some researchers contend that the Milankovitch theory works well for the early, relatively short, and less intense Pleistocene glacial advances that ended about 1 million years ago but that it does not adequately explain the last ten major glaciations, each starting about 100,000 years apart. These scientists postulate that the 100,000-year timing relates to the periodic slight tilt of about 2.5 degrees of the plane of Earth's orbit with respect to the orbits of the other planets. They propose that during these times of tilting, Earth moves through a region of denser interplanetary dust. The dust blocks some solar radiation from reaching Earth's surface.

Support for the theory comes from studies of sea-floor sediments. Within the sediments the amount of the isotope helium 3, a tracer of extraterrestrial dust, increases and then decreases over 100,000 year cycles. Furthermore, the amount of helium 3 in the sediments dramatically increased between 2 million and 1 million years ago. But why did the amount of extraterrestrial dust in that region of the solar system change? One idea is that large asteroids collided about 1 million years ago and produced large clouds of dust in the inner solar system.

Skeptics contend, however, that the variations in the amount of dust are too small to have influenced Earth's climate. Also, scientists do not understand well how interplanetary dust affects Earth's climate.

Earth-Related Causes for Ice Ages

Some of the more interesting Earth-related theories for what causes ice ages include changing configurations of continents, changing atmospheric compositions, volcanism, the ice-free Arctic Ocean theory, massive releases of icebergs into the North Atlantic Ocean, high elevations of continental landmasses, and human activities.

CONFIGURATIONS OF CONTINENTAL LANDMASSES

Periods of continental glaciation have been the exceptions to the average global climatic conditions during the last several billion years. The earth has experienced only four episodes of continental glaciation, the most recent during the Pleistocene epoch. During most of the earth's history, broad, open oceans likely covered the polar regions. Seawater circulated unrestricted, allowing warm water from equatorial regions to flow toward the poles and moderate the cooler polar seawater. However, landmasses near polar regions would prevent warm currents from reaching the existing polar seas. This would allow glaciers to form at high latitudes on parts of continents. The configuration of continental landmasses and their latitudinal locations near the poles must have played a major role in the formation of continental glaciers.

About 3.5 million years ago, North and South America became connected. Although this configuration predated the beginning of the Pleistocene epoch, the connection clearly affected oceanic circulation patterns and, according to paleontologist Steve Stanley, may have triggered the Pleistocene ice ages. He reasons that prior to the formation of the Isthmus of Panama, relatively saline and warm water from the Atlantic Ocean flowed into the Pacific Ocean while, beneath this current, less salty but cooler and thus denser water flowed from the Pacific Ocean to the Caribbean Sea on the Atlantic Ocean side. The result was an equalization of salinities in the Caribbean Sea

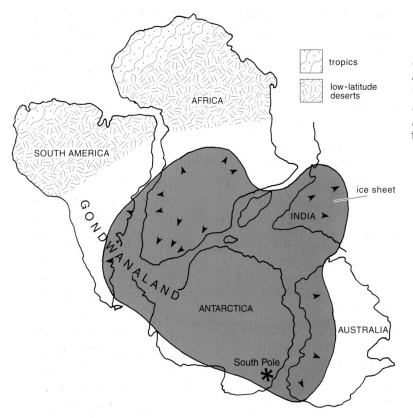

	tropics
	low-latitude deserts

Location of glacial ice and direction of ice movement over Gondwanaland with the continents of the Southern Hemisphere in their premovement, late Paleozoic positions —Modified from Holmes, 1965

and Pacific Ocean. At the same time, the Gulf Stream flowed north as the North Atlantic Current and eventually delivered its mass of relatively warm water to the Arctic Ocean.

The formation of the Isthmus of Panama halted the homogenization of Pacific and Atlantic Ocean waters on either side of the Panamanian strait. With high evaporation rates and without Pacific Ocean water to dilute it, the Gulf Stream became saltier and consequently more dense. Because of its high density and cooling during its travel northward, the Gulf Stream sank between Norway and Greenland, depriving the Arctic Ocean of relatively warm water. This may have triggered the Pleistocene ice ages. According to Stanley, the cooling of Arctic Ocean water, coupled with the Milankovitch cycles and the high

reflectivity of solar radiation from Arctic Ocean pack ice, may have been responsible for the initial cooling of the Northern Hemisphere and the start of glacial times.

Evidence for this concurrence of events includes a change in animal life on both sides of the Isthmus of Panama approximately 3 million years ago—about when the first ice-rafted debris appeared in the North Atlantic seafloor's sedimentary record. Ratios of oxygen isotopes in the siliceous shells of marine organisms also show water temperatures starting to decrease about 3.2 million years ago. Finally, a shift of both carbon and oxygen isotopes in deep-sea microorganisms such as foraminifera indicate that the Caribbean Sea started to grow saltier about 3.5 million years ago.

If we look at the present configuration of continents, which resembles the continental configuration of Pleistocene time, we see the continent of Antarctica located at the South Pole and the bulk of the remaining continental landmasses in the Northern Hemisphere ringing the Arctic Ocean. While these polar regions are cold, they do not presently receive a lot of precipitation in the form of snow—which was also the situation during the Pleistocene epoch. In fact, the nucleus of the Pleistocene ice sheets started their development at least 1,000 miles (1,600 kilometers) south of the Arctic Ocean.

CHANGES IN THE ATMOSPHERE'S COMPOSITION

Changes in the composition of the earth's atmosphere can heat or cool the earth's surface. For instance, increases in atmospheric carbon dioxide, water vapor, and methane produce the well-known greenhouse effect. These gases partially trap the long-wavelength solar radiation, or infrared heat, that has reached the earth's surface. Once caught, the heat cannot radiate back into space. The glass panes of a greenhouse or the windows of a parked car do the same thing, so that on sunny days the interior is considerably warmer than the ambient temperature outside. Conversely, decreases in the amounts of these atmospheric gases lead to global cooling.

Scientists found that atmospheric carbon dioxide concentrations changed very rapidly—in just a few thousand years—between 15,000 and 10,000 years ago as the ice sheets retreated northward. Atmospheric carbon dioxide increased from about 210 to 280 parts per million. Researchers attribute the change to deposition of the remains of organisms that contained both phosphate and carbon on the submerging continental shelves as sea level rose. The result was a reduced ratio of phosphate to carbon in the water. Phosphate is the limiting nutrient in photosynthesis, so its reduction would have impeded marine photosynthesis. Because the process of photosynthesis consumes carbon dioxide, a decrease in photosynthesis would increase carbon dioxide in both the surface seawater and the atmosphere. This could have ultimately led to global warming.

How do scientists determine the amounts of these gases in the atmosphere for past ages? One way is to analyze gas trapped in bubbles in ancient glacier ice and in amber or sap from dead and ancient, living trees. Cores from deep drill holes into the glaciers of Greenland and Antarctica show lesser amounts of both carbon dioxide and methane gases in Pleistocene ice than are present in the atmosphere today. But the low level of carbon dioxide seems to predate the expansion of the ice sheets. It appears that the lower levels of these gases can account for perhaps one-half of the global cooling that took place during Pleistocene time.

The data from glacier ice cores also demonstrate that the atmosphere contained more dust during Pleistocene time than it does today. Dust impedes the penetration of the Sun's radiation to Earth's surface, exacerbating atmospheric cooling. What increased the concentrations of atmospheric dust? It appears that the ice ages were not only cooler but also windier than now, which increased amounts of windborne dust. The dust came from arid regions and lands that droughts left barren. Other sources include dust blown away from glacial deposits and dust liberated from erupting volcanoes. Many researchers now think the increased dust in the the atmosphere was a result rather than cause of the ice ages.

VOLCANISM

Scientists have long recognized volcanic activity as a possible mechanism for causing continental glaciation. Large volcanic eruptions not only produce significant quantities of sulfur dioxide gas and the greenhouse gas carbon dioxide but also blow high into the atmosphere fine volcanic ash and acidic mist called aerosols. Both the ash and the aerosols cool the atmosphere by scattering solar energy before it reaches the earth. The effect of volcanic dust is more short-lived than that of aerosols.

Some researchers who study data from deep-sea cores believe that volcanoes were more active during the Pleistocene epoch than both before and after. Why might volcanoes have been more active? We don't know, but the ultimate cause could be increased rates of movement of the earth's lithospheric plates. Volcanism would then increase where plates spread at mid-oceanic ridges and where one plate dives beneath another along the edges of some continents. That major volcanic eruptions produce short-term atmospheric cooling is well documented. For example, the 1990 eruption of Mount Pinatubo in the Philippines lowered the average annual world temperature by about 1 degree Fahrenheit (0.5 degree Celsius) for about three years.

EWING-DONN, OR ICE-FREE ARCTIC, THEORY

The big Pleistocene ice sheets originated at high latitudes on land in the Northern Hemisphere. But these regions of northwestern Europe and north-central Canada south of the Arctic Ocean do not presently receive much yearly precipitation. So how could these areas have received enough precipitation for glaciers to form? The Ewing-Donn, or ice-free Arctic Ocean, theory provides one explanation. This theory, developed in 1956 and modified in 1966 by Maurice Ewing and William L. Donn at Lamont-Doherty Geological Observatory, goes like this.

Should the Arctic Ocean lose all or a significant part of the pack ice that covers it most of the year, evaporation over the dark water would increase significantly. This would bring increased precipitation, mainly in the form of snow, on the lands south of the ocean.

But how could the Arctic Ocean get rid of its relatively permanent pack ice, in some places dozens of feet (several meters) thick? One very convenient mechanism would be to change the course of the Gulf Stream. This river of warm water within the Atlantic Ocean originates in the Gulf of Mexico. After passing through the strait separating Florida from Cuba, the current heads northeastward along the east coast of the United States and across the Atlantic Ocean toward Norway. It then curves south along the west coast of Europe, bringing mild, wet winter weather to western Europe.

Now suppose that instead of making that curve off the coast of Norway, the Gulf Stream continued north between Iceland and Spitsbergen into the Arctic Ocean. Great volumes of warm water would be available to raise the temperature of the Arctic Ocean above the freezing point of seawater, 27 degrees Fahrenheit (-3 degrees Celsius). The Arctic Ocean could thus be freed of pack ice.

The relatively shallow (several hundred feet) depth of the ocean between Iceland, the Danish Faeroe Islands, and northern Scotland would make the process self-regulating: as the continental glaciers in western Europe and North America grew, sea level would lower to the point that exposed land would block the Gulf Stream's delivery of warm water to the Arctic Ocean. The ice pack would then re-form, and the continental glaciers would starve for snow and wither away.

A variation on this theory would be for the Gulf Stream to change direction from its present course in the North Atlantic to a more southerly, central Atlantic crossing. With this scenario, the Arctic Ocean would retain its ice pack, and the southern limit of pack ice would shift farther south, closer to the new path of the warm Gulf Stream. This would bring much cooler temperatures to western Europe and northern North America and perhaps start an ice age. The CLIMAP study of what the world was like 21,000 years ago (see Chapter 3, page 45) supports at least the idea of a more southern limit of Atlantic Ocean pack ice and a cold western Europe.

HEINRICH EVENTS

Scientists have detected a correlation between late Pleistocene glacial advances in the western United States, Chile, and elsewhere with massive discharges of icebergs into the North Atlantic Ocean from the Laurentide ice sheet, which was centered over eastern Canada. These huge floods of icebergs are called Heinrich events after German scientist Hartmut Heinrich, who discovered them while examining cores of deep-sea sediment from the North Atlantic Ocean.

There have been at least six Heinrich events over the past 60,000 years or so, with approximately 10,000 years between each episode. The events took place during or following short-term growth of the Laurentide ice sheet when the North Atlantic Ocean was coldest. Each huge flotilla of icebergs dumped a prominent layer of sediment—the ice-rafted debris— on the floor of the North Atlantic Ocean. The layers thin from 1 foot (0.33 meter) to 1 inch (2.5 centimeters) or less along the icebergs'

route between the Labrador Sea in the western Atlantic and the coast of Europe. The sand-sized fragments in the sedimentary layers contain few foraminifera shells but much limestone detritus that could only have come from northeastern Canada.

Researchers have found a striking correlation between climatic variations, iceberg armadas, and cold Atlantic Ocean water. The evidence includes the southern geographical extent of polar foraminifera, the depleted oxygen-18 isotope in foraminifera shells, and oxygen isotope data from dated Greenland ice cores. The low number of forams and low oxygen-18 values of their shells probably mean the animals grew in low-salinity seawater diluted by freshwater from the melting icebergs.

Scientists believe the surface layer of cold freshwater stopped the formation of dense, cold, salty water off the coast of southern Greenland. When heavy saltwater forms off the coast of Greenland, it sinks and flows southward along the ocean bottom, only to be replaced by warm surface water of the Gulf Stream flowing north from the tropics. This north-flowing warm water eventually warms northern Europe. Without dense saltwater, this surface-subsurface flow system would have stalled, immediately chilling northern Europe. This, in turn, could precipitate a general worldwide cooling.

Beginning about 12,000 to 11,700 years ago, another catastrophic event hit North America and northern Europe. Called the Younger Dryas, this was the last cold period before the warmer Holocene epoch of the present day. The thousand-year-long frigid period, named for a tundra flower that extended its range southward in Europe during this time, appears to have resulted from another mechanism that affected the North Atlantic Ocean.

Lake Agassiz was the largest known glacial lake to have existed in North America. The lake covered parts of present-day North Dakota, South Dakota, Minnesota, Ontario, Manitoba, and Saskatchewan. Catastrophic drainage of the lake may have veneered the western North Atlantic Ocean with enough freshwater to trigger the Younger Dryas worldwide cooling event. —Modified from Elston, 1967

About 13,000 years ago, a huge body of freshwater called Lake Agassiz existed in a glacier-depressed basin in south-central Canada, just south of the retreating ice sheet. The 96,500-square-mile (250,000-square-kilometer) lake was as much as 650 feet (200 meters) deep, but it was short-lived. The lake initially drained to the south into the Mississippi River. By about 12,000 years ago, however, the Canadian-born ice sheet had retreated far enough northward to allow for an immense, catastrophic draining of the lake eastward across central Canada through the St. Lawrence River Valley and into the Atlantic Ocean. This huge flood of freshwater onto North Atlantic saltwater had the same effect as the melting of one of the iceberg armadas. The flood appears to have initiated—or at least correlates in time with—the Younger Dryas worldwide cooling period.

Most researchers currently believe that Heinrich events occurred. But did the Heinrich events cause climatic change or merely respond to it? Did the events reflect some as yet unknown internal feature of the Laurentide ice sheet? Heinrich events evidently occurred at major climatic boundaries, but both at transitions from interglacial to glacial times and from glacial to interglacial times. Also, the 10,000-year separations of the Heinrich events are roughly equivalent to about half the length of Earth's precession cycles.

HIGH-ELEVATION LANDMASSES

Some researchers think that high-elevation landmasses in nonequatorial regions caused some significant changes in "normal" weather and may have brought on the ice ages. According to one theory, the worldwide average annual temperature started to decline about 40 million years ago—about the time India,

brought northward by plate tectonic movement from its former location as part of Gondwanaland, crashed into Asia. The collision folded and faulted the rocks, creating the India-Asia suture zone and producing the world's highest mountain range, the Himalaya.

One consequence of having elevated landmasses such as the Himalaya, Tibetan Plateau, and Andes Mountains of South America at this time was increased rates of mineral and rock weathering or in-place rock disintegration. Weathering releases large amounts of debris, including dissolved calcium, that rivers carry to the oceans. This increases the calcium concentrations in the sea. The calcium then combines with carbon dioxide and forms the mineral calcite, which makes up marine limestone. This reaction removes greater amounts of carbon dioxide than normal from the atmosphere. This process, therefore, reverses the greenhouse effect and lowers temperatures. The decline in average temperatures worldwide accelerated starting about 5 million years ago and coincided with accelerated rates of high mountain uplift and erosion. While not proving this hypothesis, these data are clearly consistent with the theory.

HUMAN ACTIVITIES

In 1997, R. G. Johnson of the University of Minnesota theorized that increasing salinity of the Mediterranean Sea could cause continental glaciers to return to high-latitude areas of Canada, possibly precipitating a new ice age. Diminished flow of river water into the Mediterranean Sea, especially into the sea's more arid eastern end, could be the culprit behind the saltier water.

Because sea level remains essentially constant, the inflow of water from the Atlantic Ocean through the Strait of Gibraltar compensates for the evaporative loss of water in the Mediterranean Sea. But heavy, dense, salty Mediterranean Sea water also flows out into the Atlantic Ocean under the cooler but less dense Atlantic in-flowing water. In fact, until the perfection of sonar, World War II German submariners in the Mediterranean sought the appropriate depth, turned off the engines, and rode these same currents through the strait—right under the noses of the British.

But how could this saltier Mediterranean Sea trigger an ice age? As the last major glacial advance started, at least the northwestern part of the Labrador Sea and Baffin Bay warmed. Scientists discovered this by analyzing the oxygen-18 isotopic values and pollen content of ancient glacier ice on Devon and Ellesmere Islands. A strong, northward current of water originating in the Mediterranean Sea wells up off the coasts of Ireland and Scotland. This upwelling, if intense, will divert the relatively warm Gulf Stream into the Labrador Sea. The influx of warm water into the Labrador Sea in turn brings greater snowfall to that region and leads to the formation of massive ice sheets on the adjacent land. Furthermore, this diversion of the Gulf Stream from its normal path along the west coast of northern Europe could initiate dramatic cooling in Europe, and then the world.

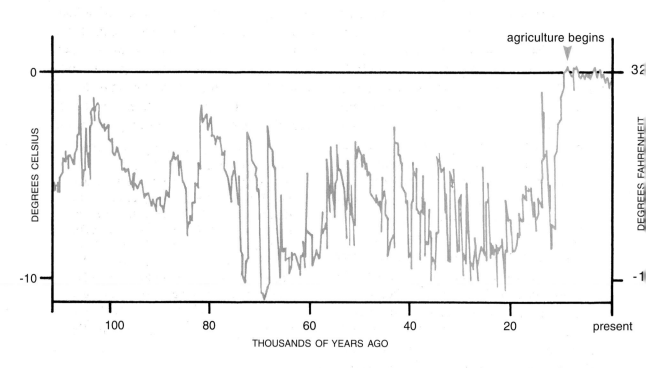

Average annual world temperature differences during the past 100,000-plus years compared with the present average annual temperature. Note that the peaks in the curve have asymmetrical, sawtooth shapes, demonstrating that continental glaciation takes longer to develop than to disappear. —Modified after Broecker, 1995

This realization leads us to ask how human activities in that region might cause the next ice age. Currently, agricultural, domestic, and industrial users withdraw increasing volumes of water from rivers, primarily the Nile, that flow to the Mediterranean Sea. Diminishing volumes of river water ultimately reach the sea, so the Mediterranean Sea is growing saltier. Global warming compounds this human effect by increasing the evaporation of freshwater from the sea's surface. Therefore, the growing use of freshwater in the region might create conditions similar to those during the last major ice age.

Understanding Ice Ages— Understanding the Future

Understanding the cause(s) of ice ages, as well as the rates of temperature change leading both to and away from ice ages, may give us insight into the rate of human-induced climate change. By analyzing ancient glacier ice from Greenland, researchers have demonstrated that the transition from the cold, dry, and windy Younger Dryas time near the end of the Pleistocene epoch to the warmer Holocene climate of today spanned only about 40 years. But it took about 1,500 years from 11,700 to 10,200 years ago for the ratios of oxygen isotopes within the glacial ice to reach the values of the warmer present-day. The bottom line, if this research is valid, is that ice ages may start and end within a few decades—much less than a human lifetime and much faster than scientists ever imagined.

But the stability and health of our civilization and most of the earth's plants and animals depend on climates that remain relatively constant in any particular area. This, for humanity, is borne out by the concurrent rise of agriculture, cities, and civilizations starting about 10,000 years ago, when the world's average annual temperatures and climates stabilized. Should rapid warming or cooling occur, most of us could be in big trouble because we have adjusted our life-support systems to the present, rather stable, climatic conditions.

Imagine the effects of such rapid climate changes on plants and animals in northern and temperate latitudes. Most animals can generally move to new environments. Plants, on the other hand, take much longer to migrate to more suitable habitats, if such habitats exist. Many might become extinct, taking down with them the herbivores that depend on them for food. The demise of carnivores that eat the plant eaters would soon follow. Such was the situation at the end of the Pleistocene epoch. Was the extinction of animals at the end of the Pleistocene epoch due to deglaciation and the warming climate? Or did human activities, such as hunting and habitat destruction, contribute to the animals' demise? We will explore the lives and extinctions of Ice Age animals in the following pages.

References: Broecker, 1982, 1994, 1995, 1999; Brouwer, D., and A. J. J. Van Woerkom, 1950; Campbell, 1984; Clark and Bartlein, 1995; Covey, 1984; Croll, 1875; Elston, 1967; Eyles and Young, 1994; Gates, 1976; Hays et al., 1976; Heinrich, 1988; Imbrie, J., and J. Z. Imbrie, 1979, 1980; Johnson, 1997; Ledley et al., 1999; Morrison, 1991; Muller and MacDonald, 1997; Raymo, et al., 1988; Reid, 1979; Severinghaus and Brook, 1999; Stanley, 1995; Taylor, et al., 1997

5

THE PLEISTOCENE ANIMALS

Scientists may not know exactly how conditions combined to cause the ice ages, but they do know that the Pleistocene epoch was a period of environmental stress. And periods of environmental stress can trigger rapid evolutionary changes in plant and animal species to help them meet the challenges. It was apparently just such rapid changes that resulted in the development of some strange Ice Age animals.

The transition from the Pleistocene climate to today's climate presented another challenge to the survival of certain plant and animal species. Many North American mammals and birds of late Pliocene and Pleistocene time went extinct within the past 10,000 to 12,000 years. At least thirty-one genera of animals that weighed 100 pounds (44 kilograms) or more and lived during the Ice Age—less than an instant ago geologically speaking—are no longer with us. However, many other animals, including humans, survived the change from the cold climate of the late Pleistocene epoch into the warmer climate of Holocene time today.

Placing these animals in the context of ice ages helps us understand some of their adaptations, such as large size and heavy fur coats. For example, a larger animal has less surface area relative to its body mass than a smaller animal of similar design. The advantage for the larger animal is that it loses proportionally less heat and so can stand cold temperatures better than its smaller relative. Look for these traits as you read about Pleistocene animals.

What follows are descriptions and illustrations of many of the mammals that lived in North America during the last Ice Age. This book cannot possibly describe all the extinct Pleistocene animals. Instead, it describes the large, the most interesting, and the just plain weird animals—the ones you might like to see strolling down the street, but at a distance. Some would pay you no mind as you wandered by. Some you could easily outpace by walking. Still others might try to eat you on sight. The book also includes some of the mammals that lived during the Pleistocene epoch and are still with us today. This book

BIG ANIMALS

The Pleistocene epoch was a time of oversized animals. Why did some get so large? What are the advantages of large size? Conversely, what are the disadvantages of bigness? And when discussing size, what scale should be used? Is length, height, or weight the best parameter? Length is great for snakes, but what about giraffes or bears or sloths? Mass or weight is most commonly used for animals that have relatively the same geometry. For example, dogs, bears, cats, sloths, and humans have roughly similar geometries, so weight is appropriate for comparing them.

The largest animal ever, as far as we know, is the great blue whale, which can measure more than 100 feet (30 meters) long and weigh more than 100 tons (90,000 kilograms). One of the largest land animals was the 80-ton brachiosaurus dinosaur. The largest land mammal appears to have been the 30-ton *Baluchitherium,* a relative of the modern rhinoceros that lived 35 million years ago. It stood more than 16 feet (5 meters) tall at the shoulder.

Living sloths tip the scales at up to 12 pounds (5 kilograms), but the late, great sloths called megathere sloths weighed as much as 3 tons (2,700 kilograms). Why did they get so large? It turns out that the evolutionary tendency within certain animal lineages seems to be toward greater size. Scientists call this phenomenon phyletic size increase or Cope's Rule, after the late nineteenth-century American paleontologist Edward Drinker Cope.

Some advantages of greater size are easy to envision. For example, as the volume of an animal increases, its surface area increases but at a rate of only about two-thirds the rate that volume increases. Big animals, therefore, lose proportionally less body heat than smaller ones. Bigger animals are also better insulated because they have thicker skin with or without more body fat beneath. This further contributes to their ability to retain heat. So, a smaller dog or sloth will lose proportionally more heat than will a larger one. Larger animals, then, are generally better adapted than smaller animals are to lower temperatures, such as those of the ice ages.

With increased size and insulation, metabolic rates decrease. Larger animals breathe more slowly, and their hearts beat fewer times per minute. A good example is the comparison between the resting metabolic rates of elephants and mice. Elephants average 6 breaths and 30 heartbeats per minute; mice average 150 breaths and 600 heartbeats per minute. Interestingly, an elephant's heart beats about the same number of times during its 40- to 50-year life span as a mouse's heart beats during its 3-year life.

musk ox
(Ovibos moschatus)

American lion
(Panthera leo atrox)

glyptodont
(Doedicurus)

yak
(Bos grunniens)

6 feet

The consideration of longevity leads us to another advantage of size, at least in mammals: the bigger ones generally live longer than their smaller friends and enemies. A correlation between longevity and brain size also seems to exist, although scientists do not know if this is truly a cause-and-effect relationship. The apparent correlation may be due to the fact that intelligence often increases along with brain size.

Another major advantage of size is safety. The bigger the beast, the fewer the types of predators it has to worry about. For example, consider the predation hazards the modern 12-pound sloth confronts compared with those his late 3-ton relative faced.

How about some disadvantages? Well, it takes more fuel, in the form of food, to keep a big animal going, so large animals require more forage area. But the big guys have longer strides than the wee ones and so use proportionally less fuel to obtain food. It is more efficient to move one pound or kilogram of a larger animal than one pound or kilogram of a smaller one.

Another disadvantage is that, generally, the bigger the animal, the lower the density or abundance of animals on the land surface. A large animal, then, might have to search more widely for a mate, and there would be no surplus of the species to survive adverse conditions and diseases. This rule applies to both vegetarians and meat eaters. Clearly, gravity also comes into play with the big guys. The pull of gravity works against the pumping of fluids such as blood.

Size also influences an animal's ability to jump and its tendency to fall. Rats and cats can jump up to or down from places many times their length. Really big animals—more than a few hundred pounds—do not have that luxury and can critically or mortally injure themselves by tripping while running or by falling from small heights.

Another disadvantage of large size is increased vulnerability of offspring. Big animals begin life small compared to their final, adult size. Although all young, whether large or small, are vulnerable to predation, big animals cannot hide their offspring in nests or holes as easily as small animals can hide their young. Larger animals typically have lower birth rates and longer gestations than do smaller animals.

Steven Stanley, a renowned paleontologist, has found that as bodies become bigger, they become structurally more complex. With complexity comes more specialization. And specialization can make a species less

Harlan's ground sloth
(*Paramylodon harlani*)

Long-horned giant bison
(*Bison latifrons*)

Yesterday's camel
(*Camelops hesternus*)

Titanis
bird

adaptable to changes in habitats, such as the climate swings of the ice ages. Some of the little guys, such as rats, adapt well to change and typically survive adverse conditions.

Scientists who statistically examined the extinction of South American mammals at the end of Pleistocene time found that size was the only factor correlatable with probability of extinction. It made no difference whether the animals were marsupials or placentals. Researchers could not conclude, however, whether either human predation or climate change caused the extinction of these large animals.

Much has been written concerning animal size. A good place to find such information is in *Scaling: Why Is Animal Size So Important?* by Knut Schmidt-Nielsen. Other works include those by paleontologists Stephen Jay Gould and Steven Stanley.

References: Gould, 1966; Lessa and Farina, 1996; Quammen, 1995; Schmidt-Nielsen, 1984; Stanley, 1998

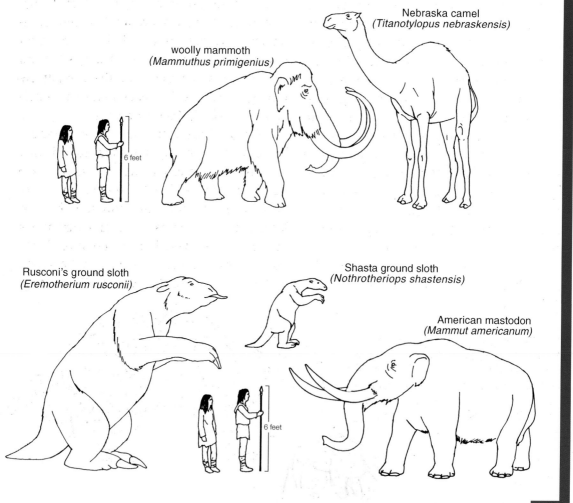

Nebraska camel
(*Titanotylopus nebraskensis*)

woolly mammoth
(*Mammuthus primigenius*)

6 feet

Rusconi's ground sloth
(*Eremotherium rusconii*)

Shasta ground sloth
(*Nothrotheriops shastensis*)

American mastodon
(*Mammut americanum*)

6 feet

focuses on sloths and armadillos of the order Xenarthra; deer, moose, elk, and their relatives of the order Artiodactyla; horses, rhinos, and tapirs of the order Perissodactyla; mammoths and mastodons of the order Proboscidea; wolves, bears, cats, and other members of the order Carnivora; and beavers, porcupines, and capybaras of the order Rodentia.

The book does not discuss marsupials, those animals such as opossums with pouches in which to carry their young; the order Insectivora, insect-eating small animals such as shrews and moles; the order Chiroptera, containing hordes of bat species; the order Lagomorpha, containing hares, rabbits, and pikas, all of which have two pairs of ever-growing front teeth; and the order Sirenia, containing sea cows and manatees, which today are fighting extinction. The order Primates—apes, monkeys, and us—will be neglected except for a brief discussion of the arrival of the first humans to the New World.

The descriptions of the animals include the scientific name (genus, and species when known), approximate weight, and details about how the animal lived. The carbon-14 absolute age dating technique provides approximate time periods of when each animal lived, although the technique is useable only for animals that lived within the past 50,000 years.

For more information about the animals, please refer to the references at the end of each section. .

Let's begin with some really different animals, the endentates or, perhaps more precisely, animals within the Magnorder Xenarthra.

Xenarthrans or Edentates
ORDER XENARTHRA
Sloths and Armadillos

The order Xenarthra contains some of the largest and most bizarre animals of the Pleistocene epoch—or of any age for that matter. The order includes armadillos and pampatheres, glyptodonts, tree sloths, extinct giant ground sloths, and anteaters. The fossil record indicates that ancestors of these relatively primitive animals date back to about 55 million years ago in South America.

The word edentate means "without teeth," but in this order only anteaters truly fit that definition. Some armadillos and sloths have simple, peglike teeth. All the members, however, are xenarthrous, meaning they have at least secondary joints or extra articulations between certain vertebrae of the lower backbone. This trait gives them excellent flexibility and helps support the back while digging.

The northern pampathere, Holmesina septentrionalis, *weighed as much as 600 pounds (273 kilograms). Compare this to its cousin, the living nine-banded armadillo* (Dasypus novemcinctus), *which weighs in at about 17 pounds (7.7 kilograms).*

Other archaic mammalian features that paleontologists recognize within the order include poor regulation of and low body temperature and teeth without enamel. Many species had short, massive limbs with huge claws.

Most species, including all the largest varieties, became extinct around the same time at the end of the Wisconsinan ice age, approximately 10,000 to 11,000 years ago. Of the few species of the order still living, some such as armadillos are thriving.

Xenarthrans evolved in South America from insectivorous ancestors into very specialized creatures. Most species only ventured into North America during late Pliocene and early Pleistocene time, about 3 to 2 million years ago. This was before or just after the land bridge was established between the two continents.

This isolation for most of the Cenozoic era no doubt explains in large part the bizarre nature and specialized features of many South American animals. They lived far from the mainstream of mammalian evolution, which was centered in the Old World with connections to North America. South American carnivores were marsupials and birds, plus a whole range of evolutionarily convergent horse-, camel-, elephant-, and hippo-like animals that stemmed from some very primitive mammalian ancestors.

Conditions were therefore appropriate for evolution of strange-looking animals, by Old World standards, that retained many archaic features of early mammals, features that vanished long ago in the rest of the world.

The demise of most species in this order, especially the large ones, probably stemmed from a combination of factors. Their small brain size, slow and clumsy movements, and apparently solitary lifestyle would have made them easy prey for groups of human hunters with spears and other projectiles. Many apparently required quite specific habitat and/or food types, so sudden climate changes probably also brought significant hardship. During Pleistocene time, there were seven families of Xenarthrans containing at least thirty-four species. Today, four families of Xenarthrans, containing a total of twenty-nine species, exist.

Xenarthrans are divided into two main groups: the armored cingulates, which include armadillos and glyptodonts; and the hirsute pilosans, which include anteaters, ground sloths, and tree sloths. The armadillos, glyptodonts, and ground sloths extended their range into the southern United States, while the sloth species of the genus *Megalonyx* made the long trip to Alaska before going extinct.

ARMADILLOS
Family Dasypodidea

The largest and most specialized armadillo ever, the extinct northern pampathere (*Holmesina septentrionalis*) of the subfamily Pampatheriinae, reached 6 feet (2 meters) long and 3 feet (1 meter) tall. Adults must have weighed as much as large black bears—close to 600 pounds (273 kilograms). With such dimensions, this beauty would be a real road hazard today.

Remains of the extinct, giant northern pampathere have been found in a belt from Florida west to Texas and Kansas. The sparse fossil record leaves us to only speculate about the nature of their lives. These animals probably ate insects and invertebrates and lived much like the modern nine-banded armadillo. Northern pampatheres were extinct by approximately 9,880 years ago.

Eight genera containing twenty-one species of armadillos presently inhabit the region from

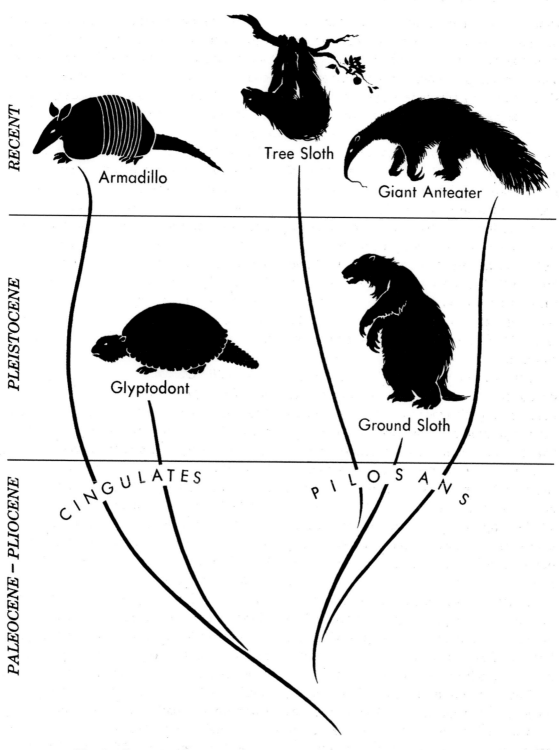

The family tree of Edentates from early Tertiary time until the present
—Reprinted with permission from John Wiley and Sons

Kansas to Argentina, but only the small and common nine-banded armadillo *(Dasypus novemcinctus)* resides in North America today. It ranges from Texas, Oklahoma, and southeastern Kansas southeastward to southern Georgia and all but the southern tip of Florida, and south into Central America. These sparsely haired animals are entirely encased in a jointed armor, with nine bands around the middle of the body. They eat insects and small invertebrates. The Spanish coined the name armadillo because upon first encounter with the animal, they thought it resembled "a little man in armor." Ancestors of these armadillos date back to late Paleocene and Eocene time, about 60 to 55 million years ago.

Living armadillos have three to five toes on their front feet and five toes on the rear. They are mainly insectivorous, preferring ants and termites, but they also eat small animals, carrion, and plants. They chew this food with seven or more peglike teeth on each side of each jaw. While cursed with poor eyesight, they have a good sense of smell. All living species sleep and live in self-dug burrows, where they raise from one to twelve identical young of the same sex. The nine-banded armadillo is about 2.5 feet (80 centimeters) long

Two glyptodonts, the South American Doedicurus, *with the medieval-looking spiked tail, and* Glyptotherium arizonae, *a North American inhabitant*

and may weigh 17 pounds (7.7 kilograms). New babies weigh 3 ounces and resemble miniature piglets.

GLYPTODONTS
Family Glyptodontidae

These large, clumsy-looking animals probably descended from ancestors of their relatives the armadillos. In terms of shape, speed, brains, and armor, the glyptodonts were clearly the tanks of the mammal world. Their defense consisted of a shell, called a carapace, that covered their entire body and consisted of at least 1,800 polygonal plates. Their massive tails were flexible and probably swayed back and forth as the animals waddled. Though heavily armored, some glyptodonts apparently succumbed to large carnivores, as evidenced by saber-tooth-like puncture wounds found in one skull.

Three species inhabited the southern United States, with remains found in Texas, Florida, South Carolina, and Arizona. The animals migrated north from South America over the newly established land bridge at the end of Pliocene time or early in Pleistocene time. Glyptodonts inhabited tropical and subtropical, humid, aquatic environments where they browsed on vegetation.

The largest glyptodont that roamed North America, *Glyptotherium arizonae*, weighed at least 1 ton. It measured 10 feet (3 meters) long, and 4.5 feet (1.5 meters) tall. This glyptodont arrived in what is now the United States during the Irvingtonian Land Mammal Age, at the beginning of the Pleistocene epoch. It retreated south to Mexico and then returned to the United States in the Rancholabrean Land Mammal Age, only to become extinct everywhere by 10,000 years ago. Extinction may have resulted from the dramatic climate changes at the end of Pleistocene time.

Some researchers propose that glyptodonts used their tails as formidable weapons. The carapaces of some fossilized glyptodonts show fractures that may support that idea. A glyptodont's tail weighed as much as 88 pounds (40 kilograms). Used as a club, the tail would surely pack a wallop.

LIVING SLOTHS
Family Choloepidae—Two-Toed Sloths
Family Bradypodidae—Three-Toed Sloths

To be called a sloth has never been complimentary. Spaniard Gonzalo Fernandez de Oviedo y Valdes, one of the first Europeans to see a sloth in the wilds of South America, wrote "The sloth takes the whole day for fifty paces, is about as long as it is broad, and has four thin legs with long nails, which cannot support the body. . . . I have never seen anything uglier or more useless than the sloth." In 1825, English author Oliver Goldsmith deemed the sloth an incomplete work of nature. In 1837, French zoologist and paleontologist Georges Cuvier pronounced that nature had been pleased to produce something imperfect and grotesque in jest. Naturalist William Beeb in 1925 concluded that "the three-toed sloth was well adapted to life on Mars where the year had 600 days and because of its self-absorption . . . had no right to live on Earth."

But sloths also claim many appreciators—this author included. Even with their unique design, or perhaps because of it, they found a quiet, low-stress ecological niche to their liking in this complex world and have thrived for a long time. One sloth admirer wrote in a 1555 French travelogue that this animal had a human face and bearlike body and that only the Creator himself knew why he made such a marvelous form.

At least eight species within three families of ground sloths came north from South

America and lived in Central and North America during various parts of the Pleistocene epoch. Some of these were almost as big as an elephant, but none of the large ones survived into the Holocene epoch. Five sloth species survived the end of the Pleistocene ice ages and still inhabit tropical forests of South and Central America. These are probably descendants of the first arrivals and certainly were around during late Pleistocene time.

One of the surviving species of sloths is the brown-throated three-toed sloth *(Bradypus variegatus)*. Typical of the survivors, this fellow has a low metabolic rate and low core body temperatures (75 to 91 degrees Fahrenheit, or 24 to 33 degrees Celsius) depending on the air temperature. It can weigh up to 12 pounds (5.5 kilograms) and possesses longer front than rear legs. This sloth ranges from eastern Honduras south to Argentina.

Sloths spend days in trees, hanging upside down while eating leaves. They only descend to the ground to defecate, a curious behavior that makes them vulnerable to predators. These animals have long, stiff hair that commonly has a blue green tint due to its blue-green algal guests. The algae, of the genera *Trichophilus* and *Cyanoderma*, have a mutualistic relationship with sloths: the animal transports algae into sunlight at the tops of trees, and the algae camouflage the sloth's hairy coat.

Living sloths have five simple peglike teeth on each side of the upper jaw and four on each lower jaw. Their feet have two or three long curved claws 3 to 4 inches (8 to 10 centimeters) long for grasping branches and climbing trees. To accommodate a sloth's upside-down lifestyle, the fur grows from the belly towards the back, the reverse of most other animals. Sloths also can rotate their heads slowly up to 90 degrees right and 90 degrees

left. All modern sloths are good swimmers. They live as long as thirty to forty years and are usually solitary animals. Females generally have a single young. Sloths have a multi-compartmental stomach that contains cellulose-digesting bacteria. This arrangement allows sloths to fully digest the leaves they eat.

Today's sloths belong to one of two families. Two-toed sloths belong to the family Choloepidae, which also contained some of the late, great giant ground sloths including Jefferson's. Living species include Hoffmann's sloth *(Choloepus hoffmanni)* at 10 to 18 pounds (4.5 to 8.1 kilograms) and the southern sloth *(Choloepus didactylus)* at 10 to 19 pounds (4.5 to 8.1 kilograms).

Three-toed sloths belong to the family Bradypodidae. Besides *Bradypus variegatus* they include the pale-throated sloth *(Bradypus tridactylus)* at 7 to 13 pounds (3.3 to 6 kilograms), and the maned sloth *(Bradypus torquatus)* at 8 to 9 pounds (3.6 to 4.2 kilograms).

The families Choloepidae and Bradypodidae apparently evolved from the families Megalonychidae and Megatheriidae, respectively. Two- and three-toed sloths have distinctly different teeth, coats, microstructures of hair fibers, and numbers of vertebrae.

Now let's look at some extinct cousins of modern sloths. At least eight species within three families lived in North America at various times during the Pleistocene epoch. These include the small and medium flat-footed ground sloths of the family Megalonychidae, the medium and large browsing ground sloths of the family Megatheriidae, and the large grazing ground sloths of the family Mylodontidae. Some of these families date back to Oligocene time, approximately 35 million years ago. The ancestors of these animals originated in South America, and some species reached

Central America in the Pliocene epoch before the land bridge connected the two continents, or before about 3.5 million years ago.

FLAT-FOOTED GROUND SLOTHS
Family Megalonychidae

The remains of these small to medium ground sloths first appear in Oligocene rocks, about 35 million years old, of Patagonia in southern South America. Based on their remains, these Pleistocene sloths weighed between 300 and 1,200 pounds (136 to 545 kilograms). The animals walked on the bottoms of their hind feet rather than on the sides as other sloths did. Sometime in the Tertiary period, and prior to the establishment of the Panamanian land bridge, about 3.5 million years ago, Megalonychids made the North American scene. These vegetarians may have emigrated on rafts of edible material and possibly island-hopped.

Instead of developing body armor like their relatives the glyptodonts and armadillos, ground sloths grew huge bones, feet, tails, and claws, and they wore a coat of heavy, coarse hair. An early member of the clan, the narrow-mouthed ground sloth, *Megalonyx leptostomus*, was widely distributed in North America by middle Pliocene time, approximately 3 million years ago. Remains of the animal have been found in deposits of Blancan Land Mammal Age. This sloth was smaller than and probably ancestral to Wheatley's ground sloth, *Megalonyx wheatleyi*. Fossils of Wheatley's ground sloth have been found in Florida, with larger specimens unearthed to the north and northwest in Pennsylvania and Kansas. Researchers believe Wheatley's sloth in turn to be the ancestor to the larger Rancholabrean Jefferson's ground sloth (*Megalonyx jeffersonii*). Of the three species present in North America during the Pleistocene epoch,

SPECIAL FOSSIL SITES

Fossils, though rare in the geological record, are found throughout the world in sedimentary deposits. Special conditions are required to preserve animal and plant remains. The conditions include burial during life or shortly following death by, for example, volcanic ash, mudflows, or submergence in swamps and bogs. Without quick burial, the remains will be eaten, with the bones scattered or weathered into dust.

Even more remarkable is fossil preservation of numerous specimens of a particular species or large numbers of many species in one locality. In North America at least three Pleistocene-age sites are worthy of more than a brief explanation because of their unique nature. They are Rancho La Brea in California; Hot Springs, South Dakota; and Big Bone Lick, Kentucky.

Rancho La Brea, California

Popularly known as the La Brea tar pits, Rancho La Brea is probably the most famous fossil locality of late Pleistocene mammals, birds, insects, and plants in the world. More than 565 species have been found within the 23-acre site. Of the remains pulled from the asphaltic deposits, 40 percent, or 24 species, of large mammals and 15 percent, or 21 species, of birds are now extinct. The site was well known to indigenous peoples of the area. The first written record of the location come from Franciscan friar Juan Crespi. In 1769–70 he accompanied Spanish explorer Gaspar de Portol and described the site as *"muchos pantanos de brea,"* or "extensive bogs of tar." In 1875, the site was recognized as a fossil site. The first systematic excavations started in 1901, and the parcel, now known as Hancock Park, was given to Los Angeles County by owner G. Allen Hancock in 1924. Because of its abundance of preserved life forms, in 1951 the site became the type locality of the late Pleistocene Rancholabrean Land Mammal Age in North America. In 1963, the park was declared a National Natural Landmark, and in 1977, the George C. Page Museum of La Brea Discoveries opened.

The remains of animals are encased in hard, asphalt-impregnated clay and sand. The clay and sand are layered with stream-deposited gravel that is part of an outwash plain leading west away from the Santa Monica Mountains. The asphalt-impregnated sedimentary deposits vary from 40 to 140 feet (12 to 58 meters) thick.

The animals were trapped in asphaltic seeps like those seen in Hancock Park today and that still seep to the surface at a rate of 8 to 12 gallons (32 to 48 liters) per day. The asphalt thoroughly impregnated the bodies, thus preserving the bones and teeth of hapless animals after death. The material also preserved insects and some types of plant material.

The tar trapped more than 10,000 individual mammals, starting about 40,000 years ago. Although herbivores typically greatly outnumber carnivores in a given population, about 70 percent of the fauna are carnivorous mammals and birds of prey. This is probably because each trapped animal would have attracted a number of carnivores, who would then become trapped themselves. Animals of note include a flat-headed peccary, tapirs, horses, camels, Columbian mammoths, giant ground sloths, dire wolves, coyotes,

Bone mass discovered at Rancho La Brea in the Pit 91 excavation in 1915. Pit 91 was not excavated again until 1969. The excavation continues each summer, and visitors can watch paleontologists at work in the pit.
—Courtesy of the George C. Page Museum

and 2,500 saber-toothed cats. Dire wolves are the most abundant remains found in the pot, followed in abundance by saber-toothed cats (*Smilodon fatalis*) and coyotes. The tar pits are the type location of the California state vertebrate, the saber-toothed cat.

Of the herbivores, bison remains outnumber horses, which in turn surpass mylodont ground sloths and camels in total number. In addition, at least 138 species of birds have been removed. They include turkeys, owls, woodpeckers, songbirds, waterbirds, and the gigantic Merriam's teratorn *(Teratornis merriami).* This extinct, meat-eating relative of the stork weighed 30 pounds (14 kilograms) and had a 14-foot (4.25-meter) wingspan. At least 159 species of plants and 234 species of invertebrates have also been recovered from the site.

Excavators have recovered the remains of only one human from the tar pits: a 4-foot-10-inch-tall woman in her mid-twenties dated to 9,000 years ago. Her cause of death is unknown, although she appears to have suffered a blow to the head. Artifacts indicate that the local people used the asphalt for glue and waterproofing over the past several thousand years.

"Next year I think we should meet in Miami!"

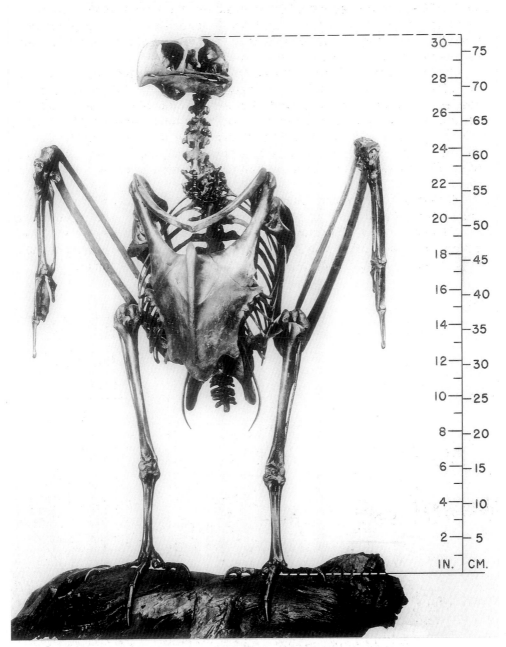

Teratorn bird, Teratornis merriami
—Courtesy of the George C. Page Museum

Excavation at the Hot Springs, South Dakota, mammoth dig
—Courtesy Larry Agenbroad, Northern Arizona University

Hot Springs, South Dakota

Hot Springs, South Dakota, first gained eminence in the late nineteenth century as a place to enjoy warm, healing mineral waters. But in 1974, the preliminary bulldozing work for a housing development revealed the remains of the first of the greatest collection of Columbian mammoths *(Mammuthus columbi)* yet discovered in the world. Work on the housing development stopped due to interest in the site and the benevolence of the landowner, Phil Anderson. The site has been preserved, and paleontological work continues.

The animal remains occupy an ancient sinkhole trap near the south end of the Black Hills of South Dakota. Absolute age dating by the radiocarbon method reveals that the natural trap was operational for between 300 and 700 years about 26,000 years ago. The depression measures 98 feet (30 meters) by 165 feet (50 meters) by 83 feet (25 meters) deep. Animals grazed on the vegetated banks or drank from the warm, water-bearing depression. At least one hundred mammoths, mainly young males, slipped in, never to climb back up the steep, slippery walls. In 1979, scientists found the first complete, articulated skeleton, with bones in life position, of a Columbian mammoth. This animal stood 13 feet (4 meters) at the shoulder, weighed 6 to 7 tons (5,400 to 6,400 kilograms), and researchers estimate its age at death as 49 years old. The remains also included very delicate tongue bones and bile or kidney stones.

The depression also contains the remains of wolves, coyotes, a giant short-faced bear, and many species of smaller animals. The remains of the bear, rare in the fossil record, was the first such find in the north-central Plains states.

The spectacular site now exists under a large building where visitors can see complete animal skeletons in life positions and learn how workers excavate and preserve these creatures.

Big Bone Lick, Kentucky

Big Bone Lick State Park, established in 1960, is located 20 miles (32 kilometers) southwest of Cincinnati, Ohio. It was the first major deposit of vertebrate fossils known in North America. In 1739, Major Charles LeMoyne de Longueuil, commander of the French and Indian troops of Canada, was the first white man known to have visited the site. Following his 1839 collecting trip, de Longueuil sent the fossils to France. Ben Franklin also visited the site, and later Thomas Jefferson, at his own expense, sent William Clark, of Lewis and Clark expedition fame, to collect fossils there in 1807. The three hundred large bones that Clark obtained were separated into three groups. One split went to the American Philosophical Society in Philadelphia, another to France's National Museum of Natural History in Paris, and Jefferson kept the third group. Some of these fossils are still on public display at Monticello, Jefferson's Virginia home.

The Big Bone Lick site is a swampy area surrounding salt- and sulfur-bearing springs. The salt and minerals attracted animals during Pleistocene time as far back as at least 18,000 years ago. Researchers have found three bone-bearing layers. The uppermost layer, the A horizon, contains recent animal bones together with pottery sherds. The middle B zone contains remains of deer, elk, bison, and reworked remains of older animals. The lowermost zone C is a blue gray sandy silt containing the late Pleistocene megafauna remains.

Harlan's musk ox *(Bootherium bombifrons)*, antique bison *(Bison antiquus)*, and stag moose *(Cervalces scotti)* were first found in North America at Big Bone Lick. Harlan's ground sloth *(Paramylodon harlani)* and Cope's tapir *(Tapirus haysii* or *Tapirus copei)* may also have been first discovered there. Other latest Pleistocene fossil remains of large animals found at the site include the American mastodon *(Mammut americanum)*, the complex-toothed horse *(Equus complicatus)*, caribou, mammoths, and deer.

Visitors to Big Bone Lick can view two full-sized replicas of Ice Age animals that provide a glimpse of life there 10,000 years ago. Many of the fossils from Big Bone Lick now reside in museums in London, Paris, and other cities worldwide, including the University of Nebraska State Museum in Lincoln, Nebraska.

References: Agenbroad, 1990; Kurten and Anderson, 1980; Marcus and Berger, 1984; Martin and Klein, 1984; Mol et al., 1993; Nelson, 1990; Schultz et al., 1963; Stock and Harris, 1992

perhaps the most interesting was Jefferson's ground sloth, named after the third president of the United States.

Jefferson's ground sloth
(Megalonyx jeffersonii)

Thomas Jefferson was forever fascinated with the sloth after receiving a gift of some sloth bones found in a cave in West Virginia. Impressed with the animal's huge claws, he named it *Megalonyx,* meaning "great claw" in Greek. Jefferson believed that *Megalonyx,* about three times the size of an African lion, was a carnivore with a "phosphorus eye" and "leonine roar." Later he realized the sloth was an herbivore. In a talk about the animal to the American Philosophical Society in 1797, Jefferson essentially initiated the study of vertebrate paleontology in the United States.

Megalonyx jeffersonii lived in North America approximately 150,000 to 9,400 years ago or from Illinoian to the end of Wisconsinan glacial time. Remains from at least seventy-five localities demonstrate that Jefferson's sloth inhabited the lower forty-eight states except for the Rocky Mountain and desert regions. The animal ranged up the west coast of North America into British Columbia, and in the interior of North America as far north as northern Canada and Fairbanks, Alaska.

The ox-sized animal (8 to 10 feet long or 2.5 to 3 meters) browsed on leaves and twigs of the woodlands and forests. For browsing, each side of the upper jaw had five peglike teeth, and each side of the lower jaw had four. Three claws on the hind feet touched the ground and, along with the strong, broad tail,

Jefferson's ground sloth, Megalonyx jeffersonii

enhanced the animal's stability when it reached high into the trees for leaves and twigs to eat.

BROWSING GROUND SLOTHS
Family Megatheriidae

In earliest Oligocene time, about 36 million years ago, browsing ground sloths made their debut in South America, where they shared a common ancestry with the flat-footed sloths, family Megalonychidae. The two major groups of Megatheriidae are the megatheres and nothrotheres, which had similar skull structure and shared many other aspects but differed greatly in size. The nothrotheres, such as the Shasta ground sloth, were slightly built, reaching a length of approximately 4 feet (1.2 meters). The megatheres, *Megatherium* and *Eremotherium,* in comparison, were huge animals that could weigh up to 3 tons (2,700 kilograms) and attain lengths of more than 20 feet (6 meters).

Rusconi's ground sloth
(*Eremotherium rusconii*)
One of the largest members of the family Megatheriidae was the elephant-sized Rusconi's ground sloth, *Eremotherium rusconii.* These huge megatheres reached North America in the late Blancan Land Mammal Age, more than 1.65 million years ago. They survived until the end of Pleistocene time, about 10,000 years ago. The best specimens have been found in El Hatillo, Panama, but remains have also been recovered from Georgia, South Carolina, Texas, and Florida, as well as Central and South America. Weighing in at more than 6,000 pounds (2,700 kilograms) and measuring 20 feet (6 meters) long, the adult males

Rusconi's ground sloth (Eremotherium rusconii), *one of the big daddies of sloths. These brutes outwardly resembled their cousin,* Megatherium.

were perhaps 50 percent larger than adult females. These animals had small heads in relation to their immense bodies. Both sexes apparently stood upright or sat, using their massive tails for balance.

Evidently the genus *Megatherium*, which inhabited South America, differed from the genus *Eremotherium* in the forefoot structure. *Megatherium* had four well-developed digits on the front feet, with the second, third, and fourth digits bearing large claws. *Eremotherium* had only three fully developed digits on the front feet, with claws located on the third and fourth. Like most other species of ground sloth, they ambled along on the knuckles of their front feet instead of on the bottoms of their front feet like most other animals. From the structure of the animals' hind feet, paleontologists speculate that *Eremotherium* probably walked less on the sides of their rear feet than *Megatherium* did.

Remains of vegetation from the stomachs of *Eremotherium* found in Peruvian and Ecuadorian tar pits show these animals browsed on twigs including thorn bushes, which are typical of a savanna environment. No evidence exists to show that *Megatherium* lived in North America.

Shasta ground sloth
(Nothrotheriops shastensis)

A much smaller member of the family Megatheriidae was the Shasta ground sloth. This nothrothere's ancestry dates back to Miocene time in South America. Shasta sloths apparently arrived in North America during the Irvingtonian Land Mammal Age about 1 million years ago. They lived as far north as southern Alberta, Canada, and became extinct about 10,780 years ago. The animal apparently preferred forests and jungles to the more open country the bigger sloths inhabited.

We know more about the Shasta ground sloth than any other extinct sloth thanks to the fortunate preservation of several specimens and dung in caves on the Colorado Plateau in the southwestern United States. Not only were some skeletons intact, but tendons still held them together. Long, coarse, pale yellowish hair, very similar to the hair of modern South American tree sloths, hung on the bones.

Likely the smallest of the now-extinct North American sloths, a full-grown Shasta measured up to 9 feet (3 meters) long and weighed between 300 and 400 pounds (135 and 180 kilograms). It was a strange animal to behold, with

Skeleton of a Shasta sloth, Nothrotheriops shastensis. *Compare this skeleton with that of the much more massive Harlan's ground sloth,* Paramylodon harlani.
—Courtesy of the George C. Page Museum

HOW DO WE KNOW HOW OLD FOSSILS ARE?

One of the most useful tools in Pleistocene research is radiocarbon, or carbon-14, absolute age dating. All formerly living things, including materials such as cloth, bone, wood, and shells, contain carbon. Other materials that may be dated because they contain some carbon include glacial ice, seawater, and groundwater. The radiocarbon dating method relies on the principle that the isotope carbon 14, with an atomic mass of 14, is radioactive and, therefore, unstable. Its instability causes it to break down or decay into what is called a daughter isotope. In this process, a neutron, which is a subatomic particle with mass but no charge, in the carbon-14 atom disintegrates into a proton, a subatomic particle with both mass and a positive charge, with the release of energy. The mass of the atom stays the same at 14, but the atom now contains 7 protons and 7 neutrons instead of the less stable 6 protons and 8 neutrons of carbon 14. The daughter isotope, nitrogen 14, is stable and generally will not change to something else.

Physicists have determined the rate of decay of carbon 14, and the system turns out to be an absolute clock useful for dating materials that have carbon in them. Carbon's rate of decay is such that if you started with one pound of carbon 14 today, you would have only one-half pound left in 5,730 years. Another 5,730 years of decay would leave only one-quarter pound, and after another 5,730 years, only half of that, or one-eighth of a pound, would be left. The halving time period of 5,730 years is called the half-life of carbon 14. Every radioactive isotope, such as the uranium 235 that atomic bombs are made from, has a different half-life length. The isotope uranium 235 decays more slowly than carbon 14, so it has a much longer half-life of about 700 million years.

The radiocarbon dating method is based on the assumption that as long as the amount of carbon 14 remains constant in the atmosphere, the living host's carbon 14 will remain fairly constant. (The production of carbon 14 has varied slightly through time.) Although the host's carbon 14 is continuously decaying, the host also takes in carbon 14 at the same time, replacing the carbon 14 that has decayed. It turns out that all living, breathing things are in equilibrium with the constant and continuously regenerating carbon 14 reservoir in the atmosphere—they have the same ratio of carbon 14 to the other, nonradiogenic carbon isotopes, carbon 12 and carbon 13. Therefore, all living organisms exposed to the atmosphere have the same ratio of carbon 14 to the stable isotopes carbon 12 and carbon 13 as in the atmosphere. When the host dies, carbon 14 no longer accumulates in its tissues and, therefore, the amount of carbon 14 begins to decline at the fixed half-life rate. Thus, researchers can use the ratio of carbon 14 to carbon 12— a stable, nonradioactive isotope of carbon—as a measure of the length of time that has passed since the host died.

Because carbon 14 has such a short half-life, geologists can use that method to date only relatively young materials. After just a few half-lives, not much carbon 14 remains. Therefore, radiocarbon dating is effective for materials from about 100 to 50,000 years old. This makes the radiocarbon scheme perfect for dating late Pleistocene and post-Pleistocene materials.

Geologists can only accurately date materials, such as bones, that have been isolated from the atmosphere since death by such geologic phenomena as burial by mud flows or volcanic eruptions, or by freezing in permafrost. Why? If the material is not removed from the atmosphere, it will tend to absorb newly made carbon 14 from the atmosphere. So, if you are digging a trench in a peat bog or permafrost in Alaska and uncover a bone fragment, quickly seal it in a plastic bag for analysis in a carbon 14 age-dating laboratory. If the material has been isolated from atmospheric contamination since burial, you should be able to obtain a date that will be very close to the original age of the material. If the sample has been exposed to the atmosphere, it will tend to reequilibrate with the atmosphere by absorbing atmospheric carbon 14. The resulting date, then, will be younger than the sample's actual age.

Pleistocene organic material that is too old to date by the radiocarbon method can be dated by the electron spin resonance (ESR) method. The system works like this. Buried fossils receive and absorb a steady dose of radiation from cosmic rays and from minerals that surround the fossil and that contain decaying radioactive elements, such as uranium. Some of the electrons liberated by the radiation from the surrounding minerals become trapped in the fossil's crystalline structure. The calcium phosphate mineral apatite, which makes up most fossils, tightly retains the electrons that the surrounding radiation continuously adds to the fossil. A researcher can calculate the age of the fossil by first using a radiation meter to measure the amount of radiation per unit of time, or flux of electrons, that the fossil is receiving at the site. Then, in the laboratory, the researcher measures the amount of electrons the specimen has accumulated in its crystal structure. Finally, researchers determine the age of the material simply by dividing the total number of electrons trapped in the fossil by the radiation flux measured at the site. This age-dating technique does not destroy the sample, so the procedure can be repeated to check accuracy.

ESR has been used to date fossilized bone, limestone, egg shells, hot spring deposits, quartz shocked or strained by meteor impact, and teeth. Teeth turn out to be among the best datable materials because the very dense nature of apatite, which makes up bones and teeth, holds the electrons tightly. The ESR technique has been applied to materials as young as 10,000 years old and as old as 500 million years.

References: Blackwell, 1995

its prehensile lips, long, slender muzzle, and small head on a long, flexible neck. This sloth walked on its knuckles while browsing on roots, stems, seeds, flowers, and fruit of globemallow, cactus, Mormon tea, century plant, catclaw, salt brush yucca, and mesquite—all plants that still grow in the animal's former range.

Some of the best information about the Shasta sloth has come from Rampart Cave in northwestern Arizona. Wonderfully preserved fossilized dung specimens called coprolites have yielded carbon-14 age dates of between 40,000 and 11,000 years before present.

GRAZING GROUND SLOTHS
Family Mylodontidae
**Harlan's ground sloth
(Paramylodon harlani)**

Another sloth that inhabited North American grasslands, including those of the Colorado Plateau region, was the huge Harlan's ground sloth, *Paramylodon harlani*. This sloth stood

Harlan's ground sloth, Paramylodon harlani.

12 feet (3.5 meters) tall and weighed as much as 3,500 pounds (1,570 kilograms). Large as it was, Harlan's ground sloth was only slightly more than half the size of the *Megatherium* and *Eremotherium*. Coarse, brownish hair covered the animal, and a protective armor of nickel-sized bony plates called dermal ossicles lay beneath its thick hide.

What distinguishes Harlan's ground sloth from the Shasta and Jefferson's sloths is its larger size, short neck, powerful chest, lobate teeth, and presence of dermal ossicles. The construction of the skull shows a small brain cavity and a good nose for smelling. What it lacked in brain power, it made up for in bulk. When mature, Harlan's ground sloths had essentially no enemies except humans.

Like the other big sloths, Harlan's apparently was a slow, clumsy walker. It ambled, or perhaps dragged itself along, on the outside of its feet. It had massive front legs and tail and impressive claws that, with its suit of armor, were its main lines of defense.

The youngest remains of Harlan's ground sloth, at 13,890 years old, were found in the Rancho La Brea tar pits in Los Angeles. However, Harlan's ground sloth may have become extinct later in Florida than in southern California. The oldest specimens date to Irvingtonian Land Mammal Age, about 1 million years ago.

Based on preserved remains, this massive animal may have been more plentiful than Shasta or Jefferson's sloths. Harlan's sloths apparently grazed in small herds on grasses,

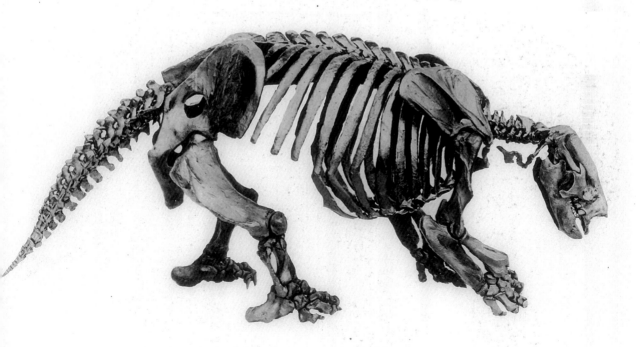

Skeleton of a Harlan's ground sloth, Paramylodon harlani —Courtesy of the George C. Page Museum

DNA AND DUNG

Deoxyribonucleic acid, or DNA, has been in the news lately for its use as a tool for fingerprinting everything from criminals to dinosaurs (á la *Jurassic Park*). DNA is usually a double-stranded molecule that spirals about its own axis. The molecule carries chemical messages or instructions for assembling proteins and, ultimately, new organisms. Animal hair, skin, and bones contain DNA. Another source of DNA is dung. For years, researchers attempted, without success, to extract DNA from feces of Ice Age animals, particularly from the well-preserved dung found in caves in arid climates.

A breakthrough came from analyzing 20,000-year-old dung from giant ground sloths in Gypsum Cave, about 19 miles (30 km) east of Las Vegas. Researchers suspected that they would find decomposed DNA in the dung. Recent research showed that usable DNA was present but camouflaged inside caramelized sugar compounds—the same types of caramelized sugars that give bread crusts and baked desserts distinctive flavors. Fortunately, these sugar compounds did not prevent researchers from analyzing the DNA.

The DNA analyses proved that the dung in Gypsum Cave came from an individual Shasta ground sloth whose fossil remains were also found in the cave. The dung-bearing DNA unexpectedly revealed that the sloth was quite the gourmet. His meals included various species of grasses, wild capers, mint, mustard plants, grapes, and yucca.

What's next for the dung researchers? They now hope to analyze 45,000-year-old feces possibly from Neanderthals who lived in caves in Gibraltar. If the feces are from Neanderthals, the DNA will further help us understand what these people ate and how similar they were to us. DNA work is also progressing on frozen mammoth remains from Siberia. An international team of researchers hopes to obtain enough usable DNA-bearing material from the mammoth remains that they can clone a woolly mammoth, using a female Indian elephant as the mother.

References: Poinar, 1999; Stone, 1999; Stokstad, 1998

The Shasta ground sloth, Nothrotheriops shastensis. *These animals apparently produced most of the sloth dung found in caves on the Colorado Plateau.*

roots, herbs, and shrubs in open country. They ranged at least across the southern United States and as far north as Washington State. The animal visited, but did not leave, at least forty fossil-bearing sites. And at least seventy-six individuals got stuck in the tar at Rancho La Brea in southern California.

References: Colbert and Morales, 1991; Emmons, 1990; Grzimek, 1990; Harrington, 1993; Jefferson, 1799; Kurten and Anderson, 1980; Martin and Wright, 1967; Mead and Meltzer, 1984; Nelson, 1990; Sheehan, 1973; Stock, 1925; Stock and Harris, 1992

Carnivores
ORDER CARNIVORA

The order Carnivora contains both living and extinct animals familiar to most people. The fossil record shows that the earliest ancestors of these animals probably were small, forest-dwelling insect eaters that date from at least as far back as Paleocene time, about 60 million to 55 million years ago. The fossil record of carnivores is generally good, and paleontological study focuses on the larger and most available specimens. While some members of this order were strict carnivores, or meat eaters, others were omnivores that ate meat and plants.

Carnivorous mammals are relatively intelligent animals—they must outsmart their next meal. They have a keen sense of smell, generally good eyesight, powerful limbs, and sharp claws. These animals also have strong incisor teeth for grasping prey, canine teeth for puncturing, and carnassial teeth for shearing flesh.

The order Carnivora originally consisted of two lineages: the creodonts and the miacids. Creodonts and miacids followed rather parallel evolutionary paths. Creodonts, the first flesh-eating, placental mammals, were the older, more primitive, and, based on their brain size, less intelligent of the two groups of meat-eating mammals. Their earliest ancestors date back about 70 million years. The evolution of creodonts peaked in early Tertiary time, about 55 million years ago, with the last of their kind living to about 10 million years ago. These animals varied from weasel- to bear-sized. Reconstructions of some of the larger species of creodonts show they probably looked like a cross between a bear and wolf. Creodonts had short, heavy limbs with respect to their body length, a long tail, and toes with claws you would not like to have sharing your bed. The skull's brow was not pronounced.

Modern carnivores descended from the other group, the miacids. Miacids were thriving in North America, Europe, and Asia by about 60 million years ago and survived until about 15 million years ago. Miacids and their evolutionary offspring lived mainly in forests, although some eventually moved into the sea. With their elongate bodies and short legs, miacids resembled weasels. Like creodonts, they had a low forehead, but had bigger brains than creodonts possessed.

Scientists use teeth, skulls, and limb bones to identify the different living and extinct species of carnivores. They divide North American carnivores into two suborders: the Fissipedia suborder, which consists of land-dwelling carnivores, and the Pinnipedia suborder, which includes seals, sea lions, and walruses. Families within the Fissipedia suborder include the families Canidae (dogs), Procyonidae (raccoons), Ursidae (bears), Felidae (cats), Hyaenidae (hyenas), and the Mustelidae with its six subfamilies that include weasels, fishers,

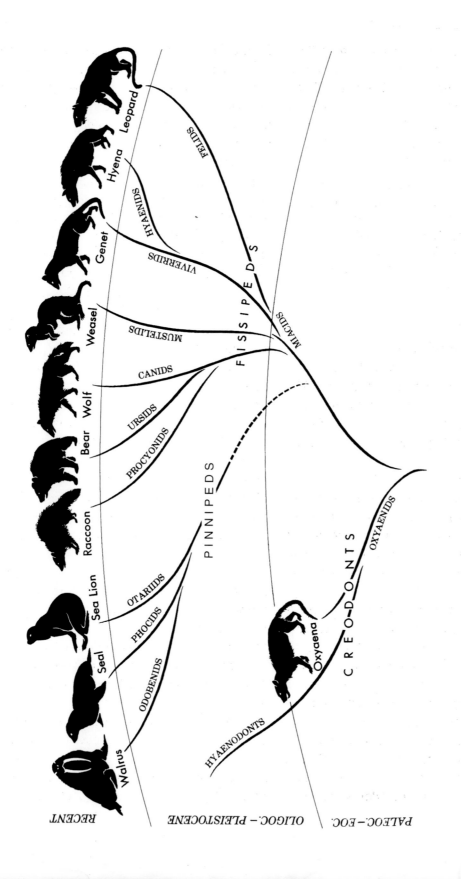

The family tree of carnivorous placental mammals, from early Tertiary time to recent time
—Reprinted with permission of Colbert and Morales, 1991

minks, martens, ferrets, wolverines, otters, badgers, and skunks.

Recognizable ancestors of our modern carnivores appeared in the Old World 35 million years ago during Oligocene time. By Pliocene time, about 5 million years ago, these animals lived on all continents except Australia and on many of the world's islands.

WOLVES, DOGS, AND THEIR RELATIVES
Family Canidae
Subfamily Caninae

The family Canidae originated in Eocene time, approximately 40 million years ago, in North America and Europe. Members of the family reached Asia in Oligocene time, about 35 million years ago, and entered South America during latest Pliocene or earliest Pleistocene time, about 2 million years ago. By the Pleistocene epoch, two main subfamilies inhabited North America: the Caninae subfamily of wolves, dogs, coyotes, jackals, and foxes, and the Simocyoninae subfamily of hyena-like dogs. The genus *Canis*, which contains true dogs and wolves, dates back to late Miocene time, about 6 million years ago in North America.

Dire wolf *(Canis dirus)* and gray wolf *(Canis lupus)*

The Caninae subfamily contained some interesting Ice Age members, including the dire wolf, whose name alone piques the imagination, especially on dark, cold nights. This wolf

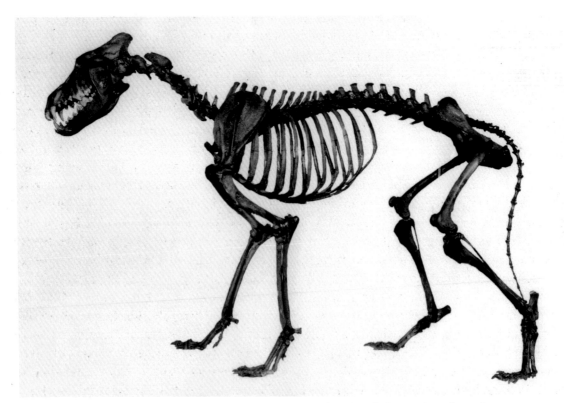

Skeleton of a dire wolf, Canis dirus. *More fossils of dire wolves have been found at Rancho La Brea than of any other mammal species.* —Courtesy of the George C. Page Museum

Dire wolf, Canis dirus

was evidently abundant during the Rancholabrean Land Mammal Age of about 100,000 to 10,000 years ago. Its remains have been found from southern Alberta, Canada, throughout most of the United States and south to Peru. The earliest evidence of this successful carnivore is in late Illinoian rocks that are slightly more than 130,000 years old.

The dire wolf had the most powerful jaws and teeth of all the wolves but a smaller brain than today's wily gray wolf. At as much as 150 pounds (68 kilograms), the dire wolf was heavier than a modern gray wolf, though about the same dimensions. Male gray wolves weigh as much as 130 pounds (59 kilograms). Researchers classify the dire wolf as a hunter/scavenger. More than 1,600 specimens have been recovered from the Rancho La Brea tar pits alone, where these and other carnivores preyed on large herbivores stranded in the muck. In pursuit of or after a hearty meal, the dire wolves also perished in the tarry goo. The last of their kind walked North America possibly as little as 8,000 years ago.

The reigns of the dire and gray wolves overlapped, as the gray wolf has prowled the North American landscape since late in the Irvingtonian Land Mammal Age, more than 500,000 years ago. Pleistocene remains have been found from Alaska and Yukon south to Virginia, Texas, New Mexico, Nevada, and California. Gray, or timber, wolves are typically a grizzled gray, but colors vary from black to white. These very intelligent and social animals travel in packs of from two to fifteen and averaging between four and seven animals. Each pack controls a territory of between 100 and 260 square miles (260 to 675 square kilometers). Within that territory, the animals hunt together, preying upon large animals such as moose, caribou, and deer. Gray wolves can reach speeds of more than 30 miles per hour (50 kilometers per hour) and live as long as 10 to 18 years.

Johnston's coyote (Canis lepophagus)

Coyotes, and possibly wolves, descended from the now-extinct Johnston's coyote (*Canis lepophagus*), which evidently originated in North America and lived between about 4 million or 3 million and 1.5 million years ago. Johnston's coyotes were generally somewhat larger and heavier than the modern species and gradually decreased in size over time to that of the modern coyote. Johnston's looked similar to the modern coyote but had slightly different teeth and bone structure. Judging by its bone structure, Johnston's coyote could not run as fast as the living species. Remains have been found in the mid-continental United States northwest to Washington and Idaho.

Coyote (Canis latrans)

A very successful survivor of the genus *Canis* is the modern coyote. The name coyote comes from the Aztec word *coyotl*. The modern species of coyote (*Canis latrans*) was apparently both common and widespread in North America during the Rancholabrean Land Mammal Age, starting about 300,000 years ago. Their remains have been found in more than one hundred North American sites. Some of the earliest remains, from the Irvingtonian Land Mammal Age, have been found in Alaska, Pennsylvania, Florida, California, Nebraska, and Mexico, a distribution that reflects the very extensive range of this animal. Coyotes weigh from 25 to more than 55 pounds (11.5 to more than 25 kilograms). They can sprint up to 40 miles per hour (65 kilometers per hour) and cruise at 25 to 35 miles per hour (40 to 50 kilometers per hour). Coyotes range from Central America north to Alaska and east to the Atlantic coast except in northeastern Canada. Coyotes are not picky eaters and consume mainly small animals and carrion. By hunting cooperatively, however, a group of coyotes can bring down antelope, deer, and bighorn sheep.

Coyote, Canis latrans

Coyotes can interbreed with dogs and wolves, although they rarely do so under normal circumstances.

Domestic dog *(Canis familiaris)*

The oldest remains of domestic dogs *(Canis familiaris)* have been dated at 11,000 and 12,000 years old, in Idaho and Iraq, respectively. Many researchers, however, believe that domesticated dogs may date to at least 20,000 years ago. Dogs may be descendants of the gray wolf that humans in Europe domesticated. Domesticated dogs have smaller brains than their wolf cousins.

BEARS

Family Ursidae

Like most animals, these magnificent creatures had humble beginnings. Bears descended from a small, tree-climbing carnivore of the Miacidae family that lived in Europe in late Eocene to early Oligocene time, 40 million to 35 million years ago. About 27 million years ago, in middle to late Oligocene time, bear ancestors were evolving from bearlike dogs in North America. By 20 million years ago, *Ursavus elemensis,* the oldest true bear, was wandering around subtropical Europe. It was a small animal, about the size of a fox terrier.

At least two bear subfamilies, containing six species, lived in North America during the Rancholabrean Land Mammal Age, from 200,000 to about 10,000 years ago. The subfamilies include Ursinae, or the living bears of Old World origin, and Tremarctinae of New World derivation. The genus *Ursus,* which includes the three modern North American species, arose about 5 million years ago in Eurasia. By 2.5 million years ago, black, grizzly, and cave bears were evolving toward their present forms in Europe from their common ancestor *Ursus etruscus,* or "modern bear." Approximately 1.5 million years ago, *Ursus etruscus* arrived in North America from Asia via Beringia, and the present North American species are its descendants.

Living bears (genus *Ursus*)

North America presently has black *(Ursus americanus),* grizzly or Alaskan brown *(Ursus arctos),* and polar bears *(Ursus maritimus).* Black bears can be traced back about 1 million years to the primitive black bear *(Ursus abstrusus),* a descendant of *Ursus etruscus.* Grizzlies date back to early Irvingtonian Land Mammal Age, 1.5 million years ago, and crossed into North America from Siberia between 200,000 and 130,000 years ago. We know little about the early history of polar bears because they live on ice and drop into the sea when dead. Over the millennia, bears have evolved toward larger size and, except for the polar bear, toward a more omnivorous diet. In general, modern male bears are usually much larger than females. Male blacks weigh up to 590 pounds (269 kilograms), grizzly males up to 1,700 pounds (700 kilograms), and male polar bears up to 1,100 pounds (500 kilograms).

Subfamily Tremarctinae

The subfamily Tremarctinae included extinct species within the genera *Tremarctos* and *Arctodus.* One species of *Tremarctos,* the spectacled bear *(T. ornatus),* still resides in South America. Extinct species of bears that roamed North America during the Ice Age until its bitter end about 10,000 years ago include the Florida cave bear *(Tremarctos floridanus)* and the so-called "bulldog bears," the giant short-faced bear *(Arctodus simus)* and the lesser short-faced bear *(Arctodus pristinus).*

Florida cave bear
(Tremarctos floridanus)

The Florida cave bear arrived in North America about 1.3 million years ago and went extinct about 8,000 years ago or later. This large but relatively small-toothed animal ranged widely in the southern United States. Its dentition suggests that it was probably vegetarian. The Florida cave bear was a large and muscular creature similar in shape, diet, and habits to the also-extinct European cave bear *(Ursus spelaeus),* and larger than its North American cousin the lesser short-faced bear *(Arctodus pristinus).*

Both Florida cave bears and European cave bears had skulls larger than those of most living bears except big grizzly bears. Their skulls, however, had a domed or vaulted forehead that is not seen in other species. Their large skulls did not contain proportionally larger brains than those of their other large cousins. The bears had large nasal cavities but small eye sockets, leading paleontologists to theorize that these cave bears probably had poor eyesight but a good sense of smell. The cave bears had the large grinding teeth of herbivores rather than the small grinding teeth of omnivorous grizzly bears, so they were most likely strict vegetarians.

Both sexes of cave bears had barrel-shaped bodies and big heads on long necks. They had short but very heavy and powerful limbs and feet, and wide paws. These massive beasts probably lumbered slowly along, swaying from side to side in their quest for tasty vegetation. Male cave bears were considerably larger than females. An average-sized male probably weighed 900 to 1,000 pounds (400 to 450 kilograms) and considerably more in the fall before hibernation.

During the Rancholabrean Land Mammal Age, the Florida cave bear inhabited swamps, lowlands, and valleys across the southern states from Florida to New Mexico and as far north as Georgia and Tennessee. Remains have been found in caves and sinkholes, commonly with those of black bears. Remains of the European cave bear are plentiful in caves across central and southern Europe from southern England and the Pyrenees Mountains of northern Spain to the Caucasus Mountains in the east.

The Florida cave bear was also similar to, but much larger than, the present-day South American spectacled bear, a 440-pound (200 kilograms) fellow that is barely surviving in mountainous regions of Panama south to Peru and Bolivia.

Short-faced bears
(genus Arctodus)

The giant and lesser short-faced bears and the spectacled bear of South America probably descended from an earlier tremarctine, *Plionarctos,* that lived between 5 million and 10 million years ago in Texas. Both short-faced bears were widespread in North America by 800,000 years ago.

The giant *(Arctodus simus)* and lesser *(Arctodus pristinus)* short-faced bears resembled each other. Their snouts appear short relative to the size of their heads—thus, the name "short-faced" bear. The width of the giant's skull was 80 percent that of the skull's length. With short faces and wide muzzles, the skulls of these two species resemble that of a big cat.

Both bears were less pigeon-toed than living bears and so walked a straight path rather than waddling from side to side. This toe-foot structure probably allowed the short-faced bears to run faster than brown and black bears. Most males were on average 15 percent larger than female bears. Studies of bones of both species show that some of these bears

Its large size and muscular build may suggest otherwise, but the Florida cave bear (Tremarctos floridanus) *was probably an herbivore.*

suffered from diseases similar to tuberculosis and syphilis.

The giant and lesser short-faced bears differed from each other in several important ways. The giant short-faced bear was not only at least several hundred pounds larger, but it also had longer legs, a shorter snout, and bigger, broader, and more crowded teeth well adapted to eating meat. The tooth structure of the lesser short-faced bear supported a more omnivorous diet than did that of its bigger cousin.

The lesser short-faced bear lived in the eastern United States and south into Mexico, preferring the wetter, forested regions. These magnificent animals lived until at least about 20,000 years ago.

The giant short-faced bear evidently preferred the more open, drier, grassy country west of the Mississippi River. Remains have been found from Alaska and Yukon south into Mexico, and from Pennsylvania west to California. Specimens of these animals found in the La Brea tar pits in southern California and elsewhere north into the Arctic show that the more northerly bears were larger than their cousins to the south. Cave remains are not uncommon, so both male and female bears may have inhabited caves for part of the year where they were available.

The giant short-faced bear, while long legged, was relatively short bodied for its leg length when compared with living bears. It also was not as heavily built as brown or grizzly bears. Even so, giant short-faced bears reached enormous sizes. At 5.5 feet tall (1.68 meters) and almost 10 feet (3 meters) long, the giant short-faced bear would dwarf the modern grizzly, which measures up to 4 feet (over 1 meter) tall and 9 feet (2.74 meters)

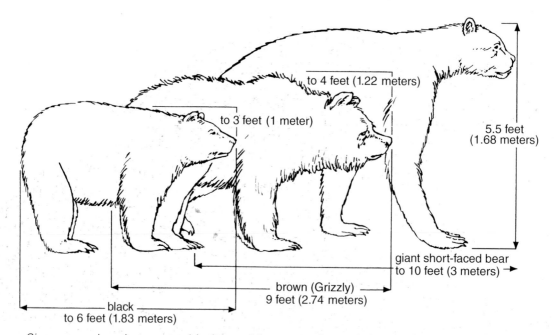

Size comparison between a black bear (Ursus americanus), *large grizzly or Alaskan brown bear* (Ursus arctos), *and the extinct giant short-faced bear* (Arctodus simus)
—Modified from Agenbroad, 1990

Skeletons of a giant short-faced bear (black) and a grizzly bear (white)
—Courtesy of the George C. Page Museum

Giant short-faced bear, Arctodus simus

long. When standing on their hind feet, the top of their head was more than 11 feet (3.4 meters) high. Male giant short-faced bears probably weighed more than 2,000 pounds (more than 900 kilograms) in the fall prior to hibernation. Compare this with a large grizzly bear, which before hibernation weighs about 1,700 pounds (770 kilograms).

The giant short-faced bear has been traced back to Irvingtonian Land Mammal Age. It may have come north from South America and coexisted with brown and grizzly bears. The youngest remains of these giant bears date at 12,650, plus or minus 350 years, before present. At least thirty specimens have been recovered from the La Brea tar pits in California and one from the Columbian mammoth burial pit at Hot Springs, South Dakota. Other important fossil localities are in Texas, Montana, Utah, and Wyoming.

What did the giant short-faced bear—the largest and most powerful of the Pleistocene bruins—eat? Whatever it was, they needed a lot. Paul Matheus, director of the Alaska Quaternary Center in Fairbanks, is convinced that these steppe-loving animals—with their very powerful jaws and large teeth capable of ripping, crushing, and gnawing—ate only meat. His proof comes from their bones. The ratio of two isotopes of nitrogen, nitrogen 15 and nitrogen 14, in bones can help researchers distinguish between carnivores, herbivores, and omnivores. Herbivore bones contain a low ratio whereas carnivore bones have a high ratio. Matheus found that the bones of giant short-faced bears have a high ratio of nitrogen 15 to nitrogen 14, supporting the contention that the animals were highly carnivorous.

Matheus's research also leads him to believe that the bone structure of this animal was not strong enough for it to bring down really large animals without getting hurt. Smaller animals such as horses, however, could evade the fast but less maneuverable bears. Matheus, therefore, thinks these animals were scavengers and that this lifestyle probably contributed strongly to their extinction. Once the other predators, such as American lions and scimitar cats, and their large prey were gone, there was not enough carrion left for the giant short-faced bear.

CATS
Family Felidae

The earliest members of the family Felidae date back about 40 million years to the forested regions of Eurasia. One of the earliest feline ancestors was *Proailurus lemanensis*. This small animal resembled the living genet, a small weasel-like carnivore related to mongooses. *Proailurus lemanensis* had short legs, a skull about 6 inches (15 centimeters) long, and more teeth than living cats have. Based on its body structure, paleontologists think the animal was a tree climber. The oldest North American cat remains are a proailurine dated at 16 million years.

The feline genus *Pseudaelurus* evolved in Europe and Africa about 20 million years ago. This genus led to the diverse lineages of the subfamilies Machairodontinae (saber-toothed cats) and the Felinae (true or conical-toothed cats). The fossil record is good for both subfamilies. While some of the saber-toothed cats became enormous beasts, the ancestors of true or conical-toothed living cats remained small until about 500,000 years ago, when lions and tigers developed.

Modern cats and those that recently became extinct, such as the saber-toothed cat, share many physical and genetic similarities because of their common ancestry. Features

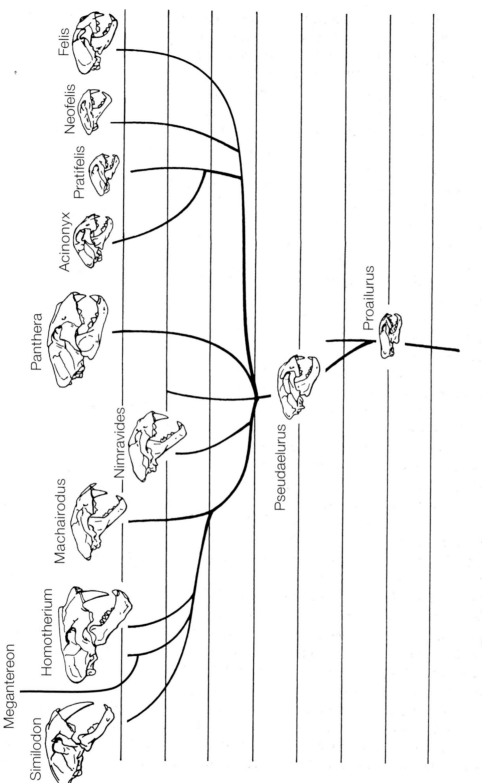

The phylogeny of cats and catlike carnivores as proposed by Van Valkenburgh, 1991.

include a shortened face when compared to bears (family Ursidae) and dogs (family Canidae). This feature, combined with large, forward-facing eyes, allows for stereoscopic vision for accurate distance determinations when hunting prey. Cats also have fewer teeth than most other carnivores and a jaw that permits only the carnassial pair of teeth to cut against each other, like scissor blades rather than the side to side grinding motion of herbivore jaws. Molar teeth behind the carnassial teeth are few. The canine teeth are long and large for grasping and killing prey.

Even with a good fossil record, much confusion exists as to the classification of cats and catlike carnivores, especially the early ones. There appear to have been two main evolutionary branches of cats and catlike animals. The earliest was probably the paleofelids or false saber-toothed beasts of the Family Nimravidae, which lived from about 35 million to possibly 5 million years ago. The other family, Neofelids of the family Felidae, originated about 25 million years ago. Some researchers believe the family Felidae arose from early members of the paleofelids. Most researchers today, however, are not in favor of this explanation.

Saber-Toothed Cats
Subfamily Machairodontinae

The machairodonts were a long-lived, widespread, and successful lineage that became extinct only at the end of the Pleistocene epoch. Species of the Machairodontinae subfamily include the western dirktooth, gracile saber-tooth, Idaho saber-tooth, false saber-tooth, saber-toothed cat, and scimitar cat. Body types varied from the long-legged *Homotherium*, the scimitar cat, to the more massive, shorter-legged *Smilodon*, the saber-toothed cat. However, all species had particularly strong forequarters for attacking and then holding prey while they used their massive teeth to dispatch the victim. The abundance of severely injured but healed bones of machairodonts supports the contention that they were social animals—that is, they helped each other. Without help and a shared food supply, the wounded animals would soon have starved.

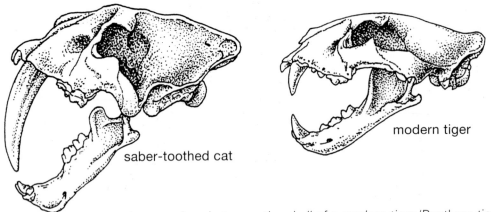

saber-toothed cat

modern tiger

A comparison between the skull of a modern tiger (Panthera tigris) *and an extinct saber-toothed cat* (Smilodon fatalis)

Saber-toothed cats had much-enlarged and flattened upper canine teeth and smaller lower canines. All members of the saber-tooth lineage appear to have died out in Eurasia by middle Pleistocene time, less than 1 million years ago, but they flourished until the end of that epoch, about 10,000 to 9,400 years ago, in the Western Hemisphere.

Dirk-toothed cat
(Megantereon hesperus)

The western dirk-toothed cat was a late Pliocene cat about the size of a puma. It weighed around 275 pounds (125 kilograms). The dirk-toothed cat had long sabers, up to 2 to 3 inches (5 to 7.5 centimeters) long, though shorter than those of its well-known descendant the saber-toothed cat (*Smilodon fatalis*). The western dirk-toothed cat evolved in Eurasia and died out in North America near the beginning of the Pleistocene epoch, about 2 million years ago. Remains of this cat have been found in Idaho, Kansas, Nebraska, and Florida. Much less is known about gracile, Idaho, and false saber-toothed cats, most of which had appreciably smaller upper canines than the saber-toothed cat. What we do know about these cats, based upon their skeletons, is that they must have looked similar to presently living big cats such as African lions. Remains of the false saber-tooth have been found in Texas, of the Idaho cat in California and Texas, and of the gracile cat in Pennsylvania, Florida, California, and Mexico.

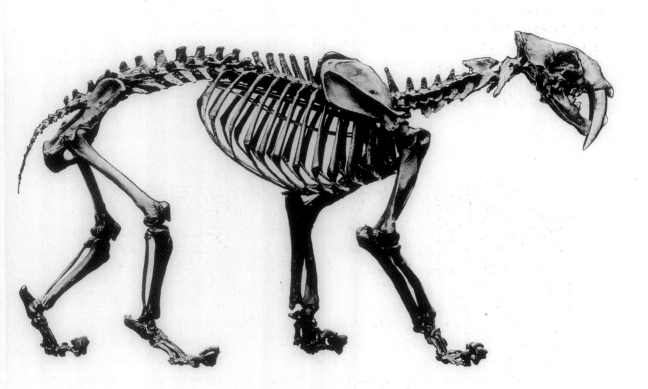

Skeleton of saber-toothed cat, Smilodon fatalis —Courtesy of the George C. Page Museum

A saber-toothed cat,
Smilodon fatalis

Saber-toothed cat
(Smilodon fatalis)

The impressive saber-toothed cat—with its fearsome front canine teeth exposed for as much as 7 inches (17 centimeters) below the upper jaw—is one of the best-known Pleistocene animals because of its abundance in the sedimentary record. Fossils date back to late Irvingtonian Land Mammal Age, about 800,000 years ago, and the last of the species probably went extinct as little as 8,000 years ago.

The distribution of at least forty Rancholabrean Land Mammal Age fossil sites in North America indicate the saber-toothed cat hunted and scavenged from southern Canada south into Peru and from Florida west to California and Oregon. The Rancho La Brea tar pits in Los Angeles, California, alone have produced more than 2,500 individuals. At the tar pits, the cats evidently feasted on large animals mired in the black, smelly goo, only to sometimes perish the same way their victims had. While the total number of animals recovered is impressive, on average only about one animal was trapped every eleven years during the existence of both the saber-toothed cat and the tar pits.

Based on the saber-tooth's skeleton and skull structure, the animal's closest living relative is the African lion. The saber-toothed cat was about 3 feet (1 meter) tall at the shoulder, which is about 1 foot (30 centimeters) shorter than the African lion. From snout to rump, the saber-tooth measured 5.5 feet (1.7 meters) compared with the 7-foot (2.1-meter) length of a lion. But, at perhaps 750 pounds (340 kilograms), the saber-toothed cat weighed nearly twice as much as the African lion. The cat's throat bones, called hyoids, indicate that it could roar like a lion. The saber-toothed cat's great bulk and relatively short legs and tail, compared with those of running cats such as leopards, lions, and cheetahs, strongly suggest that it waited in ambush for large prey, such as ground sloths, bison, and young mammoths, rather than trying to run the animals down.

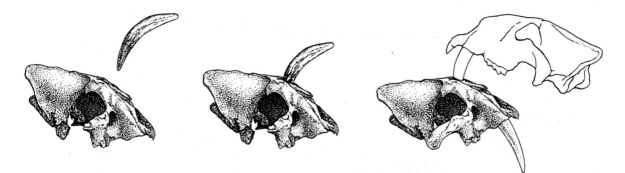

Even saber-toothed cats were not immune to the bite of other members of the clan, as this specimen retrieved from the Rancho La Brea tar pits of Los Angeles, California, shows. The attack was most likely fatal. —Modified from a photograph from Mestel, 1993

Scientists originally thought that the cats used their huge upper canines to inflict fatal wounds only to the neck and shoulders of large, slow-moving animals. However, paleontologists have found such wounds in skulls of glyptodonts, dire wolves, and even other saber-toothed cats. And research on various aspects of the 166,000 bones retrieved from the Rancho La Brea tar pits suggests the cats used their teeth for other purposes, too. The research paints the best picture to date of how the saber-toothed cat lived.

An important feature of the bone collection from the Rancho La Brea tar pits is the number of injured and deformed saber-toothed cat bones. Some animals had dislocated hips, bite wounds (some inflicted by other saber-toothed cats), and other injuries that indicate some animals were crippled and, therefore, could not run. For such injured animals to survive, saber-toothed cats probably had a social or family structure, like African lion prides. This contradicts earlier notions that

saber-tooths led solitary lives as tigers and leopards do.

Other remains of saber-toothed cats have crushed chests, fractured lower limbs, and lumpy and knobby bone growth, which are signs of repeated muscle injury. The feline hunters may have sustained such injuries while pushing and pulling large prey such as slow-moving sloths and juvenile mastodons and mammoths. The injuries also suggest to William Akersten, former curator at the George C. Page Museum at the Rancho La Brea tar pits, that the cats may have preferred to attack their victims' bellies—as do the curved-toothed Komodo dragons on the island of Timor in the East Indies—rather than attacking the animals' neck as previously believed. Attacks into the boned and strongly muscled necks of prey would have resulted in many more broken teeth than found in the cat remains recovered from the Rancho La Brea tar pits. Only two of the seven hundred skulls recovered from the tar show broken teeth with wear. Apparently, after ripping chunks of flesh from the prey animal's belly, the cat would wait until the animal bled to death before beginning its main course.

Scimitar cat
(Homotherium serum)

The scimitar cat *(Homotherium serum)* was another late member of the feline subfamily Machairodontinae that roamed North America during the Ice Age. Based on fossil finds, it was apparently less abundant than its contemporary the saber-toothed cat. Scimitar cats, however, ranged much more widely over North America than their saber-toothed relative. The scimitar cat lived in both the New and Old Worlds, including Africa. *Homotherium serum* and its Old World relative, *Homotherium ultimum,* descended during late Pliocene to early Pleistocene time from *Homotherium crenatidens,* which ranged across the northern parts of both the New and Old Worlds. Remains of the scimitar cat in the New World, first observed in Blancan Land Mammal Age deposits more than 2 million years old, have been found from ice-free central Alaska, Yukon, and the Northwest Territories south into Idaho, California, South Dakota, Nebraska, Kansas, Oklahoma, Tennessee, Texas, and Florida.

The scimitar cat was heavier than the African lion, weighing up to 620 pounds (280 kilograms) as compared with the African lion's 375 to 500 pounds (170 to 225 kilograms). This cat had slender front legs, a long neck, short tail, and powerful rear legs. It also possessed nonretractable claws on both front and rear feet (see Chapter 1, page 2, for an artist's depiction of a scimitar cat).

The scimitar cat was named for the 4-inch-long (10-centimeter), slender, curved, and serrated upper fangs or canine teeth. The serrated edges would have cut like steak knives.

The lack of wear observed on teeth from adult specimens supports the concept that the animals used them only for slashing and ripping skin and flesh. In 1824, famous French paleontologist Baron Cuvier was the first to describe the teeth of this great cat, although he believed the teeth came from a bear that once lived in France. American paleontologist E. D. Cope wrote the first description of a North American specimen in 1893.

The skull shows that the scimitar cat had a large section of the brain devoted to sight and large nasal openings for rapid air intake. The large air passages, together with the animal's slender front limbs, have led researchers to theorize that the cat probably was capable of short bursts of speeds close to 40 miles per hour (65 kilometers per hour) and was able to leap onto prey.

Researchers have found remains of both young and old scimitar cats in caves with remains of their prey in both the New World, Europe, and Asia. A remarkable cave with abundant remains is Friesenhahn in Texas. There, paleontologists have collected the intact remains of at least thirteen cubs and twenty adults, including three very old adults, and partial skeletal remains of more than six hundred other individuals. Most or all of the cubs were apparently too young to have ever left the cave before they died.

Also found in the cave are the remains of between three hundred and four hundred juvenile mammoths. Their teeth indicate that the majority were two years old or younger. This is about the age that young modern elephants in India and Africa begin to play with each other and venture away from their mothers. If mammoths behaved similarly to living elephants, which they probably did, the two-year-olds would have been vulnerable to sneak attacks from cats hiding in nearby ground cover. The idea that babies of large herbivores were a favorite food of scimitar cats also gains support from the fact that elsewhere in the world, different *Homotherium* species preyed not only on baby mammoths but also on juvenile mastodons and rhinos. Following an attack and the slashing of vulnerable throat arteries, the young animal would bleed to death. Then the cat would drag it back to the den for a family feast.

TRUE CATS

There are three subfamilies of true cats. The great cats of the subfamily Pantherinae, lions, leopards, and jaguars, roar but don't purr. Most cats belong to the subfamily Felinae, including pumas, lynxes, bobcats, and domestic cats; these cats purr but can't roar. The members of both subfamilies have color vision and night vision six times better than a human's. The sole members of the subfamily Acinonychinae, cheetahs are also the only cats without retractable claws.

Great Cats
Subfamily Pantherinae
Ice Age Lions

A most impressive extinct member of this lineage was the long-legged American lion (*Panthera leo atrox*). It was huge—males were as much as one-fourth bigger than the Indian tiger of Asia, which may weigh up to 575 pounds (260 kilograms). The American lion approached the size of the Siberian tiger, which can tip the scales at 845 pounds (385 kilograms). Although called a lion, this Rancholabrean Land Mammal Age emigrant from Eurasia was perhaps closer genetically to a giant jaguar. It survived in North America until at least 10,370 years ago.

Panthera gombaszoegensis, the earliest known ancestor of lions, including the American lion, dates from approximately 1.5-million-year-old sedimentary deposits in eastern Africa. By 500,000 years ago, primitive lions (*Panthera leo fossilis*) were roaming the steppes of Europe and Asia. About 350,000 years ago, *Panthera youngi*, which closely resembled the American lion, was living in northeastern China. Another relative, the cave lion (*Panthera leo spelaea*), lived from about 300,000 to 10,000 years ago in steppelike and desert regions of Eurasia from England to Siberia.

Ancestors of American lions apparently crossed from Asia into Alaska sometime during the Illinoian glacial stage, 187,000 to 129,000 years ago. They reached the continental United States south of the ice sheet by about 125,000 years ago. The American lion was perhaps the most widespread land mammal ever, ranging over North America and most of South America, as well as Africa and Eurasia. Only Australia, Antarctica, and islands escaped its teeth and claws.

American lions apparently were fast on their feet—researchers estimate the animals could reach top speeds of around 30 miles per hour (50 kilometers per hour). This lion had a larger brain, relative to its size, than any other lion, living or dead. It evidently had a very functional design because the animal experienced few evolutionary changes during its long reign.

Specimens are plentiful. At least eighty individuals were excavated from the asphaltic deposits at Rancho La Brea, California. The American lion's presence in the tar pits may have been due to behavior rather than sheer abundance in the area, however. Paleo-Indians hunted the American lion, and remains of hunted animals have been found in Jaguar Cave in Idaho.

Based on Paleolithic cave paintings in Europe, some researchers theorize that

American lions may have been more solitary than African lions, and looked different from their African counterparts.

In European cave art, the animal appears alone or in very small groups. Males in the paintings do not have large manes, and recent studies of African lions show that mane size correlates directly with pride size. Where large prides exist in Africa, there is much competition between males, and the males with the largest prides have the largest manes. Conversely, in areas with small prides, the males have much smaller manes. Perhaps the American lion's small mane reflected a more solitary lifestyle, or as others speculate, perhaps the paintings depict female lions. Recent work on African lions suggests to some researchers that there may be two living species of African lions—a long-maned and a short-maned form.

Jaguars

Ice Age jaguars, which date from early Irvingtonian time or about 1.5 million years ago, were at least 15 to 20 percent larger than living jaguars (*Panthera onca*), and also had a more extensive range. During pre-Wisconsinan glacial time, more than 71,000 years ago, these large predators ranged northward to Washington, Nebraska, Pennsylvania, and Maryland. During the subsequent Wisconsinan ice age (71,000 to 10,000 years ago) the northern boundary of their range stretched from Nevada, Kansas, Mississippi, and Tennessee. While jaguars were present in northern California during the Irvingtonian Land Mammal Age, 1.5 million to about 300,000 years ago, no remains have been found in younger Rancholabrean age deposits (younger than about 300,000 years) in California even though

American lion
(Panthera leo atrox)

these deposits host plentiful American lion remains. Today jaguars are restricted to an area from Patagonia and Brazil north to southernmost Texas, New Mexico, and Arizona.

Jaguars, the largest New World cat and the only one that can roar, are smaller than their close relatives the lions, and have proportionally shorter and stockier legs. While we do not know what the jaguars looked like that inhabited the United States during the Pleistocene epoch, they presumably resembled living jaguars, with beautifully spotted coats distinctly different from the tan coats of lions. Living jaguars are solitary cats that inhabit forested areas, swamps, and arid mountain scrub.

Small Cats
Subfamily Felinae

The so-called small cats include cats of substantial size, like the puma, which dates from late Rancholabrean Land Mammal Age. Smaller living cats in North and Central America today include the ocelot *(Felis pardalis)* and jaguarundi *(Felis yagouaroundi)*, which made the scene in Rancholeabrean Land Mammal Age; and the margay *(Felis wiedii)*, which arrived in North America during Holocene time.

Puma *(Felis concolor)*

The puma, also known as the cougar or mountain lion, has one of the most widespread ranges in the world. Found in the Americas, it

WEIGHTS OF LARGE MALES OF MODERN CAT SPECIES

jaguar *(Panthera onca)*	300 pounds	(136 kilograms)
puma *(Felis concolor)*	275 pounds	(125 kilograms)
ocelot *(Felis pardalis)*	40 pounds	(18 kilograms)
jaguarundi *(Felis yagouaroundi)*	18 pounds	(8 kilograms)
margay *(Felis wiedii)*	22 pounds	(10 kilograms)
lynx *(Lynx lynx)*	40 pounds	(18 kilograms)
bobcat *(Lynx rufus)*	29 pounds	(13 kilograms)

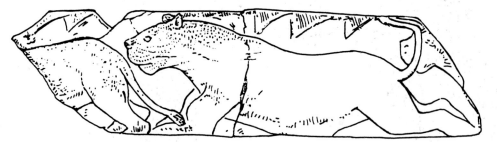

European lions carved on an animal rib, Musée des Antiquités Nationales, Saint-Germain-en-Laye, France

ranges from British Columbia and Alberta south to Patagonia in southern South America. Pumas inhabit environments that range from sea level to 15,000 feet (more than 5,000 meters) in South America. Farther north, pumas coexist with the reclusive and rare short-tailed Canada lynx *(Lynx lynx)* and the more common bobcat *(Lynx rufus)*. The oldest remains of pumas date to about 125,000 years ago. Remains of the smaller cats date to late Blancan Land Mammal Age, about 2 million years ago.

Male pumas weigh up to 275 pounds (125 kilograms), females to about 100 pounds (45 kilograms). This solitary animal, unlike most cats, hunts both day and night and can live for more than 20 years. It inhabits forested mountains, tall-grass prairies, and semi-arid terrain. Its population is increasing in the western mountain states, and pumas have been observed in some eastern states, too. Males may have a territory of 115,000 acres that they share with a harem of six or seven females. Pumas are good tree climbers and jumpers. Their diet consists mainly of large mammals, especially deer, which they can outrun for short distances. Pumas also eat raccoons, rabbits, beavers, coyotes, and even porcupines, mice, and grasshoppers.

Remains of pumas have been found in more than thirty Rancholabrean sites scattered across the southern United States from Florida to California, and north into Idaho and Wyoming. They apparently occupied habitats during the ice ages that were similar to those they live in today. The fossils indicate that the animals were larger but had smaller canine teeth than their modern descendants.

Puma, a word from the Quechua language of the Incas, means "powerful animal." The word *cougar* is derived from the Brazilian word *cuguacuarana,* and *panther* is of Greek and Latin origin. This animal has more names than almost any other animal in the world. There are eighteen South American, twenty-five North American, and forty English names for this magnificent predator.

Cheetahs
Subfamily Acinonychinae

Two species of cheetah of the genus *Acinonyx* lived in North America during the Pleistocene epoch: the larger Studer's cheetah *(Acinonyx studeri)* and the smaller descendant of Studer's cheetah, the American cheetah *(Acinonyx trumani)*. These cats differ from the other large cats in having slim, elongated legs, a relatively small head, and a light body clearly built for speed like their living African counterparts.

New World cheetahs have been classified as a more primitive subgenus, *Miracinonyx,* of their African cousins. This plus their close spatial and temporal relationships to pumas of New World derivation support the contention of some paleontologists that cheetahs originated in the New World and then spread to the Old World.

The last of the American cheetahs vanished about 20,000 years ago. Remains have been found in Nevada and Wyoming. Fossils of the older Studer's cheetah have been unearthed in Blancan and early Irvingtonian Land Mammal Age deposits in Texas, Arizona, and Pennsylvania.

HYENAS
Family Hyaenidae

Scientists long believed that the carnivorous hyena never lived in North America. Although the fossil record for this family is poor, there is evidence of the animal's existence in North America. Hyenas evolved in Asia and Africa during Miocene time, about 5 million years ago, and were suited for both scavenging and attacking live victims. Premolar teeth evolved into either conical bone smashers, as found in the living African hyenas, or slender teeth for ripping flesh, as in the extinct American species. While doglike in appearance, hyenas are anatomically closer to cats.

The American hunting hyena (*Chasmaporthetes ossifragus*) had slender teeth and long, slender legs very much like the living African cheetah. The hyena's front legs were longer than its rear legs. Built for speed, these animals ranged over what is now Arizona and Mexico during Blancan and early Irvingtonian Land Mammal Ages, between 5 million to 1.5 million years ago.

Seals, Sea Lions, and Walruses
Suborder Pinnipedia

Carnivorous marine mammals, or pinnipeds, evolved from terrestrial carnivores in middle Tertiary time. The oldest fossil remains were found in 22-million-year-old rocks in California. Early pinnipeds lived in both the North Pacific and Atlantic Oceans. Some of the living species

Artist's rendition of the American hunting hyena (Chasmaporthetes ossifragus). *In this version, the animal has spots, but we do not know what the exterior of these extinct hyenas looked like.*

attain large sizes, and all have insulating blubber and limbs that evolved into flippers. In comparison to their land-loving, meat-eating counterparts, these big animals have vision, hearing, respiratory and circulatory systems well adapted to marine water. However, their sense of smell is not that of land mammals.

WALRUSES
Family Odobenidae

These large animals evolved about 14 million years ago in temperate Pacific Ocean waters. By 8 million years ago, there were two sub-families: the Dusignathinae, which had equally large upper and lower canine teeth, and the Odobeninae, which had enlarged upper canine teeth, or tusks, and small lower canine teeth. The Dusignathinae stayed in the Pacific Ocean, and all members of the family went extinct about 4 million years ago. Members of the more successful Odobeninae family, however, spread southward along the west coast of North America, eventually making their way into the Caribbean Sea through a seaway that closed about 3.5 million years ago. Those animals that reached the Atlantic Ocean then spread northward along the east coast of North America and into Arctic waters.

Odobenus rosmarus, the only living walrus species, grew to relish cold North Atlantic waters. The species eventually spread westward through the Canadian Queen Elizabeth Islands into the northern Pacific Ocean waters less than 1 million years ago.

Walruses, which attain weights of 3,000 pounds (1,365 kilograms), have ever-growing ivory tusks, their upper canine teeth. A male's tusks may reach more than 3 feet (1 meter) long; a female's tusks can be 2 feet (60 centimeters) long. Bulls may reach lengths of 12 feet (3.7 meters) while females are about two-thirds as large.

Humankind has greatly restricted the range and numbers of these ponderously large animals. As late as the sixteenth century, walruses lived as far south as the Gulf of St. Lawrence and Nova Scotia on the western side of the Atlantic Ocean, and along the coast of Great Britain on the eastern side of the Atlantic. Pleistocene walrus remains have been unearthed as far south as Cape Hatteras, North Carolina. The southernmost Pacific Ocean specimen was dredged up off of San Francisco, California. These more southerly habitats during Pleistocene time may have reflected cooler sea temperatures, which in turn allowed for a more southerly range of particular fish stocks that walruses eat. Alternatively, the retreat northward may have been triggered by human hunting pressure.

FUR SEALS AND SEA LIONS
Family Otariidae

The Otariidae family of fur seals and sea lions came into existence by approximately 12 million years ago. These animals apparently evolved slowly until about 3 million years ago, when their rate of evolutionary development increased. Fur seals are the oldest members of this family.

By 5 million years ago, seals had reached the Southern Hemisphere and lived on both the eastern and western shores of the Pacific Ocean. Because the Isthmus of Panama had yet to rise above sea level and thereby connect North and South America, these animals likely also lived along part of the Atlantic coast of eastern South America. As a family, Otariids are noted for their gregariousness—they tend to stick together. Otariids have slender bodies when compared to their cousins in the family Odobenidae. They have long flippers, external ears, and large, pointed canine teeth.

The largest member of the family is the sea lion. Sea lions appeared in the fossil record about 3 million years ago on the coasts of both the western and eastern Pacific Ocean. Today, colonies of sea lions exist in the north Pacific Ocean and Bering Sea. The living sea lion species are Steller's sea lion *(Eumetopias jubata)* and California sea lion *(Zalophus californianus)*. The oldest remains of Steller's sea lion are between about 125,000 and 75,000 years old. Steller's males attain lengths of 11.5 feet (3.5 meters) and may weigh up to 2,420 pounds (1,100 kilograms), while females reach 9 feet (2.7 meters) and only 770 pounds (350 kilograms). Late Pleistocene fossils of Steller's sea lions have been found with *Mammuthus* and *Bison* remains in Alaska.

The oldest remains of California sea lions date from at least late Pleistocene time, approximately 20,000 years ago. Today the animals inhabit the Galápagos Islands about 600 miles (960 kilometers) off the coast of Ecuador, the west coast of North America, and the southern Sea of Japan. Males may weigh up to 615 pounds (280 kilograms) and reach 7.7 feet (2.35 meters) long, and females can reach 200 pounds (90 kilograms) and attain 6 feet (1.8 meters) in length. Pre-Holocene remains have been found only in late Pleistocene deposits in and around Los Angeles, California.

SEALS
Family Phocidae
Subfamily Monachinae

The northern elephant seal *(Mirounga angustirostris)*, one of the two biggest pinnipeds, evolved in Pleistocene time. The name refers to its monstrous proboscis, or nose, which may be more than 3 feet (1 meter) long. Elephant seals live from central Baja California, Mexico, north to southern Alaska. During the Pleistocene epoch, the distribution of glaciers undoubtedly restricted their range. Both sexes are deep feeders and may stay submerged for as long as eighty minutes.

The only Pleistocene remains of this magnificent animal have been found along the coast of southern California. Presumably,

Plants, fish, and bull and cow seals carved on a 12,000-year-old reindeer antler (14.5 inches/37 centimeters long) on display at the National Museum of Natural History in Paris, France.

early humans hunted northern elephant seals, but no kill sites have been found.

A male northern elephant seal may grow as long as 13 feet (4 meters) and weigh as much as 4,400 pounds (2,000 kilograms). At up to 1,320 pounds (600 kilograms), females are much smaller but still large by human standards. For their size, these giants of the sea do not live very long lives. Twelve to twenty years is about normal. Walruses, in comparison, live to be about forty. Elephant seal bulls fight for the right to have harems of females, which usually number about forty. However, an individual male's reign usually lasts only a very few years, and some bulls never have a chance to breed during their entire lives.

The northern elephant seal holds several noteworthy mammalian records. Females produce milk that is not only the richest in fat at 54.5 percent but also the lowest in water content at 32.8 percent. And the deepest dive ever recorded for an air-breathing vertebrate goes to a northern elephant seal. The record dive of 5,187 feet (1,581 meters) was documented in 1989.

Rendered almost extinct by whalers in the 1890s, the animal has made a spectacular recovery and now numbers more than 115,000.

References: Agenbroad, 1990; Antón and Turner, 1997; Brown, 1993; Colbert and Morales, 1990; Greiner, 2000; Guthrie, 1990; Hansen, 1992; Harington, 1996b, 1996c, 1996f; Kurten, 1968, 1976; Kurten and Anderson, 1980; Lambert, 1985; Mestel, 1993; Nelson, 1994; Novikov, 1962; Rawn-Schatzinger, 1992; Stock and Harris, 1992; Van Valkenburgh, 1991; Whitaker, 1996

Northern elephant seal,
Mirounga angustirostris

Rodents

ORDER RODENTIA

The order Rodentia is the most diversified and successful of all mammalian orders. The more than three thousand species of the order exceed in number the combined total of all other mammal species. Some of the order's species are also the most difficult to classify. Rodents apparently originated in North America in late Paleocene time. The first recognized family was the Paramyidae, and the first known rodent was of the genus *Paramys*. *Paramys* resembled a large squirrel and weighed perhaps 1 to 2.5 pounds (0.5 to 1.1 kilograms).

Rodents as an order owe their success to their small body size, frequent breeding, short gestation period, great numbers of most species, adaptability to changing environmental conditions, and range of inhabitable environments. Until humans began transporting them, they inhabited all landmasses except Australia, Antarctica, and most islands. Now they live almost everywhere.

Rodents have a pair of chisel-shaped, rootless, ever-growing incisor teeth in each jaw. They have no canine teeth, one set of premolars in the lower jaw, and three or fewer sets of molars. While most species are vegetarians, some are insectivores and others are omnivorous. Because the habitats rodents occupy are so varied—they include forests, deserts, grasslands, mountains, and watery environments—remains of these animals and their entombing sediments are good paleoecological indicators. Pollen, seeds, and spores that indicate many climatic parameters commonly accompany rodent remains.

Members of the order include squirrels, marmots, prairie dogs, and chipmunks of the family Sciuridae; pocket gophers of the family Geomyidae; kangaroo rats of the family Heteromyidae; long-tailed and large-hind-footed jumping mice of the family Zapodidae; and hamsters, voles, rats, mice, water rats, muskrats, and lemmings of the family Cricetidae. Members of the family Cricetidae, which first appeared in North America during Tertiary time, more than 25 million years ago, are especially important animals because their diversity and abundance have resulted in numerous fossil sites and specimens that provide an insight into the evolutionary changes these animals have undergone. At least 130 species of Cricetidae, both extinct and modern, have been found in Pleistocene deposits of North America. The rodent species mentioned in this book are members of the family Aplodontidae containing sewellels or mountain "beavers," family Erethizontidae containing New World porcupines, family Hydrochoeridae containing capybaras, and family Castoridae containing those wood-loving, dam-building beavers. These families contain some of the largest and most unusual-looking and -acting rodents of the Ice Age.

Sewellel (*Aplodontia rufa*)

The family Aplodontidae has lived in North America since the end of Oligocene time, about 25 million years ago. The nocturnal sewellel or mountain beaver (*Aplodontia rufa*) is the sole living member of this ancient family. Sewellels appear to have lived in the same region they inhabit today since early in the Pleistocene epoch, or about 1.5 million years ago.

The sewellel is apparently the most primitive rodent alive today, based upon the construction of its teeth and eye sockets. The family name Aplodontidae comes from the Greek words *Aploos*, meaning "simple," and *dontos*, meaning "tooth"—and simple the sewellel's teeth are. Their evergrowing, rootless teeth are nearly circular pegs. This seldom-seen animal looks like a short, stocky muskrat without a tail. Individuals weigh between 1.7 to 3.3 pounds (775 to 1,500 grams). Sewellels inhabit elevations below 7,000 feet (2,200 meters) in the Pacific Northwest of the North America, from both the Coast Range and Sierra Nevada of central California northward into southern British Columbia. These animals never travel more than a few hundred yards from home. They eat succulent plants and seedlings, dig tunnels, and den in the moist ground. Their population densities may reach up to twenty per 2.5 acres (1 hectare), and individual sewellels may live up to six years. Paleontologists think sewellels lived and looked much the same during Pleistocene time as they do now.

A sewellel, or mountain beaver (Aplodontia rufa). The name comes from the Chinook Indian word shewallal, dual, *for a blanket made of two sewellel skins sewn together. Lewis and Clark misunderstood and thought the name referred to the animal itself.*

PORCUPINES
Family Erethizontidae

Porcupines belong to the family Erethizontidae, which presently contains four genera and twelve species. In addition, three extinct species are known from fossils in North America. Members of the family have lived in South America since Oligocene time, about 30 million years ago, and in North America since late Pliocene time, about 2 million years ago. These solitary-living vegetarians wear a coat of sharp, barbed spines, called quills, for protection. However, some animals, such as pumas, can flip a porcupine over and attack its quill-free underside for an evidently fine meal. The North American porcupines generally weigh between 7.7 and 15.5 pounds (3.5 and 7 kilograms), but some individuals may reach 40 pounds (18 kilograms). The animal ranges over most of Canada, the western United States, and New England. During the Pleistocene epoch, porcupines also inhabited the southeastern United States. These animals prefer deciduous, coniferous, and mixed forests but also live in deserts and in dry scrubby areas with scattered trees. During Pleistocene time, their range was restricted to south of the ice sheet's margin. Pleistocene porcupines were the same species as the modern ones and presumably looked much like their modern descendants.

CAPYBARAS
Family Hydrochoeridae

Capybaras, of the family Hydrochoeridae, originated in South America in early Pliocene time, about 5 million years ago, and wended their way into North America in the Pleistocene. They went extinct in North America during Rancholabrean Land Mammal Age, sometime before 10,000 years ago. Today, capybaras range from Panama south to northern Argentina.

Capybaras, also known as South American water hogs, are the giants of the modern rodent world, with *Hydrochoerus hydrochoeris* weighing up to 110 pounds (50 kilograms). The animals measure about 20 inches (50 centimeters) high at the shoulder. Females are generally larger than the males. Capybaras look like giant guinea pigs and have four semiwebbed toes on the front feet and three on the rear feet. Capybaras have a vestigial tail and are covered with long, coarse but sparse hair. These tropical to semitropical animals are semiaquatic and prefer lakes, rivers, marshes, and estuaries. Capybaras eat grasses and plants. Females typically breed only once a year and have up to seven young. Both diurnal and nocturnal, these animals graze alone and in groups of up to twenty individuals. When frightened, they run like a herd of stampeding horses.

Massive as they are, modern capybaras are only about two-thirds the size of the extinct Pinckney's capybara *(Neochoerus pinckneyi)*. This rodent brute lived in North America from early to late Pleistocene time, perhaps 1.5 million to about 10,000 years ago. Pinckney's capybara weighed as much as 155 pounds (70 kilograms). Its teeth were approximately 30 percent larger than those of modern species. Remains have been found near Charleston, South Carolina, and at several sites in Florida. These capybaras probably

Pinckney's capybara (Neochoerus pinckneyi), *an extinct giant capybara of North and South America. These rodents weighed up to 155 pounds (70 kilograms) compared with the living modern species that may weigh 110 pounds (50 kilograms).*

lived much the way the modern species do today and probably inhabited similar watery environments. No human kill sites have been found, but Paleo-Indians may have relished them, as people in South America enjoy extant capybaras today. Another capybara that also inhabited Florida during the Pleistocene epoch was Holmes's capybara (*Hydrochoerus holmesi*). Little is known about these animals.

BEAVERS
Family Castoridae
The biggest of all rodents during Pleistocene time—or any time, for that matter—were beavers of the family Castoridae. These semiaquatic rodents of the Northern Hemisphere existed in North America as long ago as early Oligocene time, 35 million to 30 million years ago. Modern beavers are descendants of an early beaver called *Dipoides* that lived in North America and Eurasia about 5 million years ago. *Dipoides* gave rise to a beaver called *Procastoroides* that was larger than living beavers and approximately two-thirds the size of the giant beaver. *Procastoroides* was probably the direct ancestor of the giant beaver.

Giant beaver (Castoroides ohioensis)
The giant beaver was the size of a large black bear and weighed 330 to 440 pounds (150 to 200 kilograms). It measured at least 9 feet (3 meters) long and stood about 3 feet (1 meter) tall at the shoulder. In comparison, the modern beaver measures up to 3.5 feet (more than 1 meter) long and weighs from 20 to 86 pounds (9 to 39 kilograms). While resembling a modern beaver, the giant beaver had a longer and narrower tail. The giant beaver had huge incisors up to 6 inches (15 centimeters) long. Researchers have found no evidence to tell us whether this heavyweight built dams or felled trees, but based on the giant beaver's build,

paleontologists believe it behaved much as living beavers do. Remains have been found from in the eastern half of the United States and in Alaska, Old Crow region, Yukon, and north of the Arctic Circle, but not west of Nebraska in the lower forty-eight states or on other continents. Giant beavers may have spread north by way of lakes along the southern margin of the Canadian Shield, when the last (Wisconsinan) glaciation was waning.

The abundance of fossils suggests the giant beaver's favorite locales were ponds, lakes, and swamps south of the Great Lakes, where it ate coarse swamp vegetation. The first known remains of the giant beaver were found in the first half of the nineteenth century in a peat bog or swamp near Nashport, Ohio—hence the species name *ohioensis*. The oldest of the species date from Blancan Land Mammal Age, about 3 million years ago, and the last of their kind died late in the Wisconsinan glaciation of early Holocene time, about 10,000 years ago.

American beaver (Castor canadensis)
The living representative of the family Castoridae, the American beaver, dates back to late Blancan Land Mammal Age, at least 2 million years ago. It thrives along waterways throughout the United States except in parts of Florida, Nevada, and California. Beavers also inhabit most of Canada and central Alaska, except northeastern Canada and along the shores of the Arctic Ocean. During the Ice Age, the American beaver inhabited similar habitat and range as the giant beaver.

References: Colbert and Morales, 1991; Harington, 1996d; Kurten and Anderson, 1980; Martin and Klein, 1984; Redford and Eisenberg, 1992

Odd-Toed Ungulates
ORDER PERISSODACTYLA
Horses, Rhinos, and Tapirs

The name Perissodactyla, from the Greek *perissos*, odd, and *daktylos*, finger or toe, refers to the odd number of toes on each foot. These ungulates—hoofed herbivores—arose in the Northern Hemisphere in late Paleocene time, about 60 million years ago, and radiated rapidly in both Asia and North America during Eocene time, about 57 million to 37 million years ago. (North America was joined to Eurasia until early Tertiary time, 57 million years ago, when Greenland separated from Europe.) The order has a good assemblage of fossils. Perissodactyls evolved along three paths: the Ancylopoda lineage produced chalicotheres, which resembled clawed horses; Ceratomorpha led to tapirs and rhinos; and Hippomorpha contained now-extinct palaeotheres and titanotheres, and gave rise to today's horses.

Palaeotheres evolved rapidly in Europe during Eocene time, 57 million to 38 million years ago. By the end of that epoch, they were the size of small rhinos and had heavy legs, three-toed feet, and a tapirlike skull. They became extinct during Oligocene time, about 30 million years ago.

Titanotheres date to early Eocene time. They began as small horselike animals. By the time of their extinction in middle Oligocene

The giant beaver, Castoroides ohioensis, *measured at least 9 feet (3 meters) long and weighed up to 440 pounds (200 kilograms). The smaller, modern American beaver (left foreground) provides a size comparison.*

time, 30 million years ago, they were huge, massive animals that stood 8 feet (2.5 meters) at the shoulder and would dwarf living rhinos. Titanotheres also grew huge horns on their heads. One, *Brontotherium*, developed an impressive, branched horn on the front of its skull. Titanotheres were very successful until the end of their earthly stay. Scientists have speculated that the primitive nature of their teeth, which probably were not very useful for eating the grasses then evolving, may have led to their demise.

Perissodactyls, like artiodactyls, have hooves. Perissodactyls are distinguished by odd-toed hooves, with the axis of the foot passing through the middle toe. Very primitive perissodactyls had five toes on each foot, with their body weight distributed evenly among the toes. With evolution, the foot became elevated for running more swiftly, and the toes were later lost. Body weight concentrated on the middle toe, and the keratinized central toenail eventually became a one-toed hoof. In contrast, the ancestral artiodactyls distributed their weight evenly between digits three and four, which evolved into keratinous hooves. Perissodactyls also generally show a lengthening of legs and an increase in body size through time.

Only two Perissodactyla families survived into Pleistocene time in North America: the horses (family Equidae) and the tapirs (family Tapiridae). No member of the rhinoceros family, Rhinocerotidae, lived in North America beyond Pliocene time, about 4 million years ago. However, the woolly rhino, a species that inhabited Eurasia during the Ice Age, came very close to crossing Beringia and entering Alaska and is simply too important and unusual to ignore. So this book about North American animals includes a discussion of the woolly rhino.

HORSES
Family Equidae

This family of true Americans originated in late Paleocene time, about 55 million years ago, in North America and eventually spread throughout most of the world. By middle Tertiary time, 20 million years ago, horses had become the most abundant ungulate in North America.

A reasonably good fossil record of early ancestors of horses exists due to the resistance of horse teeth and certain bones to weathering, the relatively complete record of Tertiary sedimentary rocks in North America, and the former great abundance of these animals, which sometimes perished in herds.

Early horses

Horses are thought to have evolved either from *Hyracotherium* or *Eohippus*, also known as dawn horse. *Hyracotherium*, a paleothere, had four-toed front feet, three-toed hind feet, and was built for running. These animals had a curved back and a long, low skull. The cheek teeth had low crowns—what paleontologists call brachyodont teeth. This style of teeth allows animals to crush leaves, which makes them effective browsers. Paleontologists first discovered remains of *Eohippus* in the 1890s in both Europe and the United States. These small, forest-dwelling browsers measured 1 foot (0.33 meters) tall, and probably weighed up to about 45 pounds (20 kilograms). *Eohippus* resembled, and may have been, a tapir rather than a horse. Horses became extinct in the Old World at the end of early Eocene time, about 50 million years ago, but horse evolution continued in the New World. Subsequent species moved back and forth between North America and Asia and finally arrived in South America with the

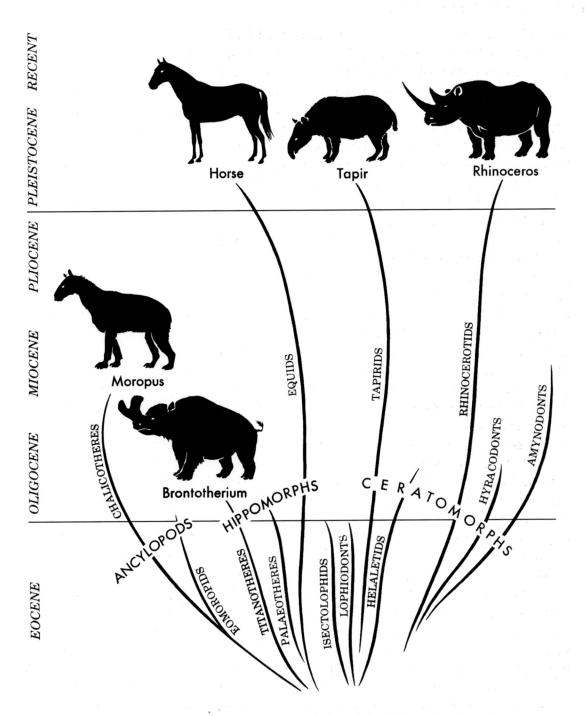

Family tree showing the evolution of the Perissodactyls, or odd-toed ungulates —Reprinted by permission of John Wiley and Sons

development of the Central American land bridge just a few million years ago.

Between Eocene and Oligocene time, approximately 55 million to 25 million years ago, horses evolved in an essentially straight genealogical line. However, during the Miocene epoch, about 20 million years ago, horse evolution branched, possibly due to the different environments horses had colonized by then: forests and grasslands. This branching also coincided with the proliferation of grasses and flowering ground plants, which may have aided the diversification of horse species. By Blancan Land Mammal Age late in the Pliocene epoch, about 3 million to 2.5 million years ago, the modern grazing horse of the genus *Equus* had evolved.

By Pleistocene time, about 1.9 million years ago, early horses had changed completely from the original small forest browsers to generally large grassland grazers. Leg and foot length and body size of Ice Age horses generally increased, with their brains increasing in size relative to their body mass. With these developments came a reduction in number of toes as the keratin-covered central toe became a

Western horse (Equus occidentalis)

HOW DO WE KNOW WHAT THESE ANIMALS REALLY LOOKED LIKE?

Most of the information we have about the extinct animals of the Ice Age comes from their skeletal parts. Sometimes, we are fortunate to have mummified remains as well. Hair, skin samples, and even preserved stomach contents tell us how they looked, what they ate, and what physical condition they were in before they died. We can tell if the animal was an aged adult or frail juvenile who perished in times of famine, or a healthy young adult brought down in its prime by a predator. Sometimes the animals are so closely related to surviving species that we can base our restoration primarily on the appearance of their modern relatives. And a few of the animals characteristic of the Ice Age in North America still survive. Some notable and perhaps familiar large survivors of the Ice Age include musk oxen, which live in the Arctic; yaks, now found only in Asia; and the North American gray wolf, black and grizzly bears, elk, and bison.

In addition to these physical clues from the animals themselves, there is another source of information about the appearance of many species. That source is art—the painting, engraving, and sculpture associated with Paleolithic cultures found across western Europe, particularly in the Dordogne and Ariège regions of France and Cantabrian, Spain. At least two hundred painted caves have been found in southern France and northern Spain, with other sites located in southern Spain and on Sicily.

The Paleolithic or Old Stone Age is the earliest period in the cultural history of *Homo sapiens.* It began about 40,000 years ago and ended about 10,000 years ago at the end of the Pleistocene epoch or Ice Age. Evidence suggests that graphic activity began in France at the beginning of the Paleolithic Age, and some of the most elaborate and important cave paintings date from that early period. The artists were a fully modern people with bone structure and brain size like ours. Scientists named these people Cro-Magnon after a cave at the Aurignac site in France. Probably the two most famous sites for cave art are Lascaux in France and Altamira in Spain. The paintings at Lascaux are Aurignacian and date from about 17,000 years ago. The Altamira cave was decorated about 14,000 years ago by a later but overlapping culture known as Magdalenean, named for the La Madeleine site in France.

The art, hidden away in caves and undiscovered until the nineteenth and twentieth centuries, provides a wealth of information about the animals of the Ice Age and the lives of the people who lived with, hunted, and painted them. And there is undoubtedly more art to be found. The Chauvet cave in France, containing an extraordinary collection of more than three hundred exciting paintings and engravings, was not discovered until 1994. The paintings are now known to be the oldest yet discovered and yield recently published radiocarbon dates of 32,000 years old. The portrayal of the animals there is among the most animated and "realistic" found anywhere. There are at least 420 animal figures, which include maneless cave lions, woolly mammoths, bison, musk oxen, an owl, deer, cave bears, charging rhinoceroses, a herd of long-horned wild oxen, a 20-foot-long (6-meter) panel

Locations of caves with Paleolithic art in western Europe
—Modified from Hadingham, 1979

of horses and parts of the human anatomy. No one apparently lived in the cave. Another group of paleolithic people revisited the cave about 6,000 years later before the entrance collapsed and sealed this treasure until modern time.

Paleolithic artists left us a veritable encyclopedia of Ice Age fauna. In western European caves, the most commonly portrayed animals are the hoofed creatures, specifically horses, bison and other bovids, reindeer and various species of deer, mammoths, bears, woolly rhinos, and large cats. The cave art also occasionally depicts birds, boar, and fish. In only a few cases are humans represented. Perhaps artists superstitiously feared making images of humans, or maybe people were simply not as important as animals in the context of cave art. We may never know the reason for their absence.

The artists may have made the animal paintings for ritualistic or mystical purposes—maybe to attract animals, ensure good hunting, or appease the animals' spirits after a hunt. But these are speculations. What we do know is that the Paleolithic artists were very good observers of nature. The paintings depict animals with a grace and elegance lacking in later Neolithic representations. The Neolithic or New Stone Age roughly corresponds to the end of the Ice Age, and the art from that time typically is geometric, more symbols than pictures of actual animals. Neolithic art tends more toward storytelling, with few descriptive elements. In contrast, Paleolithic art contains little apparent storytelling or narrative context. The artists simply presented the animals as they perceived them—living creatures, swimming, running, and fighting, sometimes pregnant, sometimes dying.

The artists went to great lengths to show the specific contour, coloration, and patterns characteristic of the animals they portrayed. This attention to detail sometimes led to a curious "double exposure" effect: animals with too many legs, as if the artist attempted to show walking, or animals with too many heads, as if the artist tried to depict nodding. Another technique was to "twist" the view of an animal, such as a bison, by showing it in profile, but turning its horns and hooves to a three-quarter view. Each segment was

This will drive them crazy in 20,000 years!

more recognizable; the parts, thus assembled, made a complete picture. Artists also tended to change scale in different parts of the same animal, as if the parts were perceived separately and assembled without concern for correct proportion. At Lascaux this mismatched scale, as seen in the famous horses with small heads and voluminous bodies, became a convention. As a result, the paintings are often astonishing in their simplicity and robust energy and may appear quite modern.

Some of the most common paintings depict the steppe bison, *Bison priscus,* which lived in Eurasia as well as North America. Although local variations within a species are likely, the Eurasian paintings help reconstruct the basic appearance of the North American bison. Consistent features of the bison paintings, such as the double hump, coloration pattern, and length of hair on the front legs and beard, tell a great deal about what the animals looked like. Portraits of woolly mammoths reveal specific details—ear size and placement, length of tail, hair length and pattern, and in some cases the absence of tusks. European lions, the same species as the extinct American lion *Panthera leo atrox,* are shown with faint stripes.

As far as we know, no cave paintings of extinct Ice Age animals exist in the Western Hemisphere. However, a likeness of a mammoth carved into a sandstone wall was found along the Colorado River on the Colorado Plateau near Moab, Utah. Such carvings, called petroglyphs, are typically etched into desert varnish, a black weathering patina on exposed rocks in the desert.

What is puzzling in North America, however, are portrayals of elephant-like trunks protruding from walls of some Mayan ruins, such as those at Chichén Itzá, Mexico. Perhaps elephant-like creatures still roamed the Western Hemisphere as recently as 1,500 years ago.

References: Balter, 1999; Clottes, 2001; Guthrie, 1990; Hadingham, 1979; Janson and Janson, 1999; Laming, 1959; Rigaud, 1988; Ucko and Rosenfeld, 1967

An artist's drawing of a painted horse from a cave at Lascaux, France, shows the tiny head and enormous body typical of the style of Neolithic artists of the time.

Petroglyph of a mammoth, found on a sandstone wall along the Colorado River on the Colorado Plateau near Moab, Utah —Courtesy Jim I. Mead

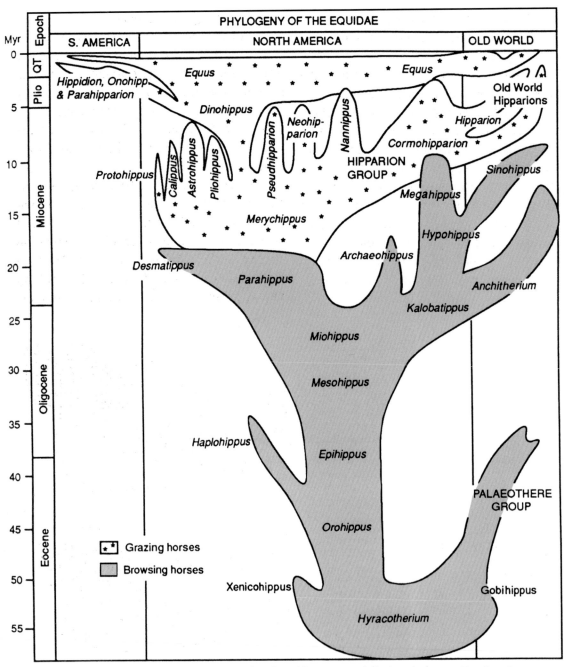

Family tree of the Equidae family of horses and their relatives —Reprinted with permission from Cambridge University Press (MacFadden, 1992)

hoof. The teeth, jaws, and skulls of Pleistocene horses also changed shape—for instance, the snout lengthened over time.

Considerable confusion exists about the number of Pliocene (Blancan Land Mammal Age) and Pleistocene species of horses, which some workers estimate at more than forty. Several factors contribute to this confusion, including an incomplete fossil record during this critical time interval of their evolution, inadequate descriptions of the fossils, and the variable characteristics of the animals' skulls, teeth, and other features. Compounding the identification problem, the teeth can vary in shape in different stages of wear, even within the same species today.

True horses (genus *Equus*)

Native horses became extinct in North America about 8,000 years ago, in Holocene time, with the youngest remains found in several localities in Alberta, Canada. Why horses died out is unclear, particularly since they have flourished in the wild since the Spaniards reintroduced them into North America five centuries ago.

The genus *Equus*, or true horse, contains all living horses, zebras, and asses, and their late Pliocene and Pleistocene ancestors. The genus appears to date back to a common ancestor, called *Dinohippus*, in late Miocene time, between 10 million and 5.5 million years ago. Today's true horses differ from one

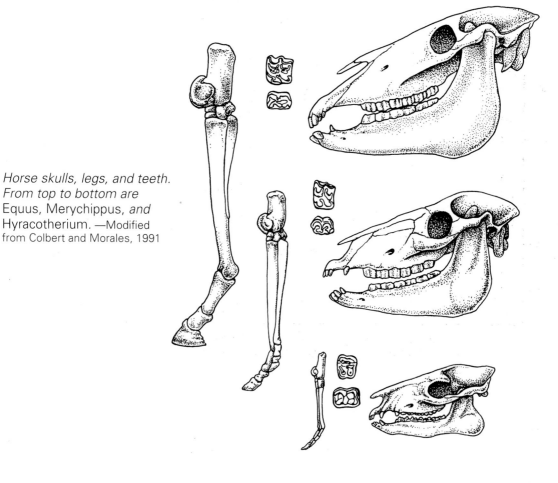

Horse skulls, legs, and teeth. From top to bottom are Equus, Merychippus, *and* Hyracotherium. —Modified from Colbert and Morales, 1991

another in the tooth appearance (which may be affected by wear patterns and animal age), tail shape, size, coat color, and ear length, as well as in differences in chromosomal makeup and gestation periods. All members of the genus can interbreed, but offspring from mixed species are usually infertile.

Pleistocene horses of North America ranged from the giant horse *(Equus giganteus)*, approximately 1,150 pounds (525 kilograms) to the small pygmy onager *(Equus tau)*, a slender-legged donkey weighing 550 pounds (250 kilograms). The giant horse is known from only one premolar tooth. Among the most common late Pleistocene horses was the small Mexican horse *(Equus conversidens)*. The Mexican horse ranged from the Valley of Mexico north to Alberta, Canada, and west to California. The most common species in the eastern and southern United States was the complex-toothed horse *(Equus complicatus)*, which lived between Irvingtonian and late Rancholabrean Land Mammal Ages. The western horse (*Equus laurentius* or *Equus occidentalis*) was the most abundant horse found in the La Brea tar pits in California, with the Mexican horse ranking a distant second in abundance.

Skeleton of the western horse (Equus occidentalis), *the most abundant horse found in the Rancho La Brea tar pits* —Courtesy of the George C. Page Museum

Scott's horse *(Equus scotti)*

Scott's horse *(Equus scotti)* was the size of a large modern horse and was widely dispersed. Remains have been found in deposits as old as about 2 million years and as young as late Pleistocene, or little more than 10,000 years ago. Remains of Scott's horse have been found in Texas, Oklahoma, Florida, and Alberta. Several complete skeletons of Scott's horse have been found. Arabian horses may be descendants of Scott's horse.

Przewalskii's horse *(Equus przewalskii)*

The most primitive horse today—the horse least changed genetically by human selective breeding—is Przewalskii's horse *(Equus przewalskii)*. This stocky animal has been around for at least 1 million years, but the first modern records of it come from the nineteenth century in Mongolia. The only living Przewalskii's horses, now numbering probably fewer than one hundred, live in zoos. When compared with domestic horses, these social animals have relatively large heads for their small but heavily built bodies. Individuals weigh between 440 and 660 pounds (200 to 300 kilograms) and may live into their early thirties.

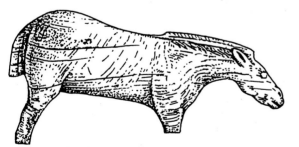

Ancient carved ivory horse, Musée des Antiquités Nationales, Saint-Germain-en-Laye, France

Modern horse *(Equus caballus)*

The modern horse is *Equus caballus*. This includes the feral (wild) horses that now roam the western United States, descendants of the horses the Spaniards and later Europeans brought to the New World. Male wild horses may weigh 860 pounds (390 kilograms), and females may weigh 750 pounds (340 kilograms), respectively. An average domestic horse weighs approximately 1,160 pounds (530 kilograms). The largest living horses, Belgian draft horses, weigh as much as 2,200 pounds (1,000 kilograms). The date of horse domestication is unknown but was at least 6,000 years ago.

TAPIRS
Family Tapiridae

Tapirs are relatively primitive browsing animals. They are neither very intelligent nor social. The tapir's roots go back to Eocene time, about 40 million years ago, in North America. These nocturnal animals that prefer dense forests and grasslands near water have changed little in the past 20 million years. They measure as much as 47 inches (120 centimeters) tall and weigh between 500 and 660 pounds (225 to 300 kilograms). Tapirs have four toes on their front feet and three on their rear feet. A prominent proboscis, or nose, is the tapir's most distinguishing facial feature. Today, three species live in Central and South America: Baird's tapir *(Tapirus bairdi)*, the mountain tapir *(Tapirus pinchaque)*, and the Brazilian tapir *(Tapirus terrestris)*. A fourth species inhabits Southeast Asia. During the Pleistocene epoch, tapirs lived from the margins of the ice sheets south to near the United States–Mexico border, including on the Colorado Plateau.

The fossil record of tapirs is poor—they inhabited woodland environments that do not favor preservation of remains. The most abundant remains have been found in deposits of Rancholabrean age in Florida. Other sites containing tapir remains exist westward from Florida into Texas.

The largest of the Ice Age members of the family included Merriam's tapir *(Tapirus merriami)*, which is known only from a single specimen at a single locality within Irvingtonian Land Mammal Age deposits, about 1.5 million years old. Remains of the Vero tapir *(Tapirus veroensis)*, which was slightly larger than the three living South American species, have been found in Rancholabrean-age deposits in the southeastern states and west to Texas. Two other extinct tapirs of similar size were Cope's tapir *(Tapirus copei)*, dating from late Blancan to Rancholabrean Land Mammal Age, and the California tapir *(Tapirus californicus)*. The California tapir closely resembled the living Brazilian tapir in size and shape. California tapirs both evolved and became extinct during Rancholabrean Land Mammal Age.

RHINOS
Family Rhinocerotidae

The family Rhinocerotidae, together with tapirs, belongs to the perissodactyl suborder Ceratomorpha. Rhinos, which continue to barely survive in parts of Asia and Africa, became extinct in North America in Pliocene time, between approximately 5 million and 2 million years ago, and in Europe and Siberia at the end of the Ice Age. Ancestors of the rhinoceros first arose in the Eocene epoch, about 50 million years ago, in Eurasia.

The name rhinoceros comes from the Greek words *rhino*, meaning "nose," and *cera*, meaning "horn," and refers to the one or two horns on the animal's snout. These horns, unlike those of artiodactyls such as sheep, goats, bison, and cattle, lack a bony core. Instead, they are an aggregation of keratin fibers that protrude from a roughened area of the skull.

The four families of rhinos that evolved were the Hyracodontidae, Amynodontidae, Rhinocerotidae, and Hyrachiidae. Little is known about this fourth family. Members of the Hyracodontidae, or running rhinos, were small and lightly built. They had long legs and were fast afoot. Hyracodontidae arose in middle to late Eocene time. Their development peaked in Oligocene time, and the last species became extinct in early Miocene time. Rhinos of the family Amynodontidae lived between late Eocene and early Miocene time. They were mainly large and heavy, and they appear to have spent much of their lives in water. *Caenopus*, which researchers think evolved from the Hyracodontidae family, lived during Oligocene time, about 30 million years ago. Scientists think the Rhinocerotidae family evolved from this family. *Caenopus* was large, approximately 4 to 5 feet at the shoulder, heavy, and hornless. With evolution, *Caenopus* rhinos generally increased in size and developed horns on the skull and broad, three-toed feet.

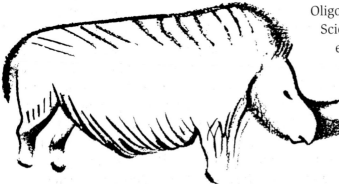

Cave painting of a wooly rhino, Font-de-Gaume, France

A depiction of what the California tapir, Tapirus californicus, *probably looked like*

The last rhino to inhabit North America was the single-horned *Teleoceras*, a hippolike, amphibious mammal. This large rhinoceros evidently thrived during Miocene and early Pliocene time before becoming extinct.

Woolly rhinoceros
(*Coelodonta antiquitatis*)

The woolly rhinoceros (*Coelodonta antiquitatis*) measured 4 to 5 feet (1.2 to 1.5 meters) tall at the shoulder, weighed 2,000 to 2,500 pounds (907 to 1,135 kilograms), and had two horns on its head. The forward horn on old males grew to as much as 3 feet (1 meter) long; the rear horn was much smaller. In comparison, the largest living rhinoceros, the white rhino (*Ceratotherium simum*) of Africa, can weigh 7,900 pounds (3,600 kilograms) and have a shoulder height of more than 6 feet (2 meters). The woolly rhino was a member of the subfamily Dicerorhinae. Today, the 2,000-pound (910-kilogram) Sumatran rhino (*Dicerorhinus sumatrensis*), which measures 4.5 feet (1.4 meters) tall at the shoulder, is the only surviving member of that subfamily.

Woolly rhinos evidently evolved in northeast Asia early in the Pleistocene epoch. Although warmly clothed with a thick, dark, wool coat, they inhabited both cold and warm climates. Remains have been found from Ireland and Great Britain to Spain, and eastward across central Europe and Asia to eastern Siberia. With lower sea level during the ice ages, Ireland and Great Britain were connected to mainland Europe, so the traverse was easy. The woolly rhinoceros never migrated from Eurasia to North America via the Beringia land bridge, although remains have been found in eastern Siberia near the Bering Strait. Why they didn't cross is a mystery. Some researchers think a lack of appropriate food in Beringia prevented the woolly rhino from crossing into Alaska. Some well-preserved woolly rhinos have been found in Siberian permafrost. A stuffed, complete specimen is mounted in the Museum of Krakow, Poland.

Rhinos were a source of food and hides for Paleolithic peoples. Along with bison, mammoths, and horses, they were popular figures in European Paleolithic cave drawings. The drawings often show the rhino with its head and neck low to the ground, an adaptation to eating short grasses and plants.

References: Clutton-Brock, 1992; Colbert and Morales, 1991; Grizimek, 1990; Kurten and Anderson, 1980; Leidy, 1847; MacFadden, 1992; Redford and Eisenberg, 1992; Stock and Harris, 1992

The extinct woolly rhino (Coelodonta antiquitatis) *of Asia*

Even-Toed Ungulates
ORDER ARTIODACTYLA
Deer, Bison, and Camels

Artiodactyls are ungulates—hoofed creatures that eat plants—with an even number of toes, either two or four. This order contains a large number of successful families and possesses an excellent fossil record. Scientists have found the remains of ancient artiodactyls in sedimentary rocks dating back to Eocene time between 57 million and 36 million years ago in both North America and Europe. Species of all the families that roamed North America during Pleistocene time, with the exception of the camels, still hoof about the continent today.

Many artiodactyls, such as deer, pronghorn, and bison, owe much of their success to the structure of their legs, ankles, and feet. Their long, slender legs and strong thigh muscles make members of these families fast runners, and some are also good leapers. The evolution of their double hoof allows them to walk and run efficiently and for sustained periods—traits that aid both escape from danger and long migrations. The double hoof can also bear great weight, so large artiodactyls have evolved. Other large artiodactyls like pigs and hippos have four toes and thicker legs.

The three living suborders of the order Artiodactyla are Ruminantia, Tylopoda, and Suina. The Ruminantia, or cud-chewers, have compound stomachs containing three or four chambers. These stomachs allow the ruminants to eat tough vegetation of low food quality. They can eat quickly and then relax as they chew their cud later. With the help of bacteria in the first stomach, they efficiently extract nutrients from plants and break down cellulose thoroughly. Ruminants also have reduced or no side toes and specialized teeth.

Ruminant families include Cervidae (deer, caribou, moose, and Wapiti or American elk), Giraffidae (giraffes), Antilocapridae (pronghorns), and Bovidae (saigas, mountain goats, sheep, oxen, musk oxen, and bison). Cervid males grow and shed their antlers yearly. Antilocaprids and bovids keep their horns throughout life, but antilocaprids shed their horn sheaths annually. Another evolutionary trend in the ruminant artiodactyls was that their upper incisor and canine teeth eventually disappeared and were replaced by a tough, bony ridge that very efficiently crops vegetation.

The suborder Tylopoda contains a single family, Camelidae, comprising camels and llamas. Camelids are also ruminants, but they differ from other ruminants in having a simpler three-chambered stomach and distinctive splayed toes with tough pads that support their weight on soft surfaces like sand. The suborder name comes from the Greek "tyle," knobby or callused, and "-pod," from "pous," meaning foot.

The Suina suborder contains piglike animals that have a simple stomach, four toes, and canine tusks. Members include peccaries of the Americas and swine and hippopotamuses of Eurasia and Africa. Unlike most Artiodactyls, pigs and peccaries are omnivorous.

Artiodactyls are among the most difficult mammals to classify. Within the order Artiodactyla, sibling or concurrent species that look alike but reproduce separately make classification difficult. Add to this an excellent but incomplete fossil record, and we can understand the problems researchers face.

The Cud-Chewers
Ruminantia Suborder
DEER
Family Cervidae

Cervids are mainly browsing animals, and the family includes deer, caribou, moose, and elk.

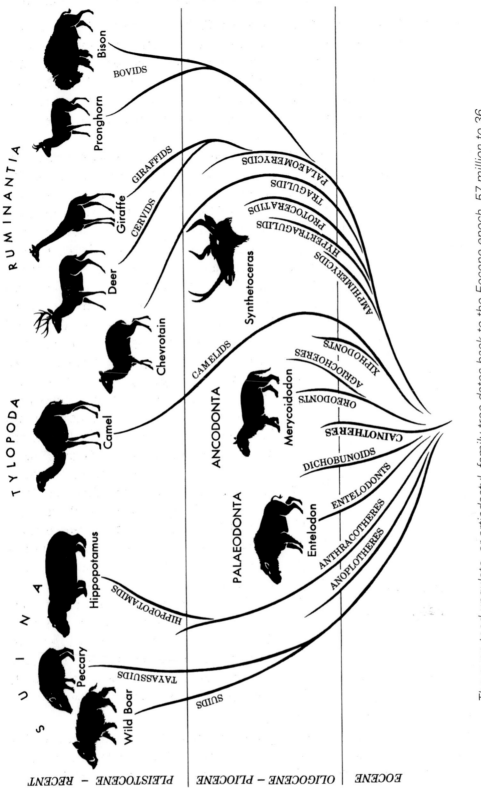

The even-toed ungulate, or artiodactyl, family tree dates back to the Eocene epoch, 57 million to 36 million years ago. —Drawing prepared by Lois M. Darling for Colbert and Morales, 1991, and reprinted with permission from John Wiley and Sons

In the Old World, their fossil record dates back to early Miocene time, about 20 million years ago. *Eumeryx* was the common ancestor of the deer family and related ruminants, the giraffes, back in Oligocene time, between 36.6 million and 23.7 million years ago. However, these two families followed genetically separate paths in the Miocene epoch, between 23 million and 5.3 million years ago. Cervids migrated to North America during the Pliocene epoch, between 5.3 million and 1.9 million years ago, and have generally proliferated since. Many members of this family are familiar to most of us. They include white-tailed deer (*Odocoileus virginianus*) and mule deer (*Odocoileus hemionus*). Others, such as the brachydont, Florida, mountain, and fugitive deer, became extinct by the end of Pleistocene time.

Subfamily Odocoileinae

The subfamily Odocoileinae contains deer, caribou, and moose. These animals differ in body size, antler shape and size, skull structure, and footprints. White-tailed deer have existed since late Pliocene time, more than 2 million years ago. They prefer woodland habitats, and their size varies greatly. Males may reach 310 pounds (140 kilograms); females can weigh 210 pounds (96 kilograms). The larger, stockier mule deer date back to late Pleistocene time, only a few thousand years ago. They prefer more open country than whitetails do. Males reach 475 pounds (215 kilograms), and females reach 160 pounds (73 kilograms).

Caribou *(Rangifer tarandus)*

Caribou are larger than deer but smaller than elk and moose. They are believed by some researchers to be descendants of South American deer, and are the only member of the deer family adapted for the cold Arctic environments of northern Europe, Asia, and North America. Caribou are also called reindeer in Europe. Their snouts are large but smaller than the ponderous muzzles of moose. Male caribou may reach 660 pounds (300 kilograms); cows weigh as much as 300 pounds (136 kilograms). Males and most females have semipalmated antlers.

Caribou date back to the Irvingtonian Land Mammal Age about 1.6 million years ago. The oldest known caribou remains were found in eastern Beringia in the Fort Selkirk region of Yukon. During the Pleistocene epoch, these animals ranged from Alaska into the continental United States as far south as Tennessee and Virginia. Researchers have found remains dated at 36,830 years near the North Carolina-Virginia border. And during the latest glacial maximum caribou ranged along the southern front of the continental ice sheets in the United States with other Arctic grazers such as woolly mammoths and musk oxen. At the other climatic extreme, 40,000-year-old caribou remains have been found in northern Greenland. Caribou are now restricted to the Arctic. Viewing the herd of a few hundred thousand strong on the North Slope of the Brooks Range in Alaska today is probably reminiscent of what the herds of Pleistocene animals that ranged across much of the grasslands of North America would have looked like a little more than 10,000 years ago.

Caribou have been hunted for food and clothing for thousands of years in Eurasia and North America. Caribou were among the first animals depicted by Paleolithic artists. Among the oldest art works are the 40,000-year-old drawings in Chauvet Cave in southern France.

Moose

Moose (*Alces alces*), the largest living cervids, are solitary animals that prefer conifer forests containing ponds and swamps. Bulls may be

7 feet (2.1 meters) high at the shoulder and weigh as much as 1,400 pounds (635 kilograms); cows may reach 1,100 pounds (500 kilograms). This majestic animal arrived from Asia to areas of North America south of the continental ice sheets during the late Wisconsinan glaciation, or less than about 20,000 years ago. Moose still inhabit parts of eastern Asia and Europe, where they are confusingly called elk.

Extinct species of moose include the broad-fronted moose *(Alces latifrons)* and the stag moose *(Cervalces scotti)*. The broad-fronted

moose was even larger than the largest modern moose that live in Alaska. It also had wider or longer-beamed antlers with palms smaller than those on the modern moose's antlers. Remains date from 33,800 years ago, plus or minus 2,000 years. These animals may have emigrated to North America from eastern Asia in Illinoian time, between 245,000 and 129,000 years ago.

Stag moose were slightly smaller in stature, and presumably in weight, than broad-fronted moose. Remains of this large inhabitant of muskegs have been unearthed in southern

The stag moose, Cervalces scotti

Canada, the Midwest, the Middle Atlantic states, and as far south as Oklahoma and Arkansas. The stag moose probably ended its stay on the earth about 10,230 years ago or less.

ELK
Subfamily Cervinae

The wapiti or American elk (*Cervus elaphus*) originated in Eurasia. The oldest North American elk remains date from the Irvingtonian Land Mammal Age, between about 1.9 million and perhaps 300,000 years ago, in Alaska and the Yukon. These are remains of the same species of elk that inhabits North America today. The European elk is called a red deer. "Elk" is the term for Old World moose, and early European settlers in North America mistakenly used the term for what the Shawnee called wapiti. American elk apparently did not inhabit the region south of the continental ice sheet until Wisconsinan glacial time, about 100,000 years ago. Researchers have found Wisconsinan-age remains that closely resemble living elk as far south as South Carolina and Tennessee and west to Arkansas and Washington State. These magnificent browsing animals inhabited grasslands, woodlands, and forests. The escalation of hunting pressure during the nineteenth century forced elk to retreat to the forests and upland regions.

Male elk may grow enormous antlers. Body weights may reach 1,090 pounds (495 kilograms) for bulls and up to 650 pounds (295 kilograms) for cows.

PRONGHORNS
Family Antilocapridae

The pronghorn family, Antilocapridae, originated in North America in middle Miocene time, about 15 million years ago, and has been with us ever since. The two recognized subfamilies are Antilocaprinae and Merycodontinae. The surviving Antilocaprinae evolved from and apparently replaced the Merycodontinae in early Pliocene time, about 5 million years ago.

Modern Pronghorn (*Antilocapra americana*)

The only survivor of the many species that lived during the ice ages is the familiar pronghorn or American antelope that ranges the grasslands of the western states, southern Canada, and north-central Mexico. The oldest remains of this species have been found in late Pleistocene, Rancholabrean Land Mammal Age, sites.

Before Europeans arrived in North America, at least 35 million pronghorns roamed what is now the United States and Canada. Today between 750,000 and 1 million animals run the range after recovering from a population low of less than 20,000 in the 1920s.

The fleet-footed pronghorn is a long-legged animal about the size of a deer. Its legs and back are light brown, and its underside is

The modern pronghorn,
Antilocapra americana

white. While often called American antelope, pronghorns are not true antelope. There is still debate on whether pronghorn belong in their own family, Antilocapridae, or should be classified with the other horned ruminants in the Bovidae family, bison, sheep, goats, cattle, and African antelope. Like the bovids, pronghorn have horns consisting of a keratinous sheath over a bony core, but unlike bovids, or any other living animals, pronghorn shed this horn sheath annually. A new sheath then grows over the bony core. Not to be confused with the antlers of members of the deer family, the horns of the pronghorn are the only branched true horns on any living species.

The pronghorn's teeth and legs place them among the most genetically advanced animals of the order Artiodactyla. The teeth allow them to browse on tough plants. Capable of running as fast as 70 miles per hour (110 kilometers per hour) and bounding as high as 20 feet (6 meters) while they run, this species is the fastest land animal in the Western Hemisphere and one of the fastest in the world. Pronghorns can cruise at a respectable 30 miles (45 kilometers) per hour for as far as 15 miles (25 kilometers). Their lives depend on their speed plus their keen eyesight, which allow them to detect and flee predators. Pronghorns graze in small groups, eating grass

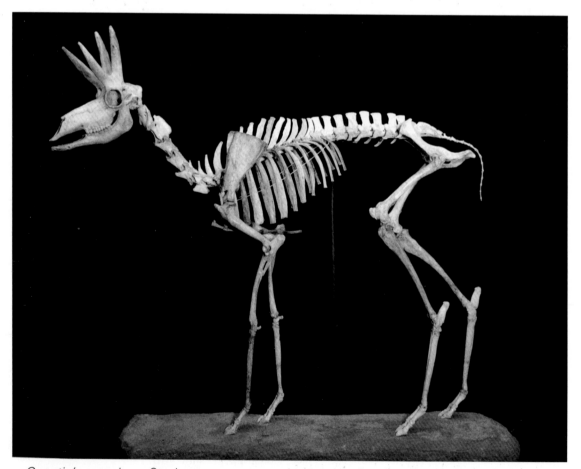

Quentin's pronghorn, Stockoceros onusrosagris, *was smaller than the modern pronghorn and had four rather than two horns.* —Courtesy of The University of Nebraska State Museum

and other plants. Males weigh 140 pounds (64 kilograms), females 105 pounds (48 kilograms). Oddly enough, considering their leaping abilities, pronghorns almost never jump fences, unlike deer and elk.

Ice Age Pronghorns

Many members of this family did not quite make it into the Holocene epoch of the last 10,000 years. Matthew's pronghorn (*Capromeryx furcifer*) ranged the southern states from Florida to California and went extinct in latest Pleistocene time, about 10,000 years ago. This animal closely resembled today's species but was about two-thirds the size. The diminutive pronghorn (*Capromeryx minor*) and the equally small Mexican pronghorn (*Capromeryx mexicana*) also survived into late Pleistocene time but died out a little more than 10,000 years ago. Male small and Mexican pronghorns probably weighed about 24 pounds (10 kilograms).

Quentin's pronghorn, Stockoceros onusrosagris

Several other species of pronghorns lived during late Pleistocene time and died near or at the end of the epoch, about 10,000 years ago. Because we lack much fossil material from these animals and because of the similar characteristics of the species, the available data about them, their ranges, and lifestyles are variably poor. Extinct species of pronghorns that lived during the Ice Age include members of the genus *Tetrameryx*, meaning "four horns" in Greek. These animals had two horns with two prongs on each stem. Two extinct members of this genus are Shuler's pronghorn (*Tetrameryx shuleri*), slightly larger than the modern pronghorn, and Mooser's pronghorn (*Tetrameryx mooseri*), which ranged from central Mexico north and was about the size of the living species.

There were also six-pronged species, with three prongs on each of two horn stems. Hay's pronghorn (*Hayoceros falkenbachi*) was a six-pronged species that inhabited North America during the Ice Age. The rear prong on each horn of Hay's pronghorn was larger than the other two. Irvingtonian Land Mammal Age remains of this species, between 1.9 million and about 300,000 years old, have been found at only one locality, Hay Spring, Nebraska.

Based on the fossil record, two species of the genus *Stockoceros* were abundant during the Rancholabrean Land Mammal Age of late Pleistocene time. Conklin's pronghorn (*Stockoceros conklingi*) and Quentin's pronghorn (*Stockoceros onusrosagris*), were smaller than modern pronghorn. From the animals' bone structures, paleontologists deduce that Quentin's was probably as fast as, and Conklin's was slower than, today's fleet-footed pronghorn.

BOVIDS
Family Bovidae

Bovids, most of which graze for a living, have true horns—head ornaments that they never shed. These horns have an unbranched bony core surrounded by a tough, permanent sheath chiefly of keratin. In many species, both sexes possess horns, but the males' horns are larger. The horns grow throughout the life of the animal. Bovids use their horns for protection, identification, and mating and territorial displays such as head bashing.

Most of the many living artiodactyls are bovids. They are descendants of an antelope-like animal that lived in early Miocene time in the Old World about 20 million years ago. Asia and Africa were the hotbeds of bovid differentiation and evolution. Starting in the Irvingtonian Land Mammal Age, members of two subfamilies, Caprinae and Bovinae, crossed Beringia and headed south to roam North America. None appear to have reached as far south as Central America. The Caprinae subfamily contains saigas, sheep, goats, and musk oxen. The Bovinae subfamily consists of bison, yaks, and oxen.

The species in the subfamily Caprinae differ greatly in size, appearance, and preferred habitat. In North America all but saigas survived the end of the last ice age and are with us today.

Saigas
Subfamily Antilopinae

Saigas (*Saiga tatarica*) are antelope about the size and shape of a pronghorn but with inflated, proboscis-like snouts for filtering dusty

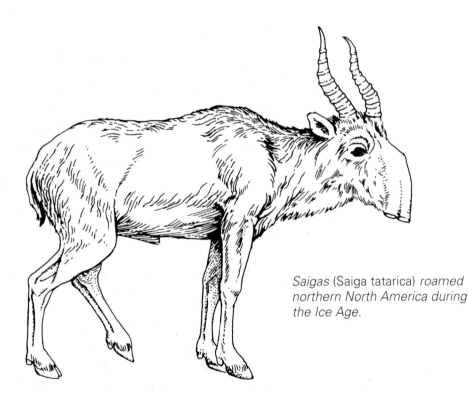

Saigas (Saiga tatarica) *roamed northern North America during the Ice Age.*

air. They presently inhabit the steppe regions of central Asia, where they originated perhaps 2 million years ago and, being nomads, subsequently spread both east and west. By about 700,000 years ago, they had made their way to western Europe, eventually reaching England during the last ice age. The Pleistocene species also spread eastward and made its way into the New World about 37,000 or more years ago. There they inhabited the dry grassland areas of Alaska, Yukon, and the Northwest Territories as far east as the Mackenzie River Delta. The Pleistocene species was about 10 percent larger than the living saiga, which stands 24 to 28 inches (60 to 70 centimeters) tall and weighs 57 to 70 pounds (26 to 32 kilograms).

New World saigas, which inhabited only steppes, were excellent paleoenvironmental indicators of their time. They became extinct about 12,000 years ago as spruce forests and tundra replaced the grasslands in the far north.

Modern saigas are fast afoot and capable of reaching more than 40 miles per hour (70 kilometers per hour) and traveling 50 to 70 miles (80 to 120 kilometers) in a day. Males possess spindly, ringed horns. Both sexes have heavy, buff-colored (white in winter), woollike coats that enable them to withstand temperatures as low as -45 degrees Fahrenheit (-43 degrees Celsius). During summers in central Asia, these animals also encounter temperatures of up to 83 degrees Fahrenheit (28 degrees Celsius). Females commonly give birth to twins.

Sheep, Goats, and Musk Oxen
Subfamily Caprinae
Goats
One of my favorite living North American animals, because of its looks, intelligence, and rigorous lifestyle, is the mountain goat

(*Oreamnos americanus*). Mountain goats are not true goats but rather goat-antelopes closely related to the European chamois of the genus *Rupicapra*. Modern mountain goats have long white coats and both graze and browse on high-elevation vegetation such as grass, shrubs, and lichens. Males reach 180 pounds (82 kilograms); females may weigh 156 pounds (71 kilograms). Mountain goats live about twelve years in the wild.

These animals have roamed the mountains of western North America since at least Sangamonian interglacial time, between 128,000 and 72,000 years ago, and probably longer. Their range extends from southern Alaska and eastern Yukon Territory south to northern Oregon and western Montana. Erosion rather than sedimentation dominates their mountainous habitat, so preservation of remains is rare, and the extent of their Pleistocene range is not known.

Harrington's mountain goat
(*Oreamnos harringtoni*)
Harrington's mountain goat is the only extinct goat from North America. Late Wisconsinan remains have been found in caves in the Grand Canyon, Glen Canyon, Natural Bridges, and Nevada. Adults were stockier and about 30 percent shorter than living mountain goats. They had shiny black horns slightly smaller than those of living goats, and sported white fur coats. Dung found in mountain caves shows they grazed on twenty-four species of grasses, small plants, rushes, globemallow, sagebrush, and yucca. They also ate fifty species of bushes and trees, including Douglas fir and limber pine, depending on the season. The youngest radiocarbon dates on dung from Harrington's mountain goat give dates of 11,160 years. This species may have evolved from mountain goats after members

Harrington's mountain goat,
Oreamnos harringtoni

of the species became isolated in high and cool parts of the southwestern United States.

Sheep

The ancestors of true sheep, including the Dall and mountain sheep, appear in Europe and Asia in Blancan Land Mammal Age deposits that date from 3.5 million to 2 million years old. The sheep arrived in mountainous regions of North America, North Africa, and Eurasia in late Pleistocene time. Illinoian glacial deposits, 187,000 to 129,000 years old, near Fairbanks, Alaska, contain the oldest North American remains.

Dall sheep *(Ovis dalli)*

Dall sheep first appear in late Pleistocene sedimentary rocks 187,000 to 129,000 years old in central Alaska and western Canada. Dalls evolved from Rupricaprini, a tribe designation of goat antelopes that were isolated from Asia by the rise of the Bering Sea, which periodically drowned the Beringia land bridge to Asia. Dall sheep typically have white coats, and both sexes have horns, with the male's being more massive. Male Dalls reach 200 pounds (91 kilograms) and females may attain 125 pounds (57 kilograms). This grazing

animal has an appetite for herbs and grasses and today lives in the northern Rocky Mountains of Canada and Alaska.

Bighorn Sheep *(Ovis canadensis)*

The muscular mountain or bighorn sheep also dates back to Sangamonian interglacial time, 128,000 to 72,000 years ago. Today mountain sheep inhabit the mountainous regions between southern British Columbia, Canada, and northern Mexico and Baja California. Their Pleistocene range was more extensive, extending as far east as Alberta, Wyoming, Colorado, and New Mexico.

Bighorns are dark brown to tan with a creamy white rump and are larger than Dall sheep. Male bighorns may weigh up to 316 pounds (143 kilograms) and reach 36 to 42 inches (91 to 107 centimeters) tall; females weigh as much as 200 pounds (91 kilograms) and measure 30 to 36 inches (76 to 91 centimeters) tall. The bighorn has larger and thicker horns than the Dall sheep possesses. The horns

Dall sheep,
Ovis dalli

Bighorn sheep,
Ovis canadensis

grow throughout the animal's life, producing a prominent check line when the growth slows in winter. Researchers can use those growth lines like tree rings to determine an animal's age. And so paleontologists use the growth rings on the horns to determine the age at death of Ice Age sheep. Bighorn sheep browse and graze on grasses, low plants, and shrubs in less steep terrain than mountain goats favor.

Dall sheep and bighorns looked the same during Pleistocene time as they do now.

Musk Oxen

The musk ox *(Ovibos moschatus)* dates back at least to Illinoian glacial time, between about 187,000 and 129,000 years ago, in Alaska. The genus name *Ovibos* contains parts of the Latin words *ovis,* meaning "sheep," and *bos,* meaning "oxen." During Wisconsinan glacial time, musk oxen ranged as far south as Montana, North Dakota, New York, and Ohio. Today, these wonderfully hardy beasts inhabit northern Canada and Greenland, as well as Alaska, where they were reintroduced after extermi-

nation. Males of these tundra-loving, stocky animals weigh up to 900 pounds (408 kilograms); females may tip the scales at 670 pounds (304 kilograms). Musk oxen eat grass, shrubs, and willows.

Both sexes have horns. The males have larger bodies than the females do, but both sexes have relatively short legs for their massive bodies and possess warm wool coats. Very long, coarse, dark hair that almost reaches the ground covers fine, soft hair that moisture cannot penetrate. These social herbivores form herds of up to one hundred animals. For protection against cold, wind, and predators such as wolves, musk oxen "circle the wagons." The adults form fortresslike rings—living walls—with heads facing out and the young and infirm protected within the circle. This behavior became their undoing when musk oxen faced human predators with long-ranging weapons.

Musk oxen appear to have originated in Europe, with the earliest remains dating from deposits of middle Irvingtonian Land Mammal Age, about 1 million years old, in Germany. The animals went extinct in Eurasia about 3,000 years ago.

Extinct North American relatives of the musk ox include the shrub ox *(Euceratherium collinum),* Soergel's ox *(Soergelia mayfieldi),* and the woodland musk ox *(Symbos cavifrons).* The shrub ox first settled North America in the Irvingtonian Land Mammal Age, less than 1 million years ago. The muscular shrub oxen weighed in at about 1,500 to 1,700 pounds (680 to 775 kilograms)—larger than musk oxen but slightly smaller than bison. Paleontologists think shrub oxen were closely related to musk oxen because they have similar bone structures. Based on the number of damaged skulls found, researchers also think that shrub oxen bulls butted heads more when rutting than musk oxen do. The last of the shrub oxen date to about 11,500 years ago, and remains have been found as far south as California, Oklahoma, and Kansas.

Soergel's ox was larger than the shrub ox and close to the bison in size. These massively built animals died out earlier than the shrub-ox in North America. The fossil record is sparse, but remains have been found as far south as Kansas. Soergel's ox may also have made the trip from Asia with the shrub ox during the Irvingtonian Land Mammal Age, less than 1 million years ago.

The woodland musk ox (*Symbos cavifrons*) was a wide-ranging animal that apparently preferred warmer and more wooded climates than other musk oxen species did. It roamed from Alaska south to Mississippi, and from New Jersey and Virginia west to Washington State. These animals were less bulky and taller than the musk oxen inhabiting the Arctic today. Their horns were mounted higher on their skulls, and their skulls were longer than those of living musk oxen. Paleontologists know little of the woodland musk oxen's ancestry, not even whether they evolved in the New World or Old World. Their oldest

Musk ox (Ovibos moschatus)

remains date from late in the Irvingtonian Land Mammal Age, about 500,000 years ago; the youngest are 11,100 years old, plus or minus 400 years.

Bison, Yaks, and Oxen
Subfamily Bovinae

The subfamily Bovinae contains large, cattlelike animals. Present in North America during the Pleistocene epoch were bison, yaks, and oxen. All males and most females have horns that grow throughout the animals' lives.

Ice Age bison

The genus *Bison* arose in Eurasia possibly as early as Blancan Land Mammal Age, more than 2 million to 3 million years ago. Paleontologists use its arrival in North America to mark the beginning of the Rancholabrean Land Mammal Age. Unfortunately, the actual date of the beginning of the Rancholabrean Land Mammal Age is not known accurately, and dates vary between 300,000 and 100,000 years ago.

Bison of the recent past include the steppe bison *(Bison priscus)*, which dates to at least 700,000 years ago in Europe. This big, large-horned animal with a hump on its shoulders was widespread in Eurasia until the end of Pleistocene time. It was one of the most popular figures of European Paleolithic artists. Cave paintings of bison show a powerful animal whose thick black mane sometimes makes it look like it has not one hump, but two.

The steppe bison reached Alaska and Yukon, its first stops in North America, in Illinoian glacial times, between 187,000 and 129,000 years ago. Steppe bison made at least two migrations to land south of the ice sheets. The end for the species came about 12,000 years ago. The famous steppe bison Blue Babe described in the Ice Age Mummies sidebar below perished about 31,000 years ago and became entombed in the permafrost of central Alaska.

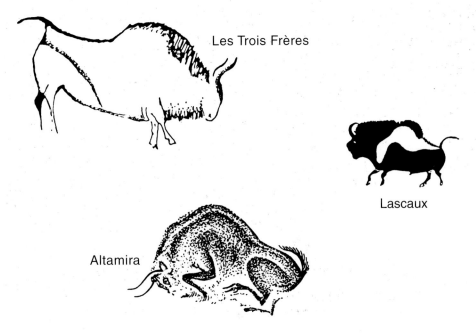

Les Trois Frères

Lascaux

Altamira

Numerous cave paintings of steppe bison have been found in Europe, including these from Les Trois Frères and Lascaux, France, and Altamira, Spain

ICE AGE MUMMIES

The word "mummy," for most people, conjures images of dead pharaohs entombed in the pyramids of Egypt. Few people realize, however, that some of the animals and humans preserved in the perennially frozen tundra, or permafrost, of northern Russia, Finland, Norway, Sweden, Canada, and Alaska have also been mummified. The process of natural mummification may be different, but the result is the same—desiccated or dried-out bodies. The remains, such as hair, skin, innards, and facial features, preserved in Ice Age mummies add greatly to our knowledge of Pleistocene wildlife.

Rather than being freeze-dried in the camping food sense, Ice Age animals mummified differently. Body moisture was not released to the atmosphere but frozen in place. With time the ice separated from the carcass, leaving behind a shrunken, dried body. The smaller the animal, the faster it cooled and, therefore, the less the body deteriorated. If the carcass was buried quickly, thereby preventing carnivores from scavenging it, complete preservation could occur.

Since about 1900, people have discovered some remarkable frozen and preserved Pleistocene animals in the northern lands. The Berezovka mammoth, found in 1900 along the Berezovka River in Russia, is one of the most famous. This animal, which had several broken ribs, a broken pelvis, and a broken shoulder blade, died so suddenly that it still had vegetation lodged between its teeth. The animal was in reasonably good health, as evidenced by the 3.6 inches (90 millimeters) of fat under its hairy hide. The

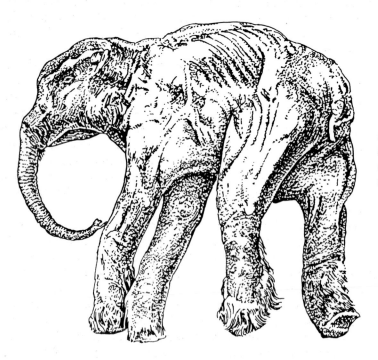

Dima, the emaciated baby mammoth found in 1977 in the frozen Russian tundra

cause of its death is still unknown, but it appears to have been catastrophic. Researchers think the fat layer, type of vegetation in the animal's mouth, and lack of fly eggs in the carcass tell them that the animal died in autumn.

Dima the baby woolly mammoth was an important mummified discovery that yielded significant information about the species. In 1977, a placer gold miner found this animal in the Russian far east about 6 feet (2 meters) into the permafrost. The mammoth, perhaps only seven or eight months old when it died, was about 3 feet (1 meter) tall and had an injured leg. The body showed very little decomposition—even its internal organs were preserved. Its stomach held silt and some of the animal's own hair, and its colon contained plant material. The carcass may be as young as 9,000 or 10,000 years old or as old as 40,000 years. Theories for Dima's demise are many. The animal may have suffered wounds as it tried to escape hunters who killed its mother, and subsequently died of starvation. Some researchers think the baby mammoth stepped into soft, organic-rich mud, became stuck, and starved to death after trying to stay alive on a diet of silt.

Another woolly mammoth calf, Baby Effie, was found near Fairbanks, Alaska, in 1948. Only the head and attached left foreleg survived the 21,300 year entombment in the permafrost. Effie now rests at the American Museum of Natural History in New York.

Other large animals found in Alaska's permafrost include three extinct stag moose specimens *(Cervalces)* and steppe bison *(Bison priscus)*. The three moose, one of which has been dated at approximately 32,000 years, were found in 1940, 1942, and 1980.

In 1952, a large male steppe bison mummy was found at Dome Creek, near Fairbanks. The Dome Creek bison, dated at about 28,000 years old, appeared to have been partly scavenged. It is now in the Smithsonian Institution's collections.

One of the most famous Ice Age mummies to be discovered in Alaska was Blue Babe, a steppe bison that died approximately 36,000 years ago. Walter Roman, a gold miner, found Blue Babe in 1979 while mining in a stream bed north of Fairbanks. The striking blue tint to the remains is due to secondary coloration by vivianite, a white iron-phosphate mineral that turns blue when exposed to air. Vivianite forms where phosphate-rich, iron-poor materials such as bones are buried in silt that is rich in iron but low in phosphate. Blue Babe's head, shoulders, and bones have a dusting of vivianite, and the thick hide also has clusters of vivianite crystals up to one-half inch across that resemble blue warts.

Comprehensive investigations of the remains of the eight- to nine-year-old bison have revealed much about Blue Babe and how he died. The bull, apparently in good health, was attacked, killed, and partially consumed by one or more American lions *(Panthera leo atrox)*. Paleontologists' evidence includes the width of the upper canine incision teeth marks, a broken lion tooth found in the hide, and the deep scratches on the rear flank that match those of African lion kills. The lions attacked the bison in the autumn just before freeze-up. During the following spring thaw, when silt commonly slides down the hillsides over the frozen earth below, sediments probably buried the carcass. Evidence for the health of Blue Babe and time of death and burial includes the thick layer of fat beneath the remaining hide and the generally good preservation and lack of flies, insect eggs, and maggots in the carcass. The mounted bull is now permanently displayed in the University of Alaska Museum in Fairbanks.

References: Arriaza, 1995; Guthrie, 1990; Menon, 1995

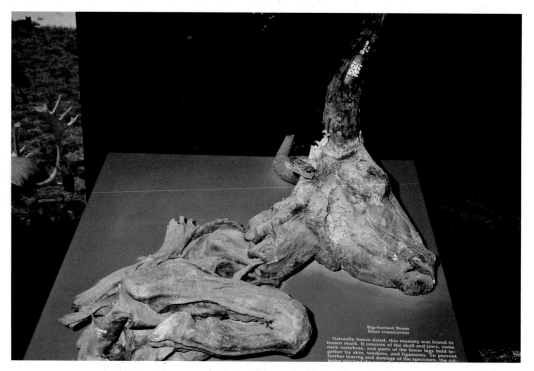

The Dome Creek steppe bison mummy, on display at the Smithsonian Institution —Courtesy Science Graphics

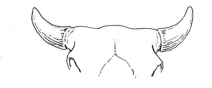

A comparison of the horns from the modern Bison bison *(top) and the* extinct Bison latifrons *(bottom)*

The biggest bison of them all was the giant bison *(Bison latifrons)*, which may have evolved from the large steppe bison *(Bison priscus)*. This animal not only was massive but also had enormous horns. Fossilized remains contain horn cores spanning 7 feet (213 centimeters). The keratinous horn sheaths are not usually preserved as fossils but were undoubtedly significantly longer than the horn cores. For comparison, large horns from an American bison *(Bison bison)* may measure as much as 3 feet (90 centimeters) across. Male giant bison were much bigger than females, as is true with the living American bison. Researchers estimate the weight of giant bison as between 2,500 pounds (1,125 kilograms) and 4,000 pounds (1,800 kilograms).

Giant bison ranged widely across the continental United States and southern Canada during Sangamonian time, the last interglacial period, which lasted from 128,000 to 72,000 years ago. The species disappeared sometime between 30,000 and 21,000 years ago, perhaps due to competition with the living species or interbreeding with it.

Bison or American buffalo *(Bison bison)*

Bison, descended from antique bison, *Bison antiquus,* or *Bison bison antiquus,* which lived in North America toward the end of the Pleis-

The extinct, long-horned giant bison, Bison latifrons

Composite skeleton of ancient bison (Bison bison antiquus) *from the Rancho La Brea tar pits, Los Angeles* —Courtesy of the George C. Page Museum

tocene epoch. Antique bison were larger than the modern bison and had horns up to 34.5 inches (88 centimeters) wide. These animals inhabited large parts of North America south of the margin of the ice sheet during the Wisconsinan glaciation 71,000 to 10,000 years ago. Some hardy individuals wandered as far south as Mexico. The many bison kill sites in the United States and Canada, some with as many as two hundred individuals, show that these animals were clearly important to Paleo-Indians.

Evolution of *Bison bison antiquus* resulted in the development of two presently living subspecies, the plains bison *(Bison bison bison)* and the slightly larger woods bison *(Bison bison athabascae)*. These animals are now the largest land animals in North America. Males reach a shoulder height of 6 feet (2 meters) and weights of 2,000 pounds (900 kilograms). Cows measure 5 feet (1.66 meters) at the shoulder and weigh 1,015 pounds (460 kilograms). These social animals have good senses of hearing and smell, can run at speeds of close to 40 miles per hour (60 kilometers per hour), and live as long as 20 years.

Bison, which numbered as many as 70 million individuals before the arrival of Europeans

The Asian yak,
Bos grunniens

in North America, ranged along the eastern slope of the Rocky Mountains from Alaska to northern Mexico and eastward to the Atlantic Ocean. Their population plummeted to less than 1,000 by 1900, thanks to the westward expansion of American settlers during the mid-nineteenth century and the policy of the United States government to promote bison extermination. Today approximately 65,000 bison live in North America.

Yak *(Bos grunniens)*

The yak, that beast of burden, milk, meat, and wool that presently inhabits the highlands of Tibet, China, and Mongolia, made its way across Beringia at least into the Fairbanks area of central Alaska, where remains have been found. Yaks migrated to Alaska during the Rancholabrean Land Mammal Age, less than 300,000 years ago. Yaks are big, hairy animals that, despite their bulky size and gawky appearance, move with agility over rocks and along ledges. Yaks are also good swimmers. Little is known about the North American yaks except that they evidently closely resembled modern yaks. Male yaks in Asia can measure 8 to 9 feet (2.4 to 2.7 meters) long and reach 2,200 pounds (1,000 kilograms), with females attaining about one-third that size. Asian yaks winter in the mountains and summer in the plains; the extinct Alaskan yaks behaved similarly. Living yaks at higher elevations eat mosses and lichens; at lower elevations they eat mosses, coarse grasses, and low shrubs. Yaks belong to the same genus as domestic cattle *(Bos taurus)* and are sometimes bred with cattle.

Suborder Tylopoda
CAMELS AND LLAMAS
Family Camelidae

Camelids have long, thin necks and legs, and no horns. They walk on large, flat feet, or more precisely, on big, thick, padded toes with large toenails. Llamas differ from camels in having larger brains, a higher domed skull, no dorsal hump, and fewer premolar teeth.

This group of Old and New World grazing animals with big lips, big soft eyes, and unmistakable figures has its roots in late Eocene time, about 40 million years ago, in North America. The earliest known camelids, such as *Protylopus*, were about the size of rabbits. They had four-toed feet and short protruding or low-crowned teeth. By Oligocene time, 37 million to 24 million years ago, the sheep-sized *Poebrotherium* had evolved. It had two toes and lived in open woodlands in what today is South Dakota. During the Miocene epoch, 24 million to 5 million years ago, camels increased in size, with their legs and necks lengthening. By approximately 5 million years ago, in early Pliocene time, some camels were huge. Camels also lived in South America then and had reached the Old World by way of the Bering Isthmus, which connected Alaska with eastern Siberia. Llamas, close relatives to camels, arose in North America in late Tertiary time and subsequently spread into South America. Modern llamas prefer the grazing environment found at high elevations.

Camels roamed North and South America, Asia, Africa, and Europe, and llamas ranged widely in North and South America by late Pliocene time, 3 million to 2 million years ago. Based on remains of the six genera of camelids that inhabited North America during the Pleistocene epoch, llamas ranged far and wide, whereas camels only inhabited what are now the western states. For unknown reasons, the

A representation of the Nebraska camel, Titanotylopus nebraskensis, *with a modern camel for scale*

apparently plentiful camels and llamas became extinct in North America at the end of the Pleistocene epoch, about 10,000 years ago. Camels also died out in South America at this time.

Camels

The largest of the camels was the huge Nebraska camel, *Titanotylopus nebraskensis*, that lived between about 5 million and 1 million years ago during at least part of Nebraska glacial time. Remains have been found in Nebraska. It reached a shoulder height of about 12 feet (3.5 meters) and weighed considerably more than 1 ton. In comparison, the living dromedary one-humped camel, *Camelus dromedarius*, reaches 6 to 7 feet (1.8 to 2.1 meters) tall at the shoulders, measures 10 feet (3 meters) long, and weighs 1,320 to 2,200 pounds (600 to 1,000 kilograms). The Nebraska camel had massive, long legs, and a large hump, but a relatively small brain. Males were larger than females. It is frightening to think how far this camel probably could spit.

An apparently slightly older species of similar size and shape also lived in the greater Nebraska region. It was *Titanotylopus spatulus*, or *Gigantocamelus fricki*, the spatulate-toothed camel. One amazingly large collection of bones has been recovered from the late Pliocene (3.5 million years old) lakebed site at Lisco, Nebraska. The more than seventy

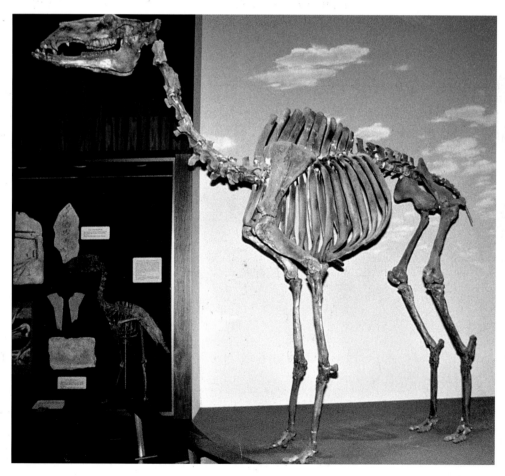

A composite skeleton of a Titanotylopus *camel* —Courtesy Science Graphics

individuals that researchers have recovered from the western Nebraskan site show that adult males were about 20 per cent taller and considerably heavier than adult females.

Males had a pair of huge canine teeth that researchers think the animals used against other males during the breeding season. The youngest remains of these camels have been found in early Pleistocene deposits of the Irvingtonian Land Mammal Age.

Camelops

Animals of the genus *Camelops* were large llamalike animals that lived in parts of western North America between central Mexico and central Alaska, and westward to Washington, Oregon, and California. Species of the genus lived between about 2 million and 10,000 years ago or less.

One big member of the genus was Yesterday's camel *(Camelops hesternus),* also called the western camel. This Rancholabrean Land Mammal Age animal evolved less than about 300,000 years ago. Abundant and widespread, Yesterday's camel traveled in herds throughout the western United States and north to the Yukon and Alaska. It was a relatively large-brained camel and possessed a slender skull. It probably both browsed and grazed on

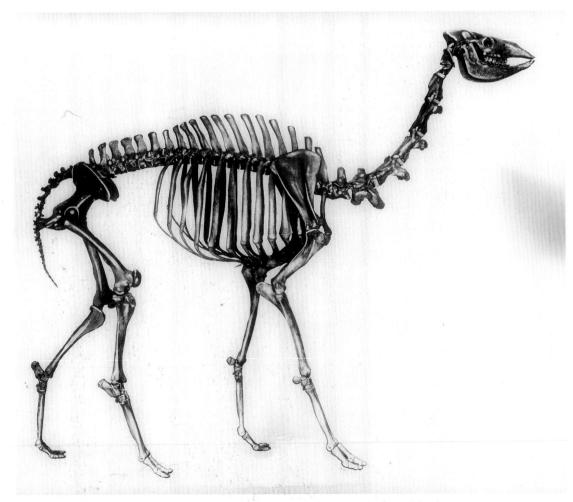

Skeleton of Yesterday's camel, Camelops hesternus, *found in the Rancho La Brea tar pits, Los Angeles, CA* —Courtesy of the George C. Page Museum

a diet of leaves, small plants, fruit, and grass. It was larger than living dromedary camels. The legs of Yesterday's camel were about 20 percent longer than those of the modern dromedary, but otherwise the two probably looked much alike. The animal went extinct for unknown reasons between 12,600 and 10,800 years ago. Well-preserved remains have been found in the southwestern states and also in the Yukon and near Fairbanks, Alaska, where miners have washed their remains out of gold placer mine diggings.

Other late Pleistocene camels include the Kansas and Huerfano camels. The Kansas camel (*Camelops kansanus*) apparently inhabited the western half of the United States between about 2 million and 10,000 years ago. Reconstructions suggest that it looked much like the living dromedary. Remains have been found in Nebraska, Kansas, and Oklahoma. The Huerfano camel (*Camelops huerfanensis*) was about the size of the Yesterday's camel. Its name comes from Huerfano County, Colorado, where first described. Remains have also been found in Idaho and Texas.

Llamas

With just a quick glance, most people recognize the camel-like faces, lips, and long legs of

Camelops *of western North America*

llamas. Llamas, however, have proportionately bigger brains housed in higher, domed skulls than camels do. They also have fewer premolar teeth and are humpless. Llamas eat grasses and leaves and buds of bushes in habitats that vary from deserts to the high mountains of South America.

Although llamas originated in North America, they have lived exclusively in South America for almost all of the last 10,000 years. The famous Hearst newspaper publishing family brought llamas to California in the 1930s. Domesticated llamas are now widespread.

Llamas are descendants of the late Miocene genus *Pliauchenia*. During late Pliocene through late Pleistocene time, approximately 2 million to 10,000 years ago, three species of the two genera *Hemiauchenia* and *Paleolama* ranged widely across North America. These genera are distinguished by their builds and teeth. *Palaeolama* lived in more rugged terrain and had a stockier structure than *Hemiauchenia*. Remains of the genus *Hemiauchenia* are found back as far as the middle Pliocene rocks of about 3 million years ago in North America. The Blanco llama (*Hemiauchenia blancoensis*) probably inhabited most of North America and reached southern South America by early Pleistocene time, approximately 1.5 million years ago. These animals were somewhat larger than living llamas (*Lama glama*), which can weigh as much as 340 pounds (155 kilograms).

Probably the best-known Pleistocene llama was the large-headed llama (*Hemiauchenia macrocephala*). Though slightly smaller than the Blanco llama, the large-headed llama was larger than the living llama. The types of sedimentary deposits that remains of the Blanco llama have been found in suggest this animal probably preferred open grasslands. It became extinct at the end of the Pleistocene epoch, about 10,000 years ago. Fossil remains are plentifully distributed across the United States.

The third extinct llama is the stout-legged llama (*Palaeolama mirifica*), which lived from Irvingtonian Land Mammal Age to late Wisconsinan time, about 1.9 million to 10,000 years ago. The distribution of this stocky animal's remains supports the contention that it inhabited rugged, mountainous areas and subsisted on grasses, leaves, and branches.

Today, the guanaco (*Lama guanicoe*) and vicuña (*Vicugna vicugna*) are the only wild llamalike animals. They inhabit parts of the Andes Mountains in South America. The more familiar llama (*Lama glama*) and alpaca (*Lama pacos*), domesticated from the guanaco, are popular pets, pack animals, stock guards, and wool producers. Guanacos weigh up to 265 pounds (120 kilograms), llamas to 340 pounds (155 kilograms), and alpacas and vicuñas to 145 pounds (65 kilograms). The selective breeding of llamas in captivity has increased their weight and size and improved the quality of their wool.

Piglike Animals
Suborder Suina
PECCARIES
Family Tayassuidae

Peccaries have been around since early Oligocene time, about 33 million years ago, in North America. They also inhabited Europe from 33 million years ago to approximately 6 million to 7 million years ago. Members of the family reached South America over the Panamanian land bridge starting about 3 million years ago. During the Pleistocene epoch, peccaries ranged from the tropics north to the southern edge of the continental ice sheet.

Related to Old World pigs, peccaries are the oldest, most primitive representative of nonruminant (non-cud-chewing) artiodactyls living today. Peccaries have short necks, snouts, and tails, as well as large heads and bristled coats. They differ from pigs in the design of their teeth and toes. In pigs the upper canine teeth or tusks curve upward; in peccaries they curve downward. All three New World peccary species have four-part stomachs and thirty-eight teeth, with one upper and one lower incisor on each side of the face. Peccary moms generally have twin infants.

The most common peccary was the flat-headed peccary *(Platygonus compressus)*, which lived from New York west to California and from Mexico north to the ice sheets. The animals were probably social because remains of groups of peccaries are commonly found in caves where collapse of the cave's roof likely trapped them. The flat-headed peccary was about the size of the European wild boar, with a shoulder height of 28 inches (72 centimeters). The youngest remains of flat-headed peccaries have been dated at 11,900 years before present, plus or minus 750 years. Human artifacts and flat-headed peccary remains have been found together at Sheridan Cave in Ohio. The remains provide dates of nearly 13,000 years before present.

Long-nosed peccary (Mylohyus nasutus), *left, and flat-headed peccary* (Platygonus compressus), *right*

Another member of the peccary clan, the long-nosed peccary *(Mylohyus nasutus)*, was about the same size as the flat-headed peccary, about 30 inches (75 centimeters) at the shoulder and weighing about 110 pounds (50 kilograms). It lived at least throughout the eastern and central portions of the United States. Fossil finds of solitary animal remains suggest that the long-nosed peccary most likely preferred a solitary lifestyle. It had a long snout and long, thin legs. The long-nosed peccary became extinct in Holocene time, less than 10,000 years ago. The earliest remains date to the Irvingtonian Land Mammal Age, about 1.5 million years ago. There is no evidence that humans hunted it.

In late Pleistocene time, the modern collared peccary *(Tayassu tajacu)* took over the range of its close relative the flat-headed peccary in what is now the southwestern United States. The collared peccary, or javelina, is a piglike animal with bristly, grayish or blackish hair. The snout has 1- to 1.5-inch-long (2.5- to 3.8-centimeter) tusks, which are the animal's canine teeth. These animals weigh between 30 and 65 pounds (13 to 30 kilograms) and stand 20 to 24 inches (50 to 60 centimeters) high. They live for 15 to 20 years.

As collared peccaries move about, musk glands on their backs emit a strong cheesy or skunky odor. This not only helps keep the group in contact but also warns others of impending danger. The perception of danger results in an involuntary discharge from the gland. At the same time, the animal emits a barking-like cough.

Collared peccaries today live from southeastern Arizona east to southwestern Texas and south to Argentina. They once roved as far north as Arkansas. Peccaries are territorial animals that travel in herds of six to thirty animals. When excited, peccaries can run as fast as 25 miles per hour (40 kilometers per hour). They are primarily herbivorous. Prickly pears are a favorite source of both food and water, but they also will eat insects, worms, and reptiles.

References: Colbert and Morales, 1991; Harrington, 1996e, 1997, 1998, 1999; Kurten, 1972; Kurten and Anderson, 1980; Martin and Wright, 1967; Meade and Meltzer, 1984; Redford and Eisenberg, 1992; Whitaker, 1996; Yukon Beringia Interpretive Center Web Site

Elephants and Their Relatives
ORDER PROBOSCIDEA

Most people are familiar with modern proboscideans. The two living species are the African elephant *(Loxodonta africana)* measuring 13 feet (4 meters) at the shoulder and weighing 5 to 7.5 tons, and the smaller Asiatic elephant *(Elephas maximus)* at 8.2 to 10 feet (2.5 to 3.1 meters) and 2.5 tons. During the Ice Age, mastodons and mammoths, also proboscideans, inhabited North America.

Proboscideans played an important role in the development of modern vertebrate paleontology, as much early work focused on the study of living elephants and their extinct kin. Paleontologists originally termed living elephants pachyderms, from the Greek word *pachydermos* meaning "thick skin." In the order Pachydermata, scientists grouped proboscideans with pigs, hippos, horses, tapirs, and hyraxes. In 1811, vertebrate paleontologist C. D. Illiger redefined the order and placed elephants in their own order, Proboscidea. The name Proboscidea comes from the Latin *proboscis,* a long trunk or snout, from the Greek "pro-," meaning before, and "boskein," to feed. Classifying the various extinct animals within the order proved difficult because of the many similarities between the species. In 1821, paleontologist J. E. Gray subdivided Proboscidea into the families Elephantidae, the elephants and mammoths, and Mammutidae, the mastodons. In 1933, American paleontologist Henry Fairfield Osborn developed the first modern classification of all proboscideans, based primarily on the shape of the teeth and secondarily on the number and shape of the tusks. Teeth are among the most common remains of extinct mastodons, mammoths, and elephants, and paleontologists rely heavily on tooth design to distinguish the species.

Of the mastodons, mammoths, and elephants, mastodons evolved first. The most obvious visual differences between mastodons and mammoths are in their teeth, skulls, and

Comparisons by shoulder height of very large male elephants. From left to right, the Indian or Asian elephant (Elephas maximus) *at 10 feet (3.1 meters), the African elephant* (Loxodonta africana) *at 13 feet (4 meters), and the Columbian mammoth* (Mammuthus columbi) *at 13 feet (4 meters). —Modified from Haynes, 1991*

body designs. While individual teeth of mast-odons have cone-shaped grinding surfaces, the eating surfaces of mammoth teeth are formed of ridges, like those of modern el-ephants. Mammoth skulls were domed while mastodon skulls were low-browed. And while mammoths were considerably taller, mast-odons had proportionally longer and more massive bodies. Both mastodons and woolly mammoths had thick coats of hair.

Remains of the earliest ancestor of pro-boscideans, the *Moeritherium,* are found in Eocene sedimentary rocks from approximately 55 million years ago in Egypt. Many paleon-tologists think *Moeritherium* was a trunkless animal about the size of a pig and that it inhabited swamps and bogs in Africa. It had an elongated skull, simple molar teeth, and enlarged incisors but no true tusks. *Moerithe-rium* lived between 55 million and 36 million years ago. Younger but still primitive probos-cideans include the Paleomastodons and *Phiomia.* They lived in forests and woodlands in the same region during Oligocene time, between about 36 million and 25 million years ago. Evolution of proboscideans brought in-creased size, shortening of the neck, elongation of the lower jaw, and specialization of teeth.

Two lineages of proboscideans followed the moeritheres: the deinothere, meaning "ter-rible beast" in Greek, and the euelephantoids, or elephant-like animals. Ancestors of elephant-like deinotheres first appear in the rock record in Eurasia about 40 million years ago; the last species became extinct during the Pleistocene epoch about 1 million years ago. Other than increasing in size to 13 feet (4 meters) at the shoulder, these forest dwellers apparently changed little during their life in Africa and Eurasia. Like modern elephants, they were long-legged and had long trunks, but unlike

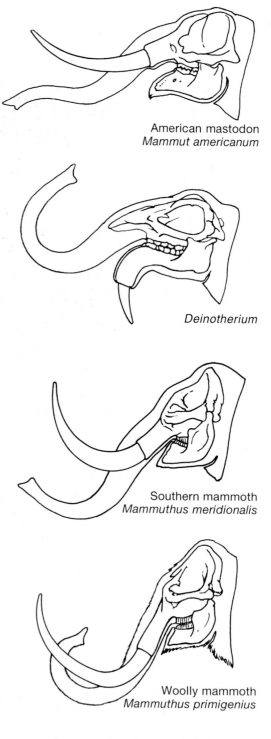

American mastodon
Mammut americanum

Deinotherium

Southern mammoth
Mammuthus meridionalis

Woolly mammoth
Mammuthus primigenius

*Comparative shapes of skulls
of extinct proboscideans.*

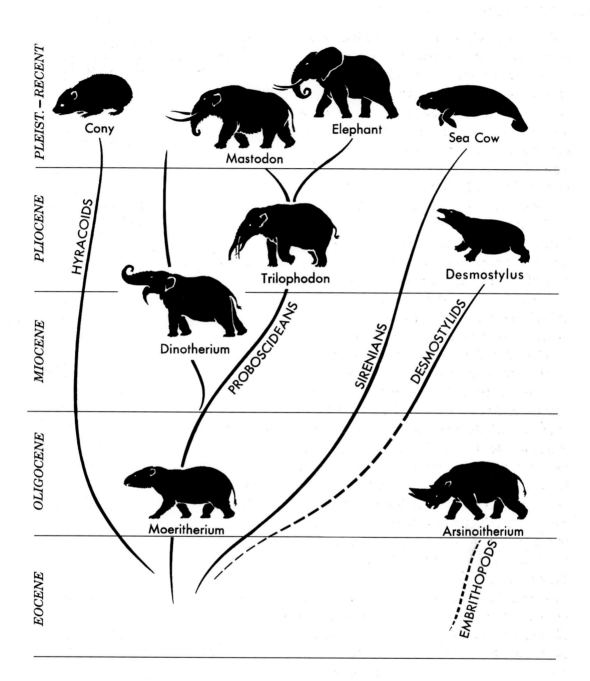

Evolutionary family tree of the proboscideans and related orders of mammals from early Tertiary time, about 55 million years ago —Reprinted with permission of Colbert and Morales, 1991·

modern elephants, they possessed a flattened skull and two tusks that curved down like giant hooks from the lower jaw back toward the chest. Tusks in probiscideans are enlarged or giant incisor teeth, whereas in most other mammals tusks are enlarged canine teeth.

Mastodons first colonized the New World in middle Miocene time, or about 15 million years ago. Mammoths arrived from Siberia via the Beringian land bridge much later, during the Irvingtonian Land Mammal Age of early Pleistocene time, about 1.9 million years ago. The Pleistocene proboscideans ranged from the tropics to the Arctic and lived on all continents except Australia and Antarctica.

MASTODONS
Family Mammutidae

Mastodons made their debut on the world stage in Egypt in early Oligocene time, about 35 million years ago. They stood 7 to 8 feet (2 to 2.5 meters) at the shoulder and had long legs and lower jaw tusks. Scientists describe their molar teeth as bunodont, meaning each tooth had rows of paired, low conical cusps rather than the sinuous, ridged grinding surface of elephant and mammoth teeth.

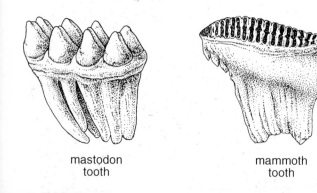

mastodon
tooth

mammoth
tooth

Comparison of the teeth of an extinct mastodon and an extinct mammoth. The design of the mammoth's tooth was very similar to that of the modern elephant.

American Mastodon
(Mammut americanum)

The American mastodon is one of the best-known fossil vertebrates. Remains of this forest dweller and open-land grazer date back to the Blancan Land Mammal Age in latest Pliocene time, a bit more than 2 million years ago. Fossils of this age have been found in northern Florida, southern Idaho, and southern Washington State. All American mastodons had upper rather than lower jaw tusks. The mastodon's molar teeth had four tooth cusps united into pairs. The American mastodon differs from other mastodons with bunodont, or cusp-shaped, teeth by having cross-crested cones rather than heavy cones along the axis of each enamel tooth.

The American mastodon had shorter legs and was more heavily muscled than mammoths and also had a longer body than woolly mammoths did. Males were larger than females. On average, the American mastodon was not as large as an African elephant but was about the same height at the shoulder (9 to 10 feet, or 2.7 to 3 meters) as an Indian elephant. Scientists estimated the weight of one large male found in New Brunswick, Canada, at about 8 tons. Both sexes had nonenamel upper-jaw tusks 6 to 9 feet (1.8 to 2.7 meters) long. The tusks, composed of dentin, exhibit annual growth rings, which researchers use to determine the animal's age when it died. Mastodon skulls were larger and had a flatter brow than mammoth skulls, and both animals had long, well-developed trunks. Compared with mammoths, American mastodons evolved little since the two diverged from a common ancestor. American and European mastodons closely resembled each other.

In North America, mastodons ranged from Alaska to central Mexico and from coast to coast. They evidently preferred the spruce forests and open woodlands of the eastern and north-central United States but lived in open country as well. Fishermen working off the eastern shoreline of the United States occasionally net remarkable "catches" of mastodon remains, scooped from the ocean bottom as much as 180 miles (300 kilometers) offshore. These catches attest to the dramatically lowered sea level during the last glacial advance and the animals' use of the coastline.

Bogs and swamps in the eastern United States have yielded strikingly intact mastodon carcasses that show the animal had long (1.25 to 7 inch or 2.75 to 18 centimeter), dark brown or black hair over a fine layer of underwool. Well-preserved specimens show that mastodons browsed on spruce needles, grass, moss, and twigs of spruce, pine, larch, and cedar. Bogs can preserve remains so well because the acidic, stagnant water pickles the animals, preventing deterioration.

In 1845, Harvard University anatomy professor John Warren bought the first complete American mastodon skeleton discovered in the United States. A dramatic find, the skeleton was standing upright in a peat bog near Newburgh, New York, with the animal's head tilted up, as if gasping for air. The "Warren Mastodon," still one of the most complete mastodon skeletons, may be seen at the American Museum of Natural History in New York City. Big Bone Lick, a swampy site in Kentucky, has produced more than one hundred mastodon remains together with an

A comparison of a Columbian mammoth (Mammuthus columbi), left, and an American mastodon (Mammut americanum)

Composite skeleton of an American mastodon (Mammut americanum) *recovered from the Rancho La Brea tar pits* —Courtesy of the George C. Page Museum

assortment of bison, horses, and moose. Once these animals ventured into the swamp, they commonly couldn't get out.

Mastodons became extinct about 8,000 years ago or later. Butchered remains show that Paleo-Indians hunted them. Some sites, such as one in western Washington State, contain mastodon bones that have healed from arrow point wounds, demonstrating that some animals escaped death at the hands of early hunters.

MAMMOTHS
Family Elephantidae

The oldest remains of the family Elephantidae were found in early Miocene sedimentary rocks from about 20 million years ago in Egypt. The three genera in this family—*Loxodonta* (African elephant), *Elephas* (Asiatic elephant), and *Mammuthus* (mammoth)—evolved rapidly. Dental and skull characteristics distinguish the genera of these highly intelligent and gregarious animals. By the end of Pliocene time, about 2 million years ago, the *Elephas* genus inhabited Eurasia, while the *Loxodonta* genus, meaning "slanting-toothed ones," remained in Africa.

Southern Mammoth
(Mammuthus meridionalis)

The mammoth lineage dates to early Pliocene time in Africa where the common ancestor of all mammoths, *Mammuthus subplanifrons,* lived between 4 million and 3 million years ago. *Mammuthus africanavus* evolved from that earlier mammoth and spread into Europe

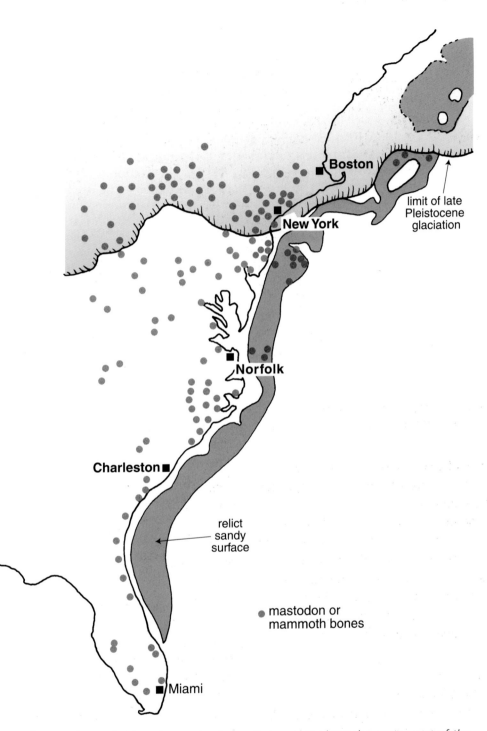

Boston

limit of late
Pleistocene
glaciation

New York

Norfolk

Charleston

relict
sandy
surface

● mastodon or
mammoth bones

■ Miami

*The locations of mastodon and mammoth remains along the east coast of the
United States* —Modified from Flint, 1971

PRESERVATION: AN UNLIKELY FATE

When an animal or plant dies, other animals and microbes typically eat it. Preservation of any of the dead organism's parts is extremely rare—to occur, the remains must be quickly removed from just about all creatures that would consume them.

One way to preserve solely hard parts, such as bone and wood, is instant burial. A mudflow or flood deposit of sand and gravel or a volcanic ashfall can encase humans, animals, and plants, isolating them from scavengers and decomposing microbes. In A.D. 79, Mt. Vesuvius erupted in a fantastic sequence of ashflows and ashfall that entombed victims in the Roman resort cities of Pompeii and Herculaneum, at the base of the mountain. The ash set up like concrete, forming molds from which researchers later made plaster casts. The problem with burial by volcanic ash is that the organism's soft tissues can be burned. If a mudflow or flood deposit buries the organism, the soft tissues generally are not preserved either. Tissues may be preserved in a mudflow only if the remains are completely cut off from air.

After an animal or plant is buried by most mudflows, tiny organisms called microbes generally consume the soft parts—the skin and organs—leaving the hard parts—the skeleton or shell—for possible preservation or replacement. Bone consists of calcium phosphate, which may be replaced atom for atom by silica. Silica may also replace wood and the calcium carbonate of shells. In rare cases, iron sulfide or copper compounds may replace bones and shells. In mineral replacement, the new compounds completely replace the original minerals and form molds and casts of the former hard parts.

Through burial and mineral replacement, the hard parts of a very small number—much less than one-tenth of 1 percent—of any species is preserved. Humans are an important exception because, at least during the past few tens of thousands of years, we have buried our dead, in some cases with some or all of their possessions. Through these processes, proportionally more human remains are being preserved.

Other less common but interesting methods can also preserve plants and animals. Amber—fossilized plant sap—can preserve insects that get trapped in the sticky stuff, but this method is only effective for little guys. Asphalt seeps preserve larger animals than amber or tree sap do, but the method is similar. However, if a larger creature such as a deer or a human drowns in a stagnant swamp or bog where the water is both acidic and oxygen-free, the remains will be pickled. Witness the recent excavations in Scandinavia of well-preserved "bog men" more than 5,000 years old. If sediment buries the bog, the next step in these environments is the transformation of the plant remains into peat deposits and, ultimately, coal.

If animal remains escape predation in a relatively dry environment—such as a cave, a desert valley, or a frozen environment such as a dry valley in Antarctica—the material will dehydrate or mummify. Bones, teeth, and fur or hair will remain, and skin will become leatherlike. Researchers have found mummified seals in Antarctica and mummified sloths in caves in the arid southwestern United States.

Preservation by freezing was a potential fate for the remains of deceased Ice Age animals that lived in frigid climates. Such cryopreservation can happen in at least two ways. An animal, tree, or human can fall into a glacial crevasse and be entombed in ice. But glaciers move and melt, eventually liberating many remains, after which they decompose. Recent finds of cryogenically preserved human remains include an Inca male found at the end of a glacier in Peru and the 5,300-year-old "Tyrolean Ice Man," who had an arrowhead in his shoulder, discovered in 1991 at the end of a glacier in the Alps. The bulk of Ice Age remains have been found in the far north were they were entombed not in glaciers but in perennially frozen ground called permafrost. All or parts of many woolly mammoths and bison were preserved that way. As permafrost melts, road and building construction proceed, and rivers cut into their banks during spring runoff, the changes expose the remains, mainly bones and tusks, of these animals, which people find almost yearly in the northernmost parts of Europe, Asia, and North America. Cryopreservation only rarely preserves flesh and hair.

References: Menon, 1995

between about 3 million and 2.5 million years ago. The southern mammoth *(Mammuthus meridionalis)* followed next along this evolutionary path and inhabited at least Europe between about 3 million and 1 million years ago. The southern mammoth was the first mammoth to reach North America, arriving by way of the Beringian land bridge early in the Irvingtonian Land Mammal Age, approximately 1.7 million to 1.5 million years ago.

The distribution of the remains of the southern mammoth show that this animal ranged over the plains and woodlands of both Europe and North America. The great beast attained a shoulder height of more than 12 feet (3.7 meters), weighed as much as 10 tons, and had large tusks with less curvature than those of subsequent mammoths. Remains have been found in southern Alberta and Saskatchewan, south to Idaho, Nebraska, Iowa, Oklahoma, and Florida.

Columbian Mammoth (*Mammuthus columbi*)

From the southern mammoth evolved the Columbian mammoth, also known as the Imperial mammoth (*Mammuthus imperator*). In 1857, Hugh Falconer (1808–1865), a prominent British geologist and botanist, first recognized the Columbian mammoth as a distinct species after studying remains found in Armenia. Some paleontologists think that Jefferson's mammoth

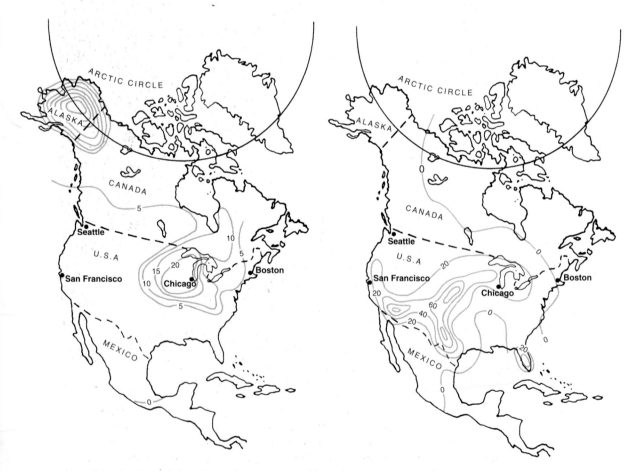

Distribution of fossil woolly (left) and Columbian (right) mammoths. The number of individual remains found within each contour is indicated, providing clues to the historic ranges of these animals. —Modified from Agenbroad, 1984

(*Mammuthus jeffersonii*) replaced the Columbian mammoth as the last of the lineage. Other elephant experts, however, do not recognize Jefferson's as a species separate from the Columbian mammoth.

How do we know that the Columbian mammoth descended from the southern mammoth? The method is relatively simple if fossils are available. It entails comparing a succession of younger and younger fossils whose geologic age is known. Especially important are comparisons of the teeth, skulls, and other prominent bones. For example, research has shown that, through time, the average number of enamel ridges on Old World mammoth teeth gradually increased.

The Columbian mammoth succeeded the southern mammoth during middle Irvingtonian Land Mammal Age, about 1 million years ago. Remains of Columbian mammoths have been

Researchers unearth entwined Columbian mammoth tusks in the badlands of northwestern Nebraska. About 10,000 years ago, two mature, approximately 40-year-old bull mammoths standing about 13 feet (4 meters) at the shoulder fought until their tusks locked. These warriors were not able to separate themselves and eventually collapsed onto and crushed a hapless coyote below. Each mammoth had one long and one short tusk. Two Soil Conservation Service employees laying an electrical line made this unique discovery in 1962 under about 8 feet (2.5 meters) of sediment. —Courtesy of The University of Nebraska State Museum

found in Mexico, the non-rain-forest areas of Central America as far south as Honduras and Nicaragua, and North America as far north as Alaska. The Columbian mammoth (or possibly Jefferson's) lived until the end of the Rancholabrean Land Mammal Age, about 11,000 to 10,000 years ago. The animal is so revered that Washington State named the Columbian mammoth its state fossil.

The Columbia mammoth was the largest of the late Pleistocene mammoth clan, with a shoulder height of between 12 and 13 feet (3.6 to 4 meters). It had a high, broad skull, massive lower jaw, and large, greatly curved tusks up to 13 feet (4 meters) long protruding from its upper jaws. Bulls had longer tusks than females did. Columbian mammoths probably had only a thin covering of hair because they lived in warmer, more temperate climates than their warmly clothed relatives, the woolly mammoths.

Jefferson's mammoth *(Mammuthus jeffersonii)*
Either the final member of the mammoth lineage or just the last of the Columbian mammoths, Jefferson's mammoth, stood between 10.5 and 11 feet (3.2 and 3.4 meters) at the shoulder. It had a concave forehead, broad skull, and large, essentially straight tusks. Scientists think Jefferson's mammoth wore a thin coat of hair. These mammoths must have preferred the abundant grasses of the Ice Age prairies because that is where their remains are most plentiful. The abundant remains of Jefferson's mammoth have been recovered from northern and western Canada south to Mexico. Numerous mammoth kill sites indicate

Skeletons of a dwarf mammoth (Elephas falconeri) *from the island of Sicily (left) and a Columbian mammoth* (Mammuthus columbi) *from Lincoln County, Nebraska —*Courtesy of The University of Nebraska State Museum

MAMMOTH TEETH, LIFE SPANS, AND DIETS

Mammoth teeth so closely resemble Indian elephant teeth that scientists have been able to estimate the ages at death of mammoth remains. Living and extinct elephants have a total of twenty-four teeth during their lifetime. Typically only four are exposed at any one time one in each of the four jaw quadrants. Six sets of four develop during the animal's life, and as the exposed teeth wear, the replacement teeth move forward on the jaw to take the place of the spent teeth. The worn-out teeth drop out of the animal's mouth.

By six years of age, mammoths had had three sets of molars. The fourth set arrived by 13 years, the fifth by 27 years, and the sixth and final set by about 43 years. The later generations of teeth were progressively larger, finally becoming about shoebox sized.

Estimates vary of how long the average modern and extinct proboscideans lived, but they range from 60 to more than 80 years. Most researchers believe that 65 years might be the best estimate. Clearly, when the last of the twenty-four teeth wore down, the animal's days were numbered.

Mammoths and mastodons had short necks that did not allow them to reach the ground with their mouths. Instead, they used their trunks to grasp food on the ground or high in trees and place it in their mouths, much the way elephants do today.

Mammoth researchers have also been curious about what extinct proboscideans, such as the Columbian mammoth, ate and the quantity of food they consumed daily. Comparison with African cousins suggests mammoths browsed on tree leaves, fruits, the woody parts of plants, and grasses. Analyses of mammoth dung from sites such as Bechan Cave, Utah, show the meals of Columbian giants in that region included grasses, sedges, cactus, blue spruce, and sagebrush wood. In the Northwest, their diet appears to have consisted mainly of grasses and sedges, with much smaller amounts of meadow-bog mosses, ferns, and various herbs and aquatic plants.

Again based on comparisons with African elephants, some researchers estimate that the 13,200-pound (6,000-kilogram) woolly mammoth would need to consume about 115,000 calories—up to 650 pounds (300 kilograms) of food per day. They figure that the 18,000-pound (8,000-kilogram) Columbian mammoth would require about 150,000 calories, or 770 pounds (350 kilograms) of food per day. That much food would require the animals to spend between 16 and 18 hours per day eating. Their relatively inefficient digestive tracts absorbed only about 44 percent of what the animals ate. In comparison, cattle, horses, and sheep digest between 50 percent and 70 percent of their food.

References: Mol et al., 1993

Paleo-Indians called Clovis people used razor-sharp obsidian as projectiles to hunt these mammoths. Jefferson's mammoths became extinct about 11,000 to 10,000 years ago, or slightly later than the dated Clovis kill sites of 11,300 to 11,150 years before present.

Woolly mammoth (*Mammuthus primigenius*)
Meanwhile back in Europe, the steppe mammoth (*Mammuthus trogontherii*), the immediate ancestor of the woolly mammoth, lived between about 750,000 and 500,000 years ago. The steppe mammoth was the largest of all mammoths. It attained shoulder heights of more than 14 feet (4.3 meters) and weighed as much as 10 tons. The steppe mammoth also may have been the first of its family to develop a thick hair coat.

By approximately 250,000 years ago, the woolly mammoth (*Mammuthus primigenius*) had evolved in northeastern Siberia. By 100,000 years ago, it had spread westward throughout Europe to Ireland and Great Britain and had crossed Beringia into North America.

With its complex tooth structure, the woolly mammoth was the most evolutionarily advanced elephant. The woolly mammoth is also the most well-known thanks to numerous cave drawings and paintings made by Paleolithic people between approximately 30,000 and 10,000 years ago in Europe. In addition, researchers have recovered several well-preserved carcasses from permafrost in Siberia and Alaska, primarily from placer gold mining operations.

Woolly mammoth,
Mammuthus primigenius

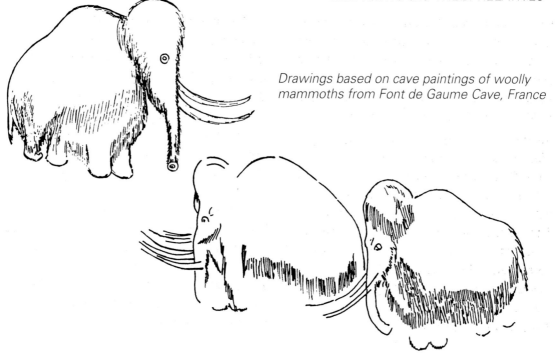

Drawings based on cave paintings of woolly mammoths from Font de Gaume Cave, France

The German scientist Johann Friedrich Blumenbach (1752–1840) first described the remains of woolly mammoths found in Europe in about 1800. He called them *Elephas primigenius,* or "the elephants which first appeared." Today they are called *Mammuthus primigenius.* Blumenbach thought that all Ice Age mammoths were huge. In reality, the woolly was one of the smallest of the clan. Still, this fellow was big, standing about 9 to 10 feet (2.7 to 3 meters) at the shoulder. Both sexes wore long, black hair together with a thick undercoat of soft fur overlying a 3-inch-thick (8-centimeter) layer of insulating fat. The animal possessed large, sweepingly curved tusks that reached lengths of more than 8.5 feet (2.6 meters). The tusks commonly show wear, suggesting that animals used them to break branches and perhaps to uproot trees and bushes. Over the last two centuries, carvers and traders have greatly sought the tusks of woolly mammoths in both Siberia and Alaska because they are ivory. More than one hundred tusks are recovered yearly in northern Russia alone, along rivers and coastal areas during the spring thaw and runoff. The first intact mammoth was found in Siberia in 1808, and more than 25,000 woolly mammoth carcasses have been found there since then. About 15,000 years ago early Arctic inhabitants in Russia constructed shelters from tusks, skulls, and the largest mammoth rib bones. The ages of the mammoth bones used in some huts span more than 8,000 years.

Detailed cave drawings from Europe and animal carcasses recovered from the tundra show that the woolly mammoth had a high, domed head and a humped, sloping back. The tail was short, and the ears were small, both probably adaptations that minimized heat loss from these body parts. The trunk was shorter than that of other mammoths, and ended in one fingerlike appendage and a protuberance that may have been used to hold vegetation. Woolly mammoth teeth, the most complex of all the elephants, had very thin, closely spaced, enameled plates. The tooth height was one-and-one-half times the tooth width. These strong, hard teeth allowed the animal to graze on coarse, siliceous grasses, tundra plants, twigs, and bark throughout its tundra-steppe range, which extended to southern Canada (British Columbia eastward), and from North Dakota eastward to New York and south to Virginia. The tooth and skull designs of these mammoths are similar to those of Asian elephants. Recent DNA analyses show that woolly mammoths are genetically closer to Asian than African elephants, confirming analysis of the teeth and skull shape.

Enemies of woolly mammoths included scimitar cats and American lions, who preyed on the young, and Paleolithic hunters. Human kill sites and cave paintings testify to the importance of mammoths to Ice Age hunters. The species probably lasted until about 10,500 to 11,000 years ago. In Europe, interactions with humans date back at least 125,000 years, or to the last interglacial time before the last major ice age.

Dwarf woolly mammoths

Dwarf or pygmy woolly mammoths evidently persisted until perhaps as recently as 3,000 years ago, on Wrangel Island off the

A comparison of a pygmy mammoth (Mammuthus exilis), which inhabited the Channel Islands off the coast of southern California, and a woolly mammoth (Mammuthus primigenius)

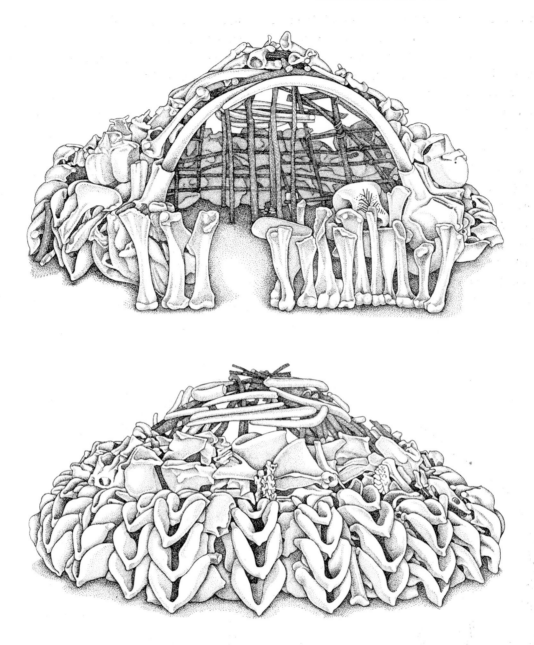

Views of one of four dwellings made from mammoth bones found in Eastern Europe, near the village of Mezhirich in Ukraine. The top view shows the entrance to the 16-foot-wide (5-meter) structure; the lower view displays the rear of the structure. Skulls, placed in a semicircle, form the interior base wall. Ninety-five mandibles, with the chins down, form the outer and upper parts of the wall. Leg bones were used in the front of the house. The roof probably consisted of a wood and bone frame covered with animal hides. Researchers estimate the total weight in bones to be 46,300 pounds (21,000 kilograms). —Courtesy of Patricia J. Wynne

coast of Siberia, and on many of the islands in the Mediterranean Sea. Pygmy mammoths *(Mammuthus exilis)* that were only a little more than 3.5 to 7 feet (1 to 2 meters) at the shoulder inhabited the Channel Islands of Santa Rosa and San Miguel off the coast of southern California from about 20,000 years ago into Holocene time, less than 10,000 years ago. In 1994 a nearly complete, fully articulated fossil skeleton of a 57-year-old male pygmy mammoth was found along the shore. This animal, which stood 5.5 feet (1.7 meters) at the shoulder, weighed about 1 ton and suffered from arthritic spurs on his feet. He evidently lay down, died, and was quickly covered by a sand dune. That postmortem burial led to the almost perfect preservation of the skeleton. Only a minor portion of the skull, right tusk, and one foot were missing. Radiocarbon dating shows this pygmy mammoth lived about 13,000 years ago.

Pygmy mammoth ancestors would have had to swim to get to these islands because even with sea level lowered by up to 328 feet (100 meters), the islands were not connected to mainland California. But modern elephants are good swimmers, so this may not have been as unlikely as it sounds. The small size of these mammoths probably resulted from adjustment to the limited food sources on the islands.

References: Barton, 1998; Colbert and Morales, 1991; Flint, 1971; Gladkin et al., 1984; Harington, 1995, 1996a; Haynes, 1991; Kurten and Anderson, 1980; Lister and Bahn, 1994; Meltzer and Mead, 1983; Mol et al., 1993; Morris, 2001; Scott, 1913; Shoshani and Tassy, 1996; Stone, 1999

6

EXTINCTIONS:
WHY ARE THE BIG GUYS GONE?

The grasslands and tundra of North America in late Pleistocene time teemed with great numbers of both large and small grazing animals and must have resembled the East African game parks of today. Vast herds of bison roamed North America along with mixed herds of mammoths and other large herbivores and their predators, the wolves, bears, lions, and saber-toothed cats. In the forests lived mastodons and various species of giant sloths. This all started to change about 14,000 years ago south of the terminus of the continental ice sheet, in what is now the continental United States. About that time, an ice-free corridor opened that linked the continental United States with the ice-free interior of Alaska. The north-south corridor allowed humans and animals—whose ancestors had come to North America over Beringia thousands to hundreds of thousands of years before—access to the open prairies and plains south of the ice sheet in the continental United States.

By the time the ice-free corridor opened, the populations of many of the large animals may have already decreased, with the decline starting possibly about 30,000 years ago. But researchers do not universally agree on this point. Some scientists believe the populations of large Ice Age animals declined not gradually but with a catastrophic plunge about 11,000 years ago. All researchers agree, however, that by approximately 10,000 years ago, North

At the Pleistocene Cafe

America and most of the other continents except Africa had lost one-half or more of their large animal species.

The extinction of the Ice Age mega-mammals was massive. North America lost at least thirty-one genera of animals weighing more than 100 pounds (44 kilograms), including several families and the entire elephant order. South America, in comparison, suffered far more genetic damage, losing at least forty-six genera in the past 3 million years. David Burney, a geoscientist interested in conservation biology and animal extinctions, states that over the last 100,000 years, North America lost 73.3 percent and South America lost 79.6 percent of all genera. Extinction rates were higher for large mammals in the Wisconsinan glaciation of Rancholabrean Land Mammal Age, and they were higher for small mammals during the earlier Blancan and Irvingtonian Land Mammal Ages. Because the earlier extinctions are more poorly known, the data are less reliable.

Extinction—defined as the end of the evolution of a genetically related group of organisms without replacement—has taken place since organisms first inhabited the earth. And extinction is the destiny of all species. Until extinction occurs, animal and plant species evolve into new species. The earth's sedimentary rocks record several mass extinctions that appear to have been relatively sudden, and they remain largely unexplained.

The greatest of all extinctions struck at the end of Permian time, 250 million years ago, when 90 percent of all ocean-dwelling species,

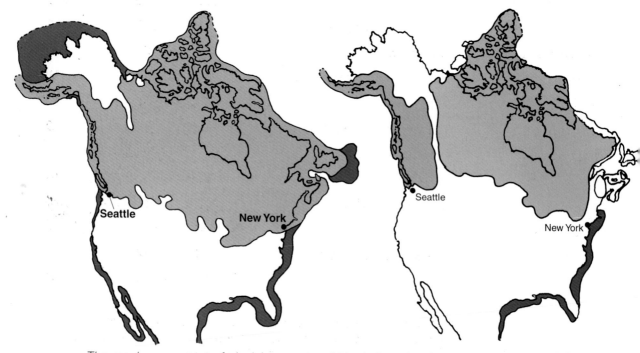

The maximum extent of glacial coverage of North America during the Wisconsinan glacial stage, 71,000 to 10,000 years ago (left); the ice-free corridor connecting Alaska with the region south of the continental glaciers, about 11,000 to 10,000 years ago. Black areas represent altered shape of continents due to lowered sea level.
—Modified from Mead and Meltzer, 1984

YOUNGEST EXTINCTION DATES FOR SELECTED GENERA

Genus	Common Name	Youngest Extinction Age Before Present	No. of Sites
Acinonyx	American cheetah	17620 +/- 1700	1
Arctodus	Short-faced bear	12650 +/- 250	2
Bootherium	Musk ox	17200 +/- 600	1
Camelops	Camel	8240 +/- 25	?
Capromeryx	Pronghorn	11170 +/- 360	3
Castoroides	Giant beaver	10230 +/- 150	2
Cervalces	Stag moose	10230 +/- 150	2
Equus	Horse	8240 +/- 960	38
Euceratherium	Shrub ox	8250 +/- 330	1
Paramylodon	Mylodont ground sloth	9880 +/- 270	9
Hemiauchenia	Llama	8527 +/- 256	3
Mammut	American mastodon	5950 +/- 300	52
Mammuthus	Mammoth	4885 +/- 160	63
Megalonyx	Megalonychid ground sloth	9380 +/- 85	10
Mylohyus	Peccary	9410 +/- 155	3
Nothrotheriops	Shasta ground sloth	9840 +/- 160	9
Panthera	American lion	10370 +/- 350	7
Platygonus	Peccary	4290 +/- 150	10
Smilodon	Saber-toothed cat	9410 +/- 155	4
Stckoceros	Pronghorn	8980 +/- 300	2
Symbos	Woodland musk ox	11100 +/- 300	1
Tapirus	Tapir	9400 +/- 250	6

Dates of the last known North American appearances of some extinct mammals calculated using the carbon-14 age-dating technique. The accuracy of some of the youngest dates is unknown. —Modified from Mead and Meltzer, 1984

30 percent of all insect orders, and 67 percent of all reptile and amphibian families perished. In total, 49 percent of all families and 72 percent of all genera vanished. Another massive extinction hit 439 million years ago, at the end of the Ordovician period. This event wiped out 57 percent of all marine genera. The most famous extinction, though not the largest, extirpated 47 percent of all genera, including dinosaurs, at the end of Cretaceous time, 65 million years ago.

Following the mass extinction of the dinosaurs came the diversification of the relatively new and opportunistic mammals, which had begun evolving well before the dinosaurs became extinct. However, the die-off of big land animals in late Pleistocene to early Holocene time passed without replacement by opportunistic animals other than humans.

Radiocarbon dates have allowed paleontologists to determine the approximate dates of the last living members of the now-extinct species of Ice Age animals. The bulk of all the terminal dates are between 12,700 and 9,400 years ago, at the very end of the Pleistocene epoch and beginning of the Holocene epoch.

While much has been written about why the dinosaurs suddenly became extinct 65 million years ago, a no less intriguing question is what caused the extinction only about 10,000 years ago, near or at the end of the Pleistocene epoch, of many of the magnificent continental Ice Age megafauna. Research into what causes massive extinctions is complex due to the combinations of factors that might lead to extinction, the possible rapid evolution of one species into another rather than extinction of the lineage, and the general lack of information available to modern-day paleontological sleuths. Compounding the mystery of what caused the extinction of megafauna at

the end of Pleistocene time are the invasions and competition by "foreigners"—animals and humans that came from Asia via the emergent Beringia land bridge, and animals that walked north from South America over the Panamanian land bridge.

Clearly, the solution to the complex problem of what caused the extinctions requires an interdisciplinary effort by geologists, paleontologists, paleoecologists, anthropologists, atmospheric scientists, paleobotanists, and other scientists. Let's examine some of the history and evolution of thinking about the extinction of the Pleistocene animals; then we'll consider the theories that are currently most popular.

Extinction—A New Idea

The concept of extinction is relatively new, having entered western thought in the latter part of the eighteenth century. Before then, the mere mention of extinction was considered an affront to God, the Creator, because it implied imperfection, flawed designs, and an attack on the principle of plenitude. For example, Thomas Jefferson's request for information from Lewis and Clark about living *Megalonyx* ground sloths stemmed from the prevalent view of the time that denied the possibility of extinction.

The earliest arguments for extinction of species, developed in the 1700s, were based upon studies of invertebrate fossils, many of which did not have any living relatives. Georges Cuvier (1769–1832), a famous French paleontologist who unearthed huge fossil bones around Paris, was one of the first to challenge scientists' thinking about extinction. He argued that it would be extremely unlikely to have animals the size of mammoths and giant ground sloths still strolling the earth unnoticed. The Creator, Cuvier believed, was fully

EXTINCTIONS OF NORTH AMERICAN MAMMAL SPECIES
BY SIZE AND LAND MAMMAL AGES

Size*	Blancan	Irvingtonian	Rancholabrean	Surviving Species	TOTAL
Small	97	55	29	181	166
Medium	31	25	33	89	50
Large	5	12	35	52	16
Very Large	1	2	6	9	1[†]

*Small=under 2 pounds (0.9 kilograms); medium=2 to 400 pounds (1 to 180 kilograms)large=400 to 3,900 pounds or 1.9 tons (181 to 1,755 kilograms); very large=over 4,000 pounds or 2 tons (1,800 kilograms)

[†]The northern elephant seal is the sole surviving mammal over 4,000 pounds

—Modified from Kurten and Anderson, 1980

capable of removing certain animals without affecting the rest, if he so desired.

In the early part of the nineteenth century, Robert Harlan, a vertebrate paleontologist building upon the works of Cuvier, reached the same conclusion in North America. Harlan listed ten late Pleistocene species, including sloths, mastodons, and mammoths, that were no longer living. The enormity of the extinctions of these gigantic, late Pleistocene animals impressed paleontologists at the time as much as they do today.

One problem paleontologists faced in the nineteenth century was correlating the ages of extinctions of the various species. Radiometric absolute age dating techniques, such as radiocarbon, were not available until after World War II. Many of the earlier researchers in the nineteenth century, however, concluded correctly that there had been relatively recent, essentially simultaneous extinctions of many very large animals, the remains of which people

were uncovering in unconsolidated stream, glacial, permafrost, and swamp deposits.

Cuvier was convinced that the late Pleistocene megamammals became extinct as a result of major but local catastrophes, unrelated to divine causes, that had struck no more than 5,000 or 6,000 years before. He based his reasoning on discoveries of mammoths frozen in Siberian permafrost and other animal carcasses found in unconsolidated swamp and stream outwash deposits in Europe. This interpretation differed from that of later scientists who proposed more widespread catastrophic processes.

Researchers in England, however, thought that the geologic and paleontologic studies in western Europe supported creation and an interactive God. Accordingly, the remains of the great, extinct Pleistocene animals found in stream, river, and other sedimentary deposits were thought to be related to flooding during Noah's time.

A major change in thinking about the Pleistocene extinctions came with the studies by the Swiss scientist Louis Agassiz (1807–1873) of glaciers and glacial deposits in and around the Alps. In his famous speech before the Swiss Society of Natural Sciences in 1837, Agassiz announced that the entire surface of the earth had been covered by glaciers that had originated at the North Pole and spread southward. The resulting drop in temperature killed the large animals. Each previous mass extinction had been glacially caused, and afterward a new divinely created assemblage of animals appeared. Agassiz never wavered in his belief that a catastrophic drop in temperature caused extinctions.

During the nineteenth century, however, other theories for extinction existed besides those of the catastrophists. Charles Lyell (1797–1875), an English geologist, was the father of the concept of uniformitarianism. According to this theory, the present is the key to the past. In other words, the processes shaping the earth today have operated in the past, but perhaps at different rates. Lyell proposed that gradual and natural changes caused the Pleistocene extinctions. He based his thesis on the observation that while some animal remains were discovered within particular horizons of sedimentary deposits, others were found in sedimentary layers above them. Therefore all animals could not have died at the same time.

An initial point of agreement between the catastrophists and uniformitarians, including Lyell, was that people arrived after the Pleistocene extinctions. Therefore, people could not have caused the extinctions.

Theories of human-caused extinctions, however, began to surface as early as the nineteenth century. Paleontologist George Turner thought the North American mastodon

to be a carnivore, the holy terror of eastern North American forests until its death at the hands of Paleo-Indians. And so by 1860, the pendulum was swinging toward human-caused extinctions, as researchers such as the English paleontologist and anatomist Richard Owen wondered if extinctions of vertebrates could be due to any cause other than human overkill. By then, the spatially associated remains of extinct Pleistocene mammals and early humans had begun to convince some researchers that the extinct mammals and humans had lived contemporaneously, and that humans may have caused at least some extinctions of Pleistocene animals.

The Reverend John Fleming, a Scottish zoologist, also concluded from his studies about the fauna of Great Britain and continental Europe in the nineteenth century that catastrophic flooding and slow climatic changes did not cause the animal extinctions. Instead he proposed that the extinction of large Pleistocene animals was quite recent, and at the hands of humans.

Once the naturalist Charles Darwin (1809–1882) presented his revolutionary research concerning evolution, other scientists began to view humans as having had a long history. Roughly contemporary with Darwin's work was that of the French scientist Jacques Boucher de Perthes. He began gathering evidence of the coexistence of people and extinct Pleistocene animals from multiple sites in the Somme River Valley in France. Boucher de Perthes, however, never wavered in his belief that the Biblical deluge had decimated the animals and humankind, and that modern animals and humans were not the descendants of those drowned but had been created later. After visiting the diggings of Boucher de Perthes, uniformitarian Lyell revised his negative view of human-caused extinctions. From then on, he believed that people not only lived during Pleistocene time but also were responsible for the extinction of the ancient beasts.

English paleontologist Robert Owen also entered the debate in the middle of the nineteenth century. Because only some of the fauna dating back to the Pleistocene epoch became extinct, Owen dismissed catastrophic theories for extinction. He also did not initially seriously consider that humans caused the extinctions of the large mammals; he thought humans were created later. By 1883, however, Owen too was convinced that the human overkill theory applied not only to Europe but to Australia as well.

As the true extent of continental glacial ice coverage became known and accepted in the latter part of the nineteenth century, more researchers rejected Agassiz's theory of catastrophic extinction by glaciation. One scientist who never supported any catastrophic theory for the great extinctions was Charles Darwin. Darwin noted in 1836 that "the American continent must have swarmed with great monsters" where only mere pygmies exist today. Because of Lyell's influence, Darwin believed in gradual extinction of at least the large South American animals. At the same time, he did not favor environmentally caused extinction. He thought, rather, that the extinct species had run their courses or outlived their time. He was "tempted to believe animals [are] created for a definite time," thus relieving the earth of an excessive number of inhabitants. Darwin, however, was not against adaptational causes of extinction. In his classic book *The Origin of Species,* he wrote about how complex the problem of extinction is. In the end, Darwin never supported any particular theory.

By the close of the nineteenth century, still no universally accepted theory had emerged to explain the cause of the great Pleistocene extinctions. The overkill hypothesis was very popular because, as late-twentieth-century archeologist Donald Grayson has stated, "the other hypotheses seemed inadequate."

Habitat and Early Humans

Cave paintings in south-central France, such as in the famous Lascaux cave, depict extinct animals and Cro-Magnon humans interacting in Europe as early as 30,000 years ago. More recent discoveries show that human hunters were also at work in the New World: many documented human kill sites are known all over North America. One important example is the Dent mammoth site along the South Platte River where it drains eastward away from Colorado's Front Range. There, about 11,000 years ago, a group of Paleo-Indians armed with spears tipped with Clovis-type points ambushed a herd of Columbian mammoths, including young animals. Within minutes, most of the animals were probably dead and subsequently butchered on the spot. The number of bones recovered at the site indicates at least thirteen mammoths died: five adults and eight juveniles, with an age span from forty-three to two years old. Work at the Dent site suggests that this particular draw may have witnessed at least two such mammoth ambushes.

But were humans the primary force leading to the extinction of the megafauna, were they partially responsible, or did they just watch the large animals die off?

Today, most of the extinction debate swirls around two of the most popular theories

CLOVIS AND FOLSOM CULTURES

Clovis refers both to a particular style of fluted stone spear tip and to the culture of the North American Ice Age people who used such spears to kill mammoths and other large game animals. The name Clovis comes from a town in New Mexico near which scientists in 1932 first discovered the points in 11,000- to 11,500-year-old sedimentary deposits and recognized them as different from the later Folsom points. The Clovis spear points were leaf-shaped and had a wide groove, or flute, on both sides of the base for fitting into short wooden and possibly bone spear shafts. Commonly, sites bearing Clovis spear points also yield mammoth remains. Petroglyphs of mammoths at two localities on the Colorado Plateau—one near Moab, Utah— also demonstrate that the Clovis people and mammoths coexisted.

Clovis kill sites, weapons caches, and individual points have been discovered across the United States and southern Canada south to northern Mexico. Where dated, Clovis kill sites in the western United States range from 11,000 to 11,500 years before present. Dated points in the eastern United States are a few hundred years younger. In 1987, orchard workers made one of the best and newest discoveries in an East Wenatchee, Washington, apple orchard. The cache of Clovis points, located during the installation of irrigation sprinklers, is within 30 feet (9 meters) of a county road. Implements recovered include the longest spear points ever found, at 9 inches (23 centimeters) long, and points fashioned from beautiful translucent quartz called chalcedony. Other materials unearthed at the site were scrapers, flaked tools called bifaces, and a decorated bone tool. Three of the implements still contained a residue of bison blood.

Where did the Clovis people and their technological skills originate? Conventional thinking has them coming from Asia by way of the Beringia land bridge and migrating southward along the ice-free corridor into the continental United States. Not all researchers agree, and for good reasons. Dr. Dennis Stanford, an archaeologist at the Smithsonian Institution who has studied the distribution of Clovis projectiles, points out that blades and blade cores are larger and more abundant in the southeastern United States than in the

Clovis point   *Folsom point*

western United States. Furthermore, none have been found in Alaska or Siberia where one would expect to find them if the people migrated southward from Siberia to inhabit North America.

Stanford recently stated that the blades are most similar to the European Solutrean culture of 23,000 to 18,000 years ago. These people left behind similar implements from about Bordeaux, France, southward around the Bay of Biscay and across northern Spain into Portugal. Not only do the implements look similar, but Stanford concludes that the method of pressure flaking their stone points must have been the same. And the distance between western Europe and the southeastern United States by foot and/or boat along the North Atlantic pack sea ice is much shorter than the long march from Siberia to Georgia.

Researchers continue searching for signs of early Americans in the eastern United States at such sites as Cactus Hill, Virginia, and the Topper site in South Carolina. Humans, possibly related to the Clovis people, may have lived there as much as 18,000 years ago.

The Folsom culture is named for Folsom, New Mexico, where fluted stone spear points of a slightly different design were first discovered together with the remains of extinct bison. Radiocarbon dates on Folsom points date to about 11,000 to 10,500 years ago and are not associated with mammoth remains. The Folsom spear points are smaller than Clovis points but have a proportionally longer flute that runs from the base to the tip. The Folsom Paleo-Indians succeeded the Clovis, or mammoth hunters, but neither group left many artifacts of their lives in North America.

References: Bozell, 1994; Frison, 1990; Hall, 2000; Holden, 1999; Mehringer, 1988; Nelson, 1990.

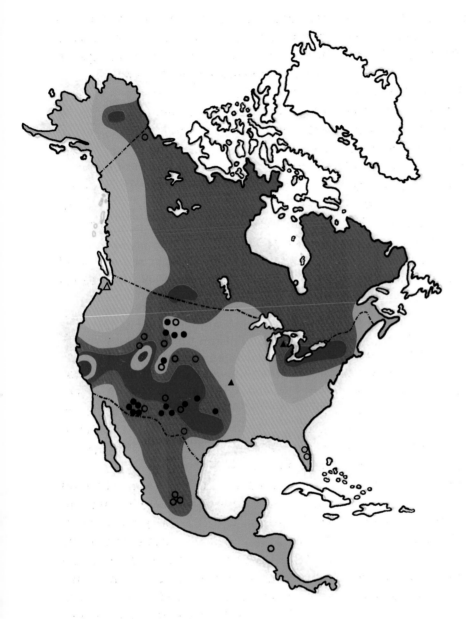

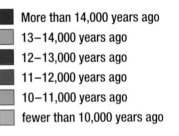

Mammoth and mastodon die-off ages in North America. The shaded areas show older extinctions in concentrated areas, while more recent extinctions are widely dispersed. Sites where evidence has been found of association between humans and mammoths and mastodons are also shown. These sites are primarily located where mammoths disappeared between 11,000 and 12,000 years ago, suggesting a possible link between human activity and mammoth extinctions. —Modified from Agenbroad, 1984

advanced in the last century. These place blame for the extinctions on dramatic habitat changes resulting from climatic shifts at the end of the last ice age, and on overkill by humans. Much evidence has accumulated since 1900 in support of both theories, and some scientists envision a combination of the two, with some modifications, for the extinction of Pleistocene megafauna. Clearly, an unprecedented spread and development of human culture throughout most of the world in the last 12,000 years coincided with the retreat of continental glaciers and the extinction of large animals.

Adherents to the theory of extinction by climatic change suggest that with the waning of the continental ice sheets as the global climate warmed, habitats necessary for the megafauna's survival became drier and less hospitable. Elsewhere, forests encroached on grasslands and tundra vegetation. As warm temperatures melted glaciers, sea level rose, accompanying the warming, and further eliminated large coastal areas for grazing. The vast coastal plain of the eastern United States is a prime example of land submerged as sea level rose. With the passing of the large plant-eating animals, many of which were easy prey for skilled human hunters, many species of Ice Age carnivores also died out in North America.

The loss of one-half or more of the large animal species in the last 30,000 years or less poses a major problem for those adherents to the climatic change hypothesis. While the earth has experienced several glacial episodes, separated by interglacial times as warm or warmer than today, during the last 2 million to 3 million years, the big animals apparently flourished. The difference between this post-glacial time and the previous interglacial times is that humankind, since about 30,000 years

ago, had adapted to living in northern climates. People developed group hunting skills at the very time climate-induced changes in habitat were stressing the large animals.

The Blitzkrieg hypothesis, advanced by statistician James Mosimann and paleoecologist Paul Martin, is one of the more creditable theories of human-caused extinction. According to this theory, hunters armed with newly developed and very lethal Clovis-type stone projectile points were able, within a few hundred years of 11,000 years ago, to decimate the North American megafauna.

Available age dates support southward extinction of the megafauna following earlier extinctions in Alaska. The big animals, not accustomed to the human threat, were exterminated first in Alaska, then farther south, and finally in the southeastern United States. Hunters would eradicate big game from a region and then move on as a front before their prey had a chance to learn evasive behavior. Compounding the problem for big animals such as mammoths was their long gestation period and resulting low birthrate.

Well fed and healthy, the hunting groups likely enjoyed reasonably high birth and survival rates. At a conceivable growth rate of 3.4 percent per year, the population would double about every 20 years. According to the calculations of Mosimann and Martin, the scenario started about 11,500 years ago with only about one hundred Paleo-Indian men and women near present-day Edmonton, Alberta, Canada. This group would have expanded in an arc, seeking new big game as they depleted a region, and their descendants would have reached the Atlantic and Gulf coasts in just 300 years. The Paleo-Indian population could have expanded to three hundred thousand hungry individuals during that time. They would have left in their wake the death and destruction of perhaps one hundred million big animals within an area of about 3 million square miles (7,800,000 square kilometers). Life after the passing of the great mammals would not be as good, so the human population would shrink to a level that could survive in the megafauna-free environment.

Support for the Blitzkrieg theory consists of the apparent last dated die-off of the animals in the southern and eastern parts of the United States, the apparent overlap of the Clovis hunters and the latest dates of the last living mammoths and other large animals, and the scattered remains of butchered mammoths and other Ice Age animals, dated at about 11,000 years ago.

The tale of megafaunal extinctions in Central America and South America is not clear. However, Mosimann and Martin think that with rates of southward migration and killing of big animals equal to that in North America, Paleo-Indians could have reached Patagonia about 1,000 years after leaving Edmonton.

Persuasive evidence for human-caused extinction of megafauna includes the persistence of many of the now-extinct animals on islands long after their disappearance on continents following the dramatic postglacial climate warming. Furthermore, animals existed on many of these islands until shortly after the arrival of humans to those islands. For example, dwarf elephants inhabited large Mediterranean islands, including the Greek island of Tilos, until about 4,000 years ago.

In 1999, Gifford Miller and coworkers at the Center for Geochronical Research at the University of Colorado reported additional support for rapid extinctions of large land animals at the hands of humans, at least in Australia. It had been known that 85 percent of Australian terrestrial genera, including huge flightless birds weighing more than 100 pounds (44 kilograms), became extinct about 50,000 years ago. The date has now been more accurately placed at 46,000 years ago. This extinction correlates closely with the arrival of humans on the continent. Reinforcing the certainty that this causal relationship exists is the fact that these same animals had lived through changing climates including much more arid conditions.

Factors beyond hunting that adversely affected animal survival in Australia would have been habitat changes wrought by human-caused fires and human introduction of non-native animals such as rats, goats, and dogs. These stresses, coupled with rising sea level as the continental ice sheets melted, would have further diminished suitable habitat.

The very recent animal extinctions in New Zealand, Hawaii, and Madagascar—some of the last areas of considerable size to be inhabited by humans—provide even more support for human-caused extinctions. In Hawaii, more species of birds became extinct in the past 1,500 years, since the arrival of the Polynesians, than survive there today. In New Zealand, the giant moa, a relative of the ostrich that was more than 10 feet (3 meters) tall and weighed at least 1,000 pounds (455 kilograms), became extinct not more than 300 years ago, or approximately 600 years after the arrival of the Maoris from the north.

It appears, then, that human hunting, in conjunction with both human- and climate-induced habitat changes, led to massive extinctions of megafauna near or at the end of the Ice Age. Add to that the arrival of exotic animal species, and these large animals faced little chance of survival.

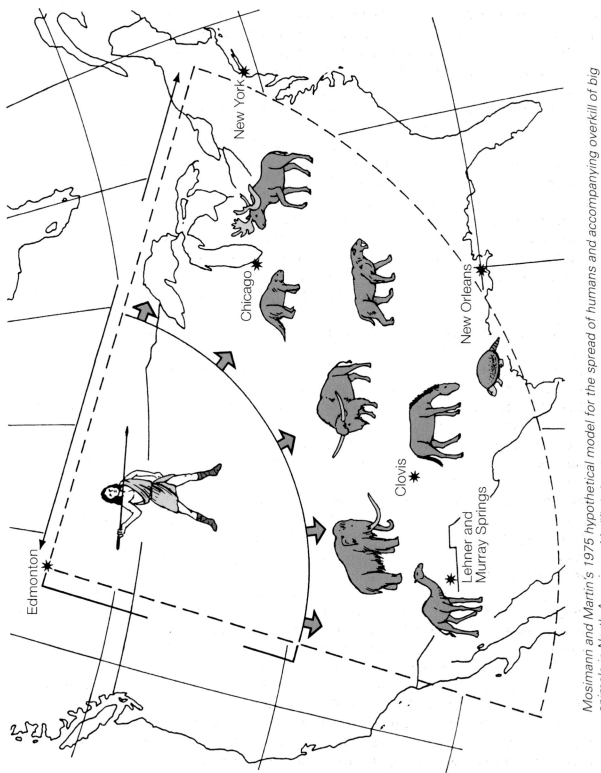

Mosimann and Martin's 1975 hypothetical model for the spread of humans and accompanying overkill of big animals in North America. —Modified after American Scientist

THE FIRST NEW WORLD HUMANS

How long have humans inhabited the New World? Some scientists believe that humans have been in North America for only about 12,000 years, or since the beginning of Clovis culture. Others present evidence that humankind may have been in the Western Hemisphere for as long as 200,000 years.

In South America, the Monte Verde site in southern Chile has the oldest accepted absolute age date of pre-Clovis artifacts in the Americas. Tom Dillehay of the University of Kentucky and his team of archaeologists did much work at the site between 1977 and 1985. The age of approximately 12,500 years is based upon about thirty radiocarbon determinations. The encampment along Chinchihuapi Creek contained nearly seventy species of plants, mastodon meat and bone, wooden tools and weapons, stone artifacts, and encampment remains. Rapid burial of the site by a peat bog preserved the artifacts and remains remarkably well.

In Brazil, radiocarbon dates on charcoal from the rock shelter Boqueirão do Sitio da Pedra Furada, if accurate, show that humans occupied the site between 32,160 years ago, plus or minus 130 years, and 6,160 years ago, plus or minus 130 years. Most evidence for human occupation, however, is in the form of stone implements, including weapons. Early peoples also used wood, bone, and plant and animal fibers for weaponry, tools, and clothing. These materials, while excellent for absolute radiocarbon age dating, decompose easily, making them rare finds. Stone implements are good evidence of human habitation, but researchers must determine an age independently. Researchers must also determine that the "implements" were really fashioned by human hands and not by some natural weathering process. Therefore, presumed implements associated with campfire charcoal are ideal for absolute age dating.

The oldest dated human skeleton in the Western Hemisphere is that of a 13,500-year-old woman found in southeastern Brazil. The skull resembles that of Africans and Australian aborigines more than that of Asians or Native Americans. At least fifty skulls found in the Americas that range in age between 8,900 and 11,600 years old are of non-Mongoloid origin. Mongoloid peoples appear to have arrived in South America approximately 9,000 years ago.

The skull characteristics of the earliest Americans have reinforced the theories of some researchers that the first Americans may not have come over the Beringia land bridge but across the Atlantic or Pacific Oceans instead. The Pacific Ocean route would have involved island-hopping eastward from Australia, where the aborigines arrived approximately 50,000 years ago, probably from Africa. The Atlantic crossing from Spain might have been made by boat and walking along the margin of the pack ice in the North Atlantic Ocean.

So where are the ancient North American sites that suggest human habitation earlier than 12,000 years ago, and what evidence supports the existence of these sites? One suspected location is the Meadowcroft rock shelter, 47 miles (76 kilometers) west of Pittsburgh, Pennsylvania. This site, perched on the steep north bank of Cross Creek, consists of a sandstone ledge projecting over an erosionally undercut shale layer beneath. The shelter measures 49 feet (15 meters) wide by 20 feet (6 meters) deep.

Researchers trenched the shelter and obtained more than one hundred radiocarbon dates on charcoal samples from the 16.5 feet (5 meters) of sedimentary layers exposed in the trench. The oldest date associated with human activities is 19,650, plus or minus 2,400 years. All dates are internally consistent with their stratigraphic position within the trench, meaning that the dates young upward as the sedimentary layers do. However, some scientists still doubt the validity of the old dates. Sites in the eastern United States that may be as old as 18,000 years include Cactus Hill, Virginia, and Topper, South Carolina.

Another famous but controversial site is along the Old Crow River in Canada's Yukon Territory. In 1966, researchers recovered four bone tools and radiocarbon dated them at about 30,000 years old. However, more recent age dating of these materials has produced dates of less than 10,000 years old. More objects, including bone flakes of mammoths, have been found yearly since the 1960s as spring runoff has further eroded the river's banks. The bone flakes give dates of 22,000 to 43,000 years old, but scientists still debate whether human hands actually shaped the flakes. Some researchers think there is no definitive evidence that people were in the area then.

At the oldest extreme is the purported age of 200,000 years for flaked stones found in the arid Calico Mountains of California. While archaeologist Alan Bryan thinks these ages are accurate, other archaeologists dispute that humans shaped these stones.

A relatively new discovery in Siberia leaves open the possibility that the first human entry into North America could have been much earlier than even 200,000 years. The Diring site on the Lena River in eastern Siberia has yielded more than four thousand stone tools within an area about the size of four football fields. These implements are at least 500,000 years old and possibly as much as 2 million years old. Did these humans cross from Siberia into North America on foot or by boat even earlier than previously suspected? Unless researchers find evidence of their emigration, we can only wonder.

References: Adovasio and Carlisle, 1984; Bower, 1986a, 1986b, 1987, 1994; Bryan, 1986; Fagar, 1977; Fiedel et al., 1996; Guidon and Delibrias, 1986; Holden, 1999a, 1999b; Meltzer, 1997; Nemecek, 2000

Geoscientist Norman Owen-Smith provides an interesting new twist to the Blitzkrieg overkill theory with his Keystone Herbivores Hypothesis. According to the theory, when the very large and slow-breeding herbivores die off, a cascade of extinctions of middle-sized browsers and grazers takes place. The large grazers destroy trees, as the elephants and rhinoceroses do in Africa today, which helps keep the savannas and grasslands open. That in turn keeps the midsized and smaller browsers and grazers in pasture. Once the large grazers become extinct, the smaller grazers and browsers soon follow. The large predators then run out of food and become extinct, too.

But perhaps the large animals died out more slowly than the Mosimann and Martin Blitzkrieg theory predicts. Since 1600 A.D., 113 species of birds and 83 species of mammals are known to have become extinct. This is a rate of 0.5 percent of living birds and 1 percent of living mammals per century, with the major driving force being habitat destruction and alteration. Statistics confirm that the greater the area of the habitat altered through cutting, burning, and/or introduction of nonnative species of plants and animals, the greater the number of extinctions. However, the extinctions don't necessarily take place immediately; some species live on but eventually succumb. It follows, then, that many species of animals alive today in limited numbers are doomed.

For a species to survive, birthrates must at least equal death rates. Obviously when death rates continually exceed birthrates, extinction is inevitable. Droughts, habitat alteration, the introduction of new predators, and harsh weather are some of the factors that decrease birthrates and increase death rates. It also follows that each species has an extinction threshold, or a minimum population below which it won't survive. But that is only part of the survival problem—if the animal population is fragmented because of habitat alteration, then the smaller animal units are even more susceptible to extinction.

Many scientists now think that the rapidly advancing killing front that Mosimann and Martin propose was not necessarily the only way to exterminate the large animals in a relatively short time. Once the minimum population threshold was passed, it was only a matter of time before the last of the giants died. For example, killing about 2 percent of the population each year would bring extinction within several centuries.

So why did the mammoths and mastodons become extinct? Scientist have proposed many plausible theories, but the extinctions happened in prehistoric time, and the fossil record, while good, doesn't appear to give a definitive answer. But maybe it does, and the answer, according to Daniel Fisher at the University of Michigan, may be found in the ivory tusks of these animals. Fisher presented his case in 1996 at the Museum of Natural History in New York City to a meeting of paleontologists. His theory follows.

Tusks are like trees in that they produce annual growth rings. The tusk rings, like tree rings, vary in width. Wide rings develop when the tusk-bearers eat well; during times of food scarcity, the rings are narrow. In addition, the tusks of female elephants also record births and the time interval between them. When the female is pregnant, her tusk rings are narrow because nutrients such as calcium go to the fetus. What Fisher has discovered in the tusks of the last mammoths and mastodons to live in Michigan and Ohio is that they were not only well fed, but they also bred frequently— females gave birth about every four years.

This matches the rate of births seen today in African elephants subjected to the pressure of heavy hunting. Many researchers now believe that the most logical predator to have put pressure on the mammoths and mastodons was the early North American human hunters.

Further support hot off the press for the overkill hypothesis is the recent computer simulation of end-Pleistocene human and large herbivore population dynamics in the continental United States by John Alroy, an evolutionary biologist at the University of California at Santa Barbara. His model predicts the extinction of large herbivores within a time period of between 801 and 1,640 years after the arrival of humans. And whether the humans invaded from the northwest, as usually assumed, or from Arizona, Florida, or Connecticut, for example, makes esentially no difference in the outcome.

Built into the computer model were modest growth rates in human population of between 1.61 and 1.7 percent per year, random rather than specific animal hunting, and variable hunting skills. Not included in the model, and which would have increased extinction rates, were such factors as human-caused habitat change, the introduction of pandemic diseases to herbivores, and selective hunting of individual species.

However, the model does not explain the survival of three large-sized species, moose (*Alces alces*), bison (*Bison bison*), and elk or wapiti (*Cervus elaphus*), and the extinction of several small species, including two species of pronghorn and two species of peccary.

Finally, for those who may underrate the hunting ability of early North Americans, remember that the Clovis hunters had to possess the skills to cross a cold, inhospitable environment to reach North America while clothing, feeding, and protecting themselves. And Paul Martin reminds us of what anthropologist Andreas Lommel said about these people: "In the beginning of hunting, a minimum of apparatus was very probably counterbalanced by a maximum of knowledge, concentration, and the gift of empathy, just as nowadays a minimum of knowledge [of animal behavior] and concentration is counterbalanced by maximum technical perfection of weapons."

The arrival of humans may have presented the large animals with yet another reason for decline: the introduction to the New World of deadly microbes against which the animals had no immunity. This was certainly the situation much later, when Europeans first encountered Native Americans during and after the voyages of Columbus. It has been estimated that smallpox wiped out up to 90 percent of the Indian population within just a few years.

Exotic and deadly microbes that accompanied animals such as dogs that the "first settlers" brought with them 12,000 or more years ago may have been partly responsible for the decimation of large animals at the end of Pleistocene time. This is an intriguing theory and more work is being done on it.

What does all of this mean for us today? Clearly the populations of remaining wild, large herbivores and carnivores are declining rapidly worldwide with little hope in sight for their long-term survival, except perhaps in zoos. As the human population continues to swell, the pressure on the remaining game parks and preserves will increase. Already many animals, such as tigers, elephants, and rhinos, are not safe even within their protected reserves in Africa and Asia. Perhaps the only hope of survival for them is a forced relocation into large preserves in safer countries with similar habitats, such as the United States, Canada, and Australia. I, for one, do not want to see them go the way of the giant ground sloths and the glypotodonts, the dire wolves and the saber-toothed cats, the woolly mammoths and all the rest of the great Ice Age animals of North America.

References: Agassiz, 1847; Alroy, 2001; Boucher de Perthes, 1847, 1864; Burney, 1993; Burns, 1990; Caloi et al., 1996; Cuvier, 1812a, 1812b; Darwin, 1859, 1871; Erwin, 1996; Flemming, 1824; Frison, 1990; Grayson, 1984; Hall, 1995; Harlan, 1825; Herbert, 1980; Hildebrand and Boynton, 1990; Hildebrand et al., 1991; Kurten and Anderson, 1980; Lommel, 1967; Lovejoy, 1964; Lyell, 1863; Mandryk, 1990; Martin, 1990; Mead and Meltzer, 1984; Miller et al., 1999; Mosimann and Martin, 1975; Owen, 1846, 1860; Owen-Smith, 1987; Pielou, 1991; Roberts et al., 2001; Rudwick, 1972; Turner, 1799; Ward, 1997

SELECTED MUSEUMS AND FOSSIL SITES
IN THE UNITED STATES AND CANADA

State or Province & Site Name*	Sights to See	Fee/No Fee
ALASKA Fairbanks University of Alaska Museum 907 Yukon Drive Fairbanks, AK 99775 907-474-7505 www.uaf.edu/museum/exhibit/index.html	36,000 B.P. mummified steppe bison—Blue Babe	Fee
ALBERTA Drumheller Royal Tyrrell Museum of Paleontology P.O. Box 7500 Drumheller, Alberta, Canada T0J0Y0 403-823-7707 www.tyrrellmuseum.com	Skulls and other bones of saber-toothed cats; bears, lions, sloth, mastodon	Fee
ALBERTA Edmonton Provincial Museum of Alberta 12845-102nd Avenue Edmonton, Alberta, T5N0M6, Canada 780-453-9100 www.pma.edmonton.ab.ca	Saber-toothed cats, Irish elk, Columbian mammoths	Fee
ARIZONA Flagstaff Museum of Northern Arizona 3101 North Fort Valley Road Flagstaff, AZ 86001 928-774-5213 www.musnaz.org	Native artifacts of the Colorado Plateau; dinosaurs	Fee
ARIZONA Sierra Vista Lehner Mammoth Kill Site BLM, 1763 Paseo San Luis Sierra Vista, AZ 85635 520-458-3559 www.az.blm.gov/tfo/spnca/lehner.html	Clovis mammoth kill site: camel, bear, about 12,000 to 13,000 B.P.	No fee
ARIZONA Sierra Vista Murray Springs Clovis Site BLM, 1763 Paseo San Luis Sierra Vista, AZ 85635 520-458-3559 www.az.blm.gov/tfo/spnca/murray.html	11,000 B.P. Clovis mammoth kill site: horse, camel, lion, dire wolf, bison	No fee

State or Province & Site Name*	Sights to See	Fee/No Fee
CALIFORNIA Berkeley Museum of Paleontology University of California 1101 Valley Life Sciences Building Berkeley, CA 94720-4780 510-642-1821 www.ucmp.berkeley.edu/	A few exhibits displayed, including *Tyrannosaurus rex*. Online exhibits include saber-toothed tiger, "long in tooth" marsupials and creodonts	No fee
CALIFORNIA Los Angeles The Page Museum at La Brea Tar Pits 5801 Wilshire Blvd. Los Angeles, CA 90036 323-934-7243 www.tarpits.org	Incredible animal/plant assemblage; more than 1,000,000 bones 40,000 B.P. to present	Fee
CALIFORNIA San Diego San Diego Natural History Museum P.O. Box 121390 San Diego, CA 92112-1390 619-232-3821 www.sdnhm.org	*Tyrannosaurus rex*; rocks, fossils, plants, and animals from southern California and Baja California	No fee
CALIFORNIA Ventura Channel Islands National Park 1901 Spinnaker Drive Ventura, CA 93001 805-658-5730 www.nps.gov/chis/pygmy.htm	Pygmy mammoth skeleton 13,000 years old	No fee
COLORADO Denver Denver Museum of Nature and Science 2001 Colorado Blvd. Denver, CO 80205-5798 303-322-7009 www.dmnh.org	La Brea Tar Pit skeletons; prehistoric journey through time exhibit	Fee
COLORADO Dinosaur Dinosaur National Monument P.O. Box 210, Dinosaur, CO 81610 303-374-2216 www.nps.gov/dino	Dinosaurs; rock art of prehistoric people	Fee

State or Province & Site Name*	Sights to See	Fee/No Fee
COLORADO Florissant Florissant Fossil Beds National Monument P.O. Box 185 Florissant, CO 80816 719-748-3253 www.nps.gov/flfo	Huge petrified redwoods; detailed fossils of ancient insects and plants	Fee
CONNECTICUT Rocky Hill Dinosaur State Park 400 West Street Rocky Hill, CT 06067-3506 860-257-7601 www.dinosaurstatepark.org	Dinosaur tracks	Fee
FLORIDA Gainesville Florida Museum of Natural History University of Florida P.O. Box 112710 Gainesville, FL 32611-7800 352-846-2000, x212 www.flmnh.ufl.edu	Mammoth, fossil horses, sloths, etc. and specimens from Leisey Shell Pit	No fee
FLORIDA Miami Miami Museum of Science 3280 South Miami Avenue Miami, FL 33129 305-646-4200 www.miamisci.org	Pleistocene exhibits	Fee
FLORIDA Naples Caribbean Gardens: the Zoo in Naples 1590 Goodlette-Frank Rd. Naples, FL 34102-5260 239-262-5409 www.napleszoo.com	Upcoming Ice Age exhibit	Fee
ILLINOIS Chicago The Field Museum of Natural History 1400 South Lake Shore Drive Chicago, IL 60605-2496 312-922-9410 www.fmnh.org	"Teeth, Tusks and Tar Pits" exhibit	Fee
ILLINOIS Springfield Illinois State Museum Spring & Edwards Streets Springfield, IL 62706-5000 217-782-7387 www.museum.state.il.us	16,000 B.P. midwest United States; rich in Pleistocene fossils	No fee

State or Province & Site Name*	Sights to See	Fee/No Fee
KANSAS Hays Sternberg Museum of Natural History Fort Hays State University 3000 Sternberg Drive Hays, KS 67601 785-628-4286 www.fhsu.edu/sternberg	Tyrannosaurus, "fish-within-a-fish," sharks, plesiosaurs, mosasaurs, flying reptiles, and more	Fee
KANSAS Oakley Fick Fossil and History Museum 700 West Third Street Oakley, KS 67748 913-672-4839 www.oakley-kansas.com/fick	Shark teeth, dinosaurs, mammals, plant fossils, mineral and rock collection	No fee
KENTUCKY Union Big Bone Lick State Park 3380 Beaver Road Union, KY 41091-9627 859-384-3522 www.state.ky.us/agencies/ parks/bigbone.htm	Sloths, mastodons, mammoths, etc., and bison trapped in marsh	No fee
MICHIGAN Ann Arbor University of Michigan Museum of Paleontology 1109 Geddes Road Ann Arbor, MI 48109-1079 313-763-6085 www.ummp.lsa.umich.edu/index1.html	Internationally recognized repository for collections of fossil specimens	No fee
MICHIGAN East Lansing Michigan State University Museum West Circle Drive East Lansing, MI 48824-1045 517-355-7474 http://museum.msu.edu	Natural history collections: mammalogy, herpetology, ornithology, ichthyology, and vertebrate paleontology	Parking fee
MISSOURI Imperial Mastodon State Historical Site 1551 Sechman Road Imperial, MO 63052 314-464-2976 www.mostateparks.com/mastodon.htm	Mastodons and prehistoric humans	No fee

State or Province & Site Name*	**Sights to See**	**Fee/No Fee**
MONTANA Bozeman Museum of the Rockies Montana State University 600 West Kagy Blvd. Bozeman, MT 59717-2730 406-994-2251 http://museumoftherockies.org	Mammoth, mastodon, saber-toothed cat, ground sloth, other fossils	Fee
MONTANA Missoula Museum of Paleontology Geology Department University of Montana Missoula, MT 59812 406-243-2341 www.cs.umt.edu/GEOLOGY/ Museum/Welcome.htm	Saber-toothed cat, dire wolf, other fossils	No fee
NEBRASKA Crawford Trailside Museum of Natural History Fort Robinson State Park P.O. Box 462 Crawford, NE 69339 308-665-2929 www.museum.unl.edu/trailside	Site of 600 bison that died about 10,000 years ago possibly due to human hunting; excavations continue	No fee
NEBRASKA Harrison Agate Fossil Beds National Monument 301 River Road Harrison, NE 69346-2734 308-668-2211 www.nps.gov/agfo	Mammal fossils, Indian artifacts	Fee
NEBRASKA Hastings Hastings Museum of Natural and Cultural History 1300 North Burlington Avenue Hastings, NE 68901 402-461-2399; 800-508-4629 www.hastingsnet.com/museum	Large Ice Age animal remains: mammoth, sloth, mastodon	Fee

State or Province & Site Name*	Sights to See	Fee/No Fee
NEBRASKA Lincoln University of Nebraska State Museum 307 Morrill Hall University of Nebraska Lincoln, NE 68588-0338 402-472-2642 www-museum.unl.edu	Elephant Hall (13 mounted) plus other extinct life	Fee
NEBRASKA Royal Ashfall Fossil Beds State Historical Park P.O. Box 66, Royal NE 68773 402-893-2000 www-museum.unl.edu/ashfall	Some of the best-preserved fossil rhinos, horses, camels, and birds	Fee
NEVADA Austin Berlin-Ichthyosaur State Park Route 1, Box 32 Austin, NV 89310 702-964-2440 www.state.nv.us/stparks/bi.htm	North America's most abundant and largest known Ichthyosaur fossils	Fee
NEVADA Carson City Nevada State Museum 600 North Carson Street Carson City, NV 89701-4004 775-687-4810 http://dmla.clan.lib.nv.us/docs/ museums/cc/carson.htm	America's largest Columbian mammoth plus other Pleistocene remains	Fee
NEVADA Las Vegas Nevada State Museum and Historical Society 700 Twin Lakes Drive Las Vegas, NV 89107 702-486-5205 http://dmla.clan.lib.nv.us/ docs/museums/lv/vegas.htm	Ice Age Las Vegas	Fee
NEVADA Las Vegas Floyd Lamb State Park 920 Tule Springs Road Las Vegas, NV 89131 702-486-5413 www.state.nv.us/stparks/fl.htm	Site of mammoths, camels, sloths, etc. and early North Americans	No fee

State or Province & Site Name*	Sights to See	Fee/No Fee
NEW MEXICO Portales Blackwater Draw Museum and Archaeological Site Station 3, Eastern New Mexico University Portales, NM 88130 505-562-2202 www.enmu.edu/~durands/ bwdraw/blackwater.html	Paleo-Indian (Clovis and Folsom) mammoth and bison kill site 11,200 B.P.	Fee
NEW YORK Bear Mountain Trailside Museum and Wildlife Center Bear Mountain State Park Bear Mountain, NY 10911 914-786-2701 www.geocities.com/ pipark_10911/trlside.html	Mastodon remains, fossils and rocks common to area	Fee
NEW YORK New York American Museum of Natural History Central Park West and 79th Street New York, NY 10024-5192 212-769-5378 www.amnh.org	Warren mastodon; vertebrate fossils displayed according to "family tree" rather than chronology	Fee
NORTH CAROLINA Raleigh North Carolina State Museum of Natural Sciences 11 West Jones Street Raleigh, NC 27601-1029 919-733-7450 www.naturalsciences.org	Giant ground sloth and other animals	No fee
OHIO Cincinnati Cincinnati Museum Center Union Terminal, 1301 Western Avenue Cincinnati, OH 45203 513-287-7000; 800-733-2077 www.cincymuseum.org	Ice age tundra; Hall of Pleistocene Vertebrates including sloths (world class immersion environment exhibit)	Fee
OHIO Cleveland Cleveland Museum of Natural History One Wade Oval Drive University Circle Cleveland, OH 44106-1767 216-231-4600; 800-317-9155 www.cmnh.org	Mastodons, mammoths, and more	Fee

State or Province & Site Name*	Sights to See	Fee/No Fee
OREGON Kimberly John Day Fossil Beds National Monument H.C.R. 82, Box 126 Kimberly, OR 97848 541-987-2333 www.nps.gov/joda	Well-preserved fossil record of the "age of mammals and flowering plants"	Fee
PENNSYLVANIA Philadelphia The Academy of Natural Science 1900 Ben Franklin Pkwy. Philadelphia, PA 19103 215-299-1000 www.acnatsci.org	Treasures of the Tar Pits (La Brea, CA) exhibit	Fee
PENNSYLVANIA Pittsburgh Carnegie Museum of Natural History 4400 Forbes Avenue Pittsburgh, PA 15213 412-622-3131 www.carnegiemuseums.org/cmnh	Fossil mammal hall	Fee
SOUTH CAROLINA Columbia South Carolina State Museum 301 Gervais Street Columbia, SC 29201-3041 803-898-4921 www.museum.state.sc.us	Mastodon, beaver, glyptodont, and other ice age creatures	Fee
SOUTH DAKOTA Hot Springs The Mammoth Site Museum P.O. Box 606 Hot Springs, SD 57747-0606 605-745-6017 www.mammothsite.com	Greatest number of Columbian mammoths in the world plus other ice age animals trapped in a pit	Fee
TENNESSEE Knoxville Frank H. McClung Museum The University of Tennessee 1327 Circle Park Drive Knoxville, TN 37996-3200 423-974-2144 http://mcclungmuseum.utk.edu/ permex/geology/geology.htm	Fossils of saber-toothed cats, dire wolf, mastodons, giant ground sloth, giant beaver	No fee

State or Province & Site Name*	Sights to See	Fee/No Fee
TEXAS Dallas Dallas Museum of Natural History 3535 Grand Avenue in Fair Park P.O. Box 150349 Dallas, TX 75315 214-421-3466 www.dallasdino.org	Collections showcasing the natural history of Texas	Fee
TEXAS Georgetown Inner Space Cavern P.O. Box 451 Georgetown, TX 78627-0451 512-931-2283 www.innerspace.com	Cave contains mastodons, dire wolves, etc.	Fee
TEXAS Houston Houston Museum of Natural Science One Hermann Circle Drive Houston, TX 77030 713-639-4629 www.hmns.org	Giant armadillo, mastodon, giant ground sloth, plus dinosaurs, etc.	Fee
TEXAS Waco Strecker Museum Baylor University, Department of Museum Studies P.O. Box 9715 Waco, TX 76798-7154 254-710-1233 www3.baylor.edu/Museum_Studies/ strecker.htm	Waco Mammoth Site: remains of 15 animals that died suddenly not due to people	Fee
UTAH Price College of Eastern Utah Prehistoric Museum 155 East Main Price, UT 84501 435-613-5111; 800-817-9949 www.ceu.edu/museum	98 percent of Columbian mammoth found in 1988 at 9,000 feet plus other, older animals	No fee
UTAH Salt Lake City Utah Museum of Natural History University of Utah President's Circle Salt Lake City, UT 84112 801-581-4303 www.umnh.utah.edu	Mammoth, dinosaurs	Fee

State or Province & Site Name*	Sights to See	Fee/No Fee
UTAH Vernal Utah Field House of Natural History 235 East Main Street Vernal, UT 84078-2605 435-789-3799 http://parks.state.ut.us/parks/www1/utaf.htm	Ancient fossil skeletal reproductions, archaeological and geological exhibits	Fee
VIRGINIA Martinsville Virginia Museum of Natural History 1001 Douglas Avenue Martinsville, VA 24112 276-666-8600 www.vmnh.org	Age of Mammals exhibit	Fee
WASHINGTON Seattle Burke Museum of Natural History and Culture University of Washington Box 353010 Seattle, WA 98195 206-543-6450 www.washington.edu/burkemuseum	Giant ground sloth, cats	Fee
WASHINGTON, D.C The National Museum of Natural History at the Smithsonian Institution Tenth Street and Constitution Avenue NW Washington, D.C. 20560 202-357-2700 http://www.mnh.si.edu	Great collection of Ice Age animals: giant ground sloths, mammoths, etc.	No fee
WYOMING Kemmerer Fossil Butte National Monument P.O. Box 592 Kemmerer, WY 83101-0592 307-877-4455 www.nps.gov/fobu	Paleoecosystems recorded in limestone lake bed	Fee

State or Province & Site Name*	Sights to See	Fee/No Fee
YUKON Whitehorse MacBride Museum 1124 First Avenue Whitehorse, Yukon, Canada Y1A1A4 867-667-2709 www.macbridemuseum.com	Ice age animals, prehistoric cultures	Fee unknown
YUKON Whitehorse Yukon Beringia Interpretive Centre Box 2703, Whitehorse, Yukon, Canada Y1A2C6 887-667-8855 www.beringia.com	Prehistoric history of Yukon	Fee

Web Sites

BBC: Walking with Dinosaurs
www.bbc.co.uk/dinosaurs

Dinosaur Magazine
www.dinosaurmag.com

Dinosaur Research Expeditions at Montana State University Northern
P.O. Box 7751, Havre, MT 59501
http://scimath.msun.edu/Dinosaurs/index.html

Discovery Channel: Dinosaur Guide
http://dsc.discovery.com/guides/dinosaur/dinosaur.html

MegaFauna: A List of Remarkable Prehistoric Mammals
www.kokogiak.com/megafauna/resources.asp

The Paleontology Museum Database Page
www.cyberspacemuseum.com/paleodbase.html

Pleistocene Links
http://inyo.topcities.com/manixpleistolinks.html

Sci-Info at the University of Arizona: Paleontology and Fossils Resources
http://inyo.topcities.com/manixpleistolinks.html

United States Geological Survey, Information Services
P.O. Box 25286, Denver, CO 80225
www.usgs.gov

GLOSSARY

age. A period of time in the history of the earth marked by special physical conditions or phases or organic conditions—for example, the ice ages.

artiodactyl. Any of an order (Artiodactyla) of even-toed ungulates that dates back to the Eocene. It includes peccaries, camels, llamas, deer and their kin, pronghorns, goats, sheep, oxen, and bison.

Beringia. The land bridge that periodically connected Alaska (North America) with Siberia (Asia) during the Pleistocene epoch. The connection occurred during the glacial maxima, when sea level dropped.

Blancan Land Mammal Age. Period approximately 3.5 to 1.9 million years ago marked by the appearance in North America of deer, gophers, and voles from Asia.

cladistics. A new classification system that organizes animals and plants by how closely they are related to one another evolutionarily. Compare with **Linnaean.**

Clovis. A Paleo-Indian culture (named for a New Mexico town) that used leaf-shaped, fluted spear points between about 11,500 and 11,000 years ago to hunt large game, including mammoths.

DNA. Deoxyribonucleic acid, usually a double-stranded molecule that twists helically, or spirally, about its own axis. The molecule carries chemical messages or instructions for assembling proteins and ultimately new organisms.

edentate. Animal of the Order Xenarthra or Edentata, which includes armadillos, anteaters, sloths, and glyptodonts. Edentate means "without teeth," but only anteaters truly fit that definition.

epoch. A unit of time that is shorter than and included within a period. For example, the Pleistocene and the Holocene epochs constitute the Quaternary period.

extinction. The end of the evolution of a genetically related group of organisms, or phyletic line, without replacement.

Folsom. A Paleo-Indian culture (named for a New Mexico town) of about 11,000 to 10,500 years ago that succeeded the Clovis people and used spear points that were smaller than Clovis points but had a proportionally longer flute that extended from the base to the tip of the point.

genus (pl. **genera**). A category of biological classification ranking between the family and the species, comprising organisms with structurally or phylogenetically related characteristics.

glacier. A mass of ice, snow, and eroded material that is partially or totally on land, showing evidence of present or past movement.

glacial maxima. The maximum extent of glacial ice coverage during a particular glacial event. For example, the Wisconsinan glacial maxima occurred 21,000 years ago.

Gondwana, Gondwanaland. The giant southern landmass of Pangaea comprising present-day South America, Africa, India, New Zealand, Madagascar, Antarctica, and Australia.

Holocene. The epoch following the Pleistocene and spanning from 10,000 years ago to the present.

Ice Age. Approximately the most recent three million years of Earth's history, during which large parts of the Northern Hemisphere landmasses were covered by continent-sized glaciers. Glacial coverage was also greater in South America and Antarctica, and mountain glaciers throughout the world were more extensive. The glaciers grew in response to lower average annual global temperatures.

Illinoian. The second-to-last major episode of North American glaciation. It was separated from the last, or Wisconsinan, by the Sangamonian interglacial stage.

Irvingtonian Land Mammal Age. Early Pleistocene period starting approximately 1.8 to 1.9 million years ago and ending between 300,000 and 150,000 years ago. The beginning is marked by the appearance in North America of the southern mammoth from Asia.

isotope. A species of an element—for example oxygen—that differs in the number of neutrons but not in the number of protons. The three oxygen isotopes all have eight protons but differ by having eight, nine, or ten neutrons.

Laurasia. The large northern part of the supercontinent Pangaea, composed of present-day North America, Greenland, Europe, and Asia.

Linnaean. A classification system of living organisms developed by Swedish botanist Carl von Linné, also called Carl Linnaeus, in the 18th century. Compare with **cladistics.**

lithosphere. The rigid outer part of the Earth, approximately 60 miles (100 kilometers) thick, which includes the crust and part of the upper mantle.

megafauna. Animals that exceed about 100 pounds or 45 kilograms in weight.

mammal. Any of a class of higher vertebrates comprising humans and all other animals that nourish their young with milk secreted by mammary glands and that have skin with variable amounts of hair.

marsupial. Any of an order (Marsupialia) of mammals that, with few exceptions, develop no placenta; females have a pouch on the abdomen which contains the teats and serves to carry the young.

Nebraskan. The first of the four North American glaciations, according to the first or classical scheme devised at the end of the 19th century.

Neolithic. Of or pertaining to the latest period of the Stone Age, characterized by polished stone implements.

pack ice. Sea ice (frozen sea water) that semipermanently covers vast parts of the Arctic and North Atlantic Oceans and the seas around the continent of Antarctica.

Paleo-Indian. One of the original human inhabitants of North America, dating from at least 12,500 years ago until just a few thousand years ago.

Paleolithic. Of or pertaining to the earliest period of the Stone Age, characterized by rough or chipped stone implements.

Pangaea. The supercontinent that existed between about 300 and 200 million years ago. It included Gondwana and Laurasia. About 200 to 180 million years ago it started to break apart and the process is continuing.

perissodactyls. Odd-toed ungulates of the order Perissodactyla, which originated in the late Paleocene. Perissodactyls include horses, tapirs, and rhinoceroses.

placenta. An organ in most mammals that unites the fetus to the maternal uterus and mediates metabolic exchanges between the two.

Pleistocene. The epoch of the ice ages starting about 1.8 to 1.9 million years ago and ending 10,000 years ago.

Pliocene. The epoch preceding the Pleistocene, starting about 5.3 million years ago and ending 1.8 to 1.9 million years ago.

radiocarbon dates. Absolute age dates on material containing carbon, including plants and animals, applicable back to about 50,000 years ago or into the late Pleistocene. The method is based upon the disintegration, break down, or decay of the unstable or radioactive isotope carbon 14 into a stable daughter isotope nitrogen 14.

Rancholabrean Land Mammal Age. The latest part of the Pleistocene epoch, dating from between 300,000 and 150,000 to 10,000 years ago. The beginning is marked by the first appearance of bison in North America from Asia.

Sangamonian. The interglacial stage in North America between the Illinoian and Wisconsinan glacial episodes.

scablands. The water-scoured topography west of Spokane, Washington, created by the periodic catastrophic releases about 15,000 years ago from glacially dammed Lake Missoula in Montana.

species. A grouping of individuals that have a common biological form measurably different from that of other groupings, and which can produce viable offspring that in turn can produce viable offspring.

steppe. Relatively level, treeless region within the interior of a continent, such as southeastern Europe and Asia, that witnesses temperature extremes: very hot summers and very cold winters.

Stone Age. The period of prehistoric human culture characterized by the use of stone tools.

Tertiary. The first of two periods of time in the Cenozoic Era, between 65.4 and 1.8 to 1.9 million years ago. It was succeeded by the Quaternary Period.

tundra. A level or undulating treeless plain characteristic of arctic and subarctic regions.

type location. The place where a specimen—for example, a rock, fossil, plant, or animal—was first recognized and described.

ungulates. Hoofed animals, most of which are herbivorous and many of which are horned.

Wisconsinan. The last major glacial episode of the Pleistocene epoch, which started about 71,000 years ago and ended 10,000 years ago. It followed the Sangamonian interglacial stage.

xenarthran. A member of the Order Xenarthra or Edentata. The name refers to the extra vertebrae or articulations between vertebrae of the lower backbone, which are unique to these animals. See **edentate.**

BIBLIOGRAPHY

Adovasio, J. M., and R. C. Carlisle. 1984. An Indian hunters' camp for 20,000 years. *Scientific American* 250:130-136.

Agassiz, L. 1837. *Discours prononcé a l'ouverture des séances de la Société Helvetique des Sciences Naturelles, à Neuchatel le 24 Juillet 1837.* Société Helvetique des Sciences Naturelles, Actes, 22me session (1837): V-XXXI.

Agassiz, L. 1847. Système glaciaire ou recherches sur les glaciers, Partie 1. *Nouvelles études et experiences sur les glaciers actuels.* Paris: V. Masson.

Agenbroad, L. D. 1984. New World mammoth distribution. In *Quaternary Extinctions: A Prehistoric Revolution*, ed. P. S. Martin and R. G. Klein, 90-112. Tucson, Ariz.: University of Arizona Press.

Agenbroad, L. D. 1990. The mammoth population of the Hot Springs site and associated fauna. In *Megafauna and Man: Discovery of America's Heartland*, ed. L. D. Agenbroad, J. I. Mead, and L. W. Nelson, 32-39. Hot Springs, N.Dak. and Flagstaff, Ariz.: The Mammoth Site of Hot Springs, South Dakota, Inc. and Northern Arizona University.

Alroy, J. 2001. A multispecies overkill simulation of the end-Pleistocene megafaunal mass extinction. *Science* 292:1893-1896.

Alt, D. 2001. *Glacial Lake Missoula and Its Humongous Floods.* Missoula, Mont.: Mountain Press.

Alt, D., and D. W. Hydman. 1995. *Northwest Exposures.* Missoula, Mont.: Mountain Press.

Antevs, E. 1929. Maps of Pleistocene glaciations. *Geological Society of America Bulletin* 40:636.Anton, M., and A. Turner. 1997. *The Big Cats and Their Fossil Relatives.* New York: Columbia University Press.

Arriaza, B., Jr. 1995. Chile's Chinchorro mummies. *National Geographic* 187(3):68-89.

Baker, V. 1995. Surprise endings to catastrophism and controversy on the Columbia. *GSA Today* 5:169-173.

Balter, M. 1999. New light on oldest art. *Science* 283:920-922.

Barton, B. R. 1998. Notes on the new Washington state fossil, *Mammuthus columbi. Washington Geology* 26(2/3):68-69.

Bernhardi, R. 1832. An hypothesis of extensive glaciation in prehistoric time. In *Source Book in Geology*, ed. K. T. Mather and S. L. Mason, 327-328. New York: McGraw Hill.

Blackwell, B. A. 1995. Electron spin resonance dating. In *Dating Methods for Quaternary Deposits*, ed. N. W. Rutter and N. R. Catto, 209-268. Toronto: Geotext 2, Geological Association of Canada.

Boucher de Perthes, J. 1847. *Antiquities celtiques et antediluviennes.* Memoire sur l'industrie primitive et les arts a leur origine, vol. 1. Paris: Treuttel and Wertz.

Boucher de Perthes, J. 1864. *Antiquites celtiques et antediluviennes.* Memoire sur l'industrie primitive et les arts a leur origine, vol. 3. Paris: Treuttel and Wertz.

Bower, B. 1986a. "Miami Ice" age site yields rich haul. *Science News* 129:52.

Bower, B. 1986b. People in Americas before last ice age? *Science News* 129:405-406.

Bower, B. 1987. Flakes, breaks and the first Americans. *Science News* 131:172-173.

Bower, B. 1994. Siberian site cedes stone-age surprise. *Science News* 145:84.

Bozell, J. R. 1994. Big game hunters. *Nebraskaland* 72(1):83-93.

Bretz, J. H. 1923. The channeled scablands of the Columbian plateau. *Journal of Geology* 31:617-649.

Bretz, J. H., H. T. U. Smith, and G. E. Neff. 1956. Channeled scablands of Washington: New data and interpretations. *Geological Society of America Bulletin* 67:957-1049.

Broecker, W. S. 1982. Glacial to interglacial changes in ocean chemistry. *Progress in Oceanography* 11:151-197.

Broecker, W. S. 1994. Massive iceberg discharges as triggers for global climate change. *Nature* 372:421-424.

Broecker, W. S. 1995. Chaotic climate. *Scientific American* 273:62-68.

Broecker, W. S. 1999. What if the conveyor were to shut down? Reflections on a possible outcome of the great global experiment. *GSA Today* 9(1):1-7.

Brouwer, D., and A. J. J. Van Woerkom. 1950. The secular variations of the orbital elements of the principle planets. *American Ephemeris and Nautical Almanac* 13(2):81–107. Washington D.C.: U.S. Government Printing Office.

Brown, G. 1993. *The Great Bear Almanac*. New York: Lyons and Burford.

Bryan, A. L. 1986. *New Evidence for the Pleistocene Peopling of the Americas*. Orono, Maine: University of Maine Press.

Burney, D. A. 1993. Recent animal extinctions: Recipes for disaster. *American Scientist* 81:530-541.

Burns, J. A. 1990. Paleontological perspectives on the ice-free corridor. In *Megafauna and Man: Discovery of America's Heartland*, ed. L. D. Agenbroad, J. I. Mead, and L. W. Nelson, 61-66. Hot Springs, N.Dak. and Flagstaff, Ariz.: The Mammoth Site of Hot Springs, South Dakota, Inc. and Northern Arizona University.

Butler, R. F., L. G. Marshall, R. E. Drake, and G. H. Curtis. 1984. Magnetic polarity stratigraphy and 40K-40Ar dating of late Miocene and early Pliocene continental deposits, Catamarca Province, NW Argentina. *Journal of Geology* 92:623-636.

Caloi, L., T. Kotsakis, M. R. Palombo, and C. Petronio. 1996. The Pleistocene dwarf elephants of Mediterranean islands. In *The Proboscidea*, ed. J. Shoshani and P. Tassy, 234-239. Oxford: Oxford University Press.

Campbell, P. 1984. New data upset ice age theories. *Nature* 307:688-689.

Chambers, R. L. 1971. Sedimentation in glacial Lake Missoula. Master's thesis, University of Montana.

Clark, P. U., and P. J. Bartlein. 1995. Correlation of late Pleistocene glaciation in the western United States with North Atlantic Heinrich events. *Geology* 23:483-486.

CLIMAP Project Members. 1976. The surface of the ice-age Earth. *Science* 191:1131-1137.

CLIMAP Project Members. 1981. Seasonal reconstruction of the Earth's surface at the last glacial maximum. *Geological Society of America Map and Chart Series*, MC-36.

Clottes, J. 2001. Chauvet Cave. *National Geographic* 200(2):104–121.

Clutton-Brock, J. 1992. *Horse Power*. Cambridge, Mass.: Harvard University Press.

Coates, A. G., J. B. C. Jackson, L. S. Collins, T. M. Cronin, H. J. Dowsett, L. M. Bybell, P. Jung, and J. A. Obando. 1992. Closure of the Isthmus of Panama: The near-shore marine record of Costa Rica and western Panama. *Geological Society of America Bulletin* 104:814-828.

Colbert, E. H., and M. Morales. 1991. *Evolution of the Vertebrates*. New York: John Wiley.

Conte, D. J., D. J. Thompson, and L. L. Moses. 1994. *Earth Science: A Holistic Approach*. Dubuque, Iowa: W. C. Brown.

Covey, C. 1984. The Earth's orbit and the ice ages. *Scientific American* 250:58-66.

Croll, J. 1875. *Climate and Time*. New York: Appleton and Company.

Cuvier, G. 1812a. *Recherches sur les ossemens fossiles les quadrupedes, ou l'on retablit les caracteres de plusieurs especes d'animaux que les revolutions du globe paroissent avoir detruites*. Paris: Deterville.

Cuvier, G. 1812b. *Discours preliminaire, in Recherches sur les ossemens fossiles des quadrupedes, ou les l'on retablit les caracteres de plusieurs especes d'animaux que les revolutions du globe paroissent avoir detruites*. Paris: Deterville.

Dalziel, I. W. D. 1995. Earth before Pangea. *Scientific American* 272(1):58-63.

Darwin, C. 1859. *On the Origin of Species by Means of Natural Selection, or the Preservation of Favoured Races in the Struggle for Life*. London: John Murray.

Darwin, C. 1871. On Pleistocene climate and the relation of the Pleistocene mammalia to the glacial period. *Popular Science Review* 10:388-397.

Dietz, R. S., and J. C. Holden. 1970. The breakup of Pangaea. *Scientific American* 223:30-41.

Elston, J. A. 1967. *Life, Land and Water*. Winnipeg, Manitoba, Canada: University of Manitoba Press.

Erwin, D. H. 1996. The mother of mass extinctions. *Scientific American* 275:72-78.

Erwin, D. H., and S. L. Wing, eds. 2000. *Deep Time*. Lawrence, Kans.: The Paleontology Society, Alton Press.

Eyles, N., and G. M. Young. 1994. Geodynamic controls on glaciation in Earth history. In *Earth's Glacial Record*, ed. M. Deynoux, J. M. G. Miller, E. W. Domack, N. Eyles, I. J. Fairchild, and G. M. Young, 1-28. New York: Cambridge University Press.

Fagar, B. M. 1977. *People of the Earth*. 2nd ed. Boston: Little, Brown and Company.

FAUNMAP. 1994. A database documenting late Quaternary distributions of mammal species in the United States. Illinois State Museum scientific papers, vol. XXV, nos. 1 and 2. Springfield, Ill.: Illinois State Museum.

Fiedel, S., T. D. Dillehay, B. J. Meggers, and A. C. Roosevelt. 1996. Paleoindians in Brazilian Amazon. *Science* 274:1820-1825.

Flemming, J. 1824. Remarks illustrative of the influence of society on the distribution of British animals. *Edinburgh Philosophical Journal* 11:287-305.

Flemming, J. 1826. The geological deluge, as interpreted by Baron Cuvier and Professor Buckland, inconsistent with the testimony of Moses and the phenomena of nature. *Edinburgh Philosophical Journal* 14:205-239.

Flint, R. F. 1957. *Glacial and Pleistocene Geology*. New York: John Wiley.

Flint, R. F. 1971. *Glacial and Quaternary Geology*. New York: John Wiley.

Forbes, E. 1846. On the connexion between the distribution of the existing fauna and flora of the British Isles, and the geological changes which have affected their area, especially during the epoch of the northern drift. *Great Britain Geological Survey*, Memoir 1, 336-432.

Frison, G. C. 1990. Clovis, Goshen, and Folsom: Lifeways and cultural relationships. In *Megafauna and Man: Discovery of America's Heartland*, ed. L. D. Agenbroad, J. I. Mead, and L. W. Nelson, 100-108. Hot Springs, N.Dak. and Flagstaff, Ariz.: The Mammoth Site of Hot Springs, South Dakota, Inc. and Northern Arizona University.

Gates, W. L. 1976. Modeling the Ice Age climate. *Science* 191:1138–1144.

Geikie, A. 1863. On the phenomena of the glacial drift of Scotland. *Geological Society of Glasgow Transactions* 1:1-190.

Gladkih, M. I., N. L. Kornietz, and O. Soffer. 1984. Mammoth-bone dwellings on the Russian Plain. *Scientific American* 251:164-169.

Gould, S. J. 1966. Allometry and size in ontogeny and phylogeny. *Biological Review* 41:587-640.

Grayson, D. K. 1984. Nineteenth-century explanations of Pleistocene extinctions: A review and analysis. In *Quaternary Extinctions: A Prehistoric Revolution*, ed. P. S. Martin and R. G. Klein, 5-39. Tucson, Ariz.: The University of Arizona Press.

Greiner, N. 2000. Mega Bear. *Alaska Magazine* 66:24-28.

Guidon, N., and G. Delibrias. 1986. Carbon-14 dates point to man in the Americas 32,000 years ago. *Nature* 321:769-771.

Guthrie, R. D. 1990. *Frozen Fauna of the Mammoth Steppe: The Story of Blue Babe*. Chicago: University of Chicago Press.

Hadingham, E. 1979. *Secrets of the Ice Age*. New York: Walker and Company.Hall, D. A. 1995. The Dent mammoth site. *Mammoth Trumpet* 10(4):1-6.

Hall, D. A. 2000. Seeking proof of pre-Clovis in the West. *Mammoth Trumpet* 15(2):1-7.

Hallam, A. 1975. Alfred Wegener and the hypothesis of continental drift. *Scientific American* 232(2):88-97.

Hansen, K. 1992. *Cougar the American Lion*. Flagstaff, Ariz.: Northland Publishing.

Harington, C. R. 1993. Jefferson ground sloth. Yukon Beringia Interpretive Center < www.beringia.com >.

Harington, C. R. 1995. Woolly mammoth. Yukon Beringia Interpretive Center < www.beringia.com >.

Harington, C. R. 1996a. Mastodon. Yukon Beringia Interpretive Center < www.beringia.com >.

Harington, C. R. 1996b. North American short-faced bear. Yukon Beringia Interpretive Center < www.beringia.com >.

Harington, C. R. 1996c. American lion. Yukon Beringia Interpretive Center < www.beringia.com >.

Harington, C. R. 1996d. Giant beaver. Yukon Beringia Interpretive Center < www.beringia.com >.

Harington, C. R. 1996e. Steppe bison. Yukon Beringia Interpretive Center < www.beringia.com >.

Harington, C. R. 1996f.American scimitar cat. Yukon Beringia Interpretive Center < www.beringia.com >.

Harington, C. R. 1997. Ice age Yukon and Alaska camels. Yukon Beringia Interpretive Center < www.beringia.com >.

Harington, C. R. 1998. North American saiga. Yukon Beringia Interpretive Center < www.beringia.com >.

Harington, C. R. 1999. Ancient caribou. Yukon Beringia Interpretive Center < www.beringia.com >.

Harlan, R. 1825. *Fauna Americana: Being a description of the mammiferous animals inhabiting North America*. Philadelphia: Finley.

Haynes, G. 1991. *Mammoths, Mastodonts, and Elephants*. Cambridge: Cambridge University Press.

Hays, J. D., J. Imbrie, and N. J. Shackleton. 1976. Variations in the Earth's orbit: Pacemaker of the ice ages. *Science* 194:1121-1132.

Heinrich, H. 1988. Origin and consequences of cyclic ice rafting in the northeast Atlantic Ocean during the past 130,000 years. *Quaternary Research* 29:143-152.

Herbert, S. 1980. *The Red Notebook of Charles Darwin.* London and Ithaca: British Museum (Natural History) and Cornell University Press.

Hildebrand, A. R., and W. V. Boynton. 1990. Proximal Cretaceous-Tertiary boundary impact deposits in the Caribbean. *Science* 248:843-847.

Hildebrand, A. R., G. T. Penfield, D. A. Kring, M. Pilkington, A. Z. Camargo, S. B. Jacobsen, and W. V. Boynton. 1991. Chicxulub crater: A possible Cretaceous/Tertiary boundary impact crater on the Yucatan Peninsular, Mexico. *Geology* 19:867-871.

Holden, C. 1999a. Were Spaniards among the first Americans? *Science* 286:1467-1468.

Holden, C. 1999b. Australasian roots proposed for "Luzia." *Science* 286:1467.Holmes, A. 1965. *Principles of Physical Geology.* New York: Ronald Press.

Hopkins, D. M., ed. 1967. The Bering Land Bridge. Stanford, Calif.: Stanford University Press.

Imbrie, J., and J. Z. Imbrie. 1980. Modeling the Climatic Response to Orbital Variations. *Science* 207:943–953.

Imbrie, J., and K. P. Imbrie. 1979. *Ice Ages: Solving the Mystery.* Short Hills, N.J.: Enslow Publishers.

Imbrie, J., and others. 1984. The orbital theory of Pleistocene climate: Support from a revised chronology of the marine S18O record. In *Milankovitch and Climate*, part 1, ed. A. L. Berger and others, 269-305. Dordrecht, Netherlands: Reidel Publishing Company.

Jackson, D., ed. 1978. *Letters of the Lewis and Clark Expedition with Related Documents 1783-1854.* Chicago: University of Illinois Press.Jamieson, T. F. 1862. On the ice-worn rocks of Scotland. *Geological Society of London Quarterly Journal* 18:164-184.

Jamieson, T. F. 1865. On the history of the last glacial changes in Scotland. *Quarterly Journal of the Geological Society of London* 21:161-195.

Jefferson, T. 1799. A memoir on the discovery of certain bones of a quadruped of the clawed kind in the western parts of Virginia. *Transactions of the Philosophical Society* 4(30):246-260.

Johnson, R. G. 1997. Climate control requires a dam at the Strait of Gibraltar. *Transactions of American Geophysical Union, Eos* 78(27):277-281.

Judson, S., M. E. Kauffman, and L. D. Leet. 1987. *Physical Geology.* Englewood Cliffs, N.J.: Prentice Hall.

Kurten, B. 1968. *Pleistocene mammals of Europe.* London: Weidenfeld and Nicolson.

Kurten, B. 1972. *The Age of Mammals.* New York: Columbia University Press.

Kurten, B. 1976. *The Cave Bear Story.* New York: Columbia University Press.

Kurten, B., and E. Anderson. 1980. *Pleistocene Mammals of North America.* New York: Columbia University Press.

Lambert, D. 1985. *A Field Guide to Prehistoric Life.* New York: Facts on File Publications.

Ledley, T. S., E. T. Sundquist, S. E. Schwartz, D. K. Hall, J. D. Fellows, and T. L. Killeen. 1999. Climate change and greenhouse gases. Transactions of American Geophysical Union, *Eos* 80(39):453-458.Leidy, J. 1847. On the fossil horse in America. *Proceedings of the National Academy of Sciences* 3:262-266.

Laming, A. 1959. *Lascaux Paintings and Engravings.* Middlesex: Penguin Books.Lessa, E. P., and R. A. Farina. 1996. Reassessment of extinction patterns among the late Pleistocene mammals of South America. *Palaeontology* 39:651-662.

Lister, A., and P. Bahn. 1994. *Mammoths.* New York: Macmillan.

Lommel, A. 1967. *Shamanism: The Beginnings of Art.* New York: McGraw Hill.

Lovejoy, A. O. 1964. *The Great Chain of Being.* Cambridge, Mass.: Harvard University Press.

Lyell, C. 1833. *Principles of Geology, Being an Attempt to Explain the Former Changes of the Earth's Surface by Reference to Causes Now in Operation*, vol. 3. London: John Murray.

Lyell, C. 1863. *The Geological Evidences of the Antiquity of Man, with Remarks on Theories of the Origin of Species by Variation.* Philadelphia: G. W. Childs.

MacFadden, B. J. 1992. *Fossil Horses Systematics, Paleobiology, and Evolution of the Family Equidae.* New York: Cambridge University Press.

Mandryk, C. A. 1990. Could humans survive the ice-free corridor? Late glacial vegetation and climate in west-central Alberta. In *Megafauna and Man: Discovery of America's Heartland*, ed. L. D. Agenbroad, J. I. Mead, and L. W. Nelson, 67-79. Hot Springs, N.Dak. and Flagstaff, Ariz.: The Mammoth Site of Hot Springs, South Dakota, Inc. and Northern Arizona University.

Marcus, L. F., and B. Berger. 1984. The significance of radiocarbon dates for Rancho La Brea. In *Quaternary Extinctions: A Prehistoric Revolution*, ed. P. S. Martin and R. G. Klein, 159-188. Tucson, Ariz.: University of Arizona Press.

Marshall, L. G. 1988. Land mammals and the great American interchange. *American Scientist* 76:380-388.

Marshall, L. G. 1994. The terror birds of South America. *Scientific American* 270:90-95.

Marshall, L. G., S. D. Webb, J. J. Sepkoski, Jr., and D. M. Raup. 1982. Mammalian evolution and the great American interchange. *Science* 215:1351-1357.

Martin, P. S. 1990. Who or what destroyed our mammoths? In *Megafauna and Man: Discovery of America's Heartland*, ed. L. D. Agenbroad, J. I. Mead, and L. W. Nelson, 109-117. Hot Springs, N.Dak. and Flagstaff, Ariz.: The Mammoth Site of Hot Springs, South Dakota, Inc. and Northern Arizona University.

Martin, P. S., and R. G. Klein. 1984. *Quaternary Extinctions: A Prehistoric Revolution*. Tucson, Ariz.: University of Arizona Press.

Martin, P. S., and H. E. Wright, Jr. 1967. *Pleistocene Extinctions*. New Haven, Conn.: Yale University Press.

McDonald, E. V., and A. J. Buscacca. 1988. Record of pre-late Wisconsin giant floods in the Channeled Scabland interpreted from loess deposits. *Geology* 16:728-731.

Mead, J. I., and D. J. Meltzer. 1984. North American late Quaternary extinctions and the radiocarbon record. In *Quaternary Extinctions: A Prehistoric Revolution*, ed. P. S. Martin and R. G. Klein, 440-450. Tucson, Ariz.: University of Arizona Press.Mehringer, P. J., Jr. 1988. Weapons of ancient Americans. *National Geographic* 174(4):500-503.

Meltzer, D. J. 1997. Monte Verde and the Pleistocene peopling of the Americas. *Science* 276:754-755.

Meltzer, D. J. and J. I. Mead. 1983. The timing of late Pleistocene mammalian extinctions in North America. *Quaternary Research* 19:130-135.

Menon, S. 1995. The dry iceman. *Discover* 16(1):57.

Mestel, R. 1993. Sabre-toothed tales. *Discover* 14(1):34-43.

Miller, G. H., J. W. Magee, B. J. Johnson, M. L. Fogel, N. A. Spooner, M. T. McCulloch, and L. K. Ayliffe. 1999. Pleistocene extinction of *Genyornis newtoni*: Human impact on Australian megafauna. *Science* 283:205–208.

Mol, D., L. D. Agenbroad, and J. I. Mead. 1993. *Mammoths*. Rapid City, S.Dak.: Fenske Printing.

Moore, R. C., C. G. Laticker, and A. G. Fischer. 1952. *Invertebrate Fossils*. New York: McGraw Hill.

Mosimann, J., and P. S. Martin. 1975. Simulating overkill by Paleoindians. *American Scientist* 63:304-313.

Morris, D. 2001. Pygmy mammoth update. Channel Island National Park Internet Information Center < www.nps.gov/chis/pygmy.htm > .

Morrison, R. B. 1991. Introduction. In *Quaternary Nonglacial Geology: Conterminous U.S.*, ed. R. B. Morrison, 1-12. *The Geology of North America*, vol. K-2. Boulder, Colo.: Geological Society of America.

Muller, R. A. and G. J. MacDonald. 1997. Glacial cycles and astronomical forcing. *Science* 277:215-277.

Novikov, G. A. 1962. *Fauna of USSR*. Zoological Institute of Academy of Science of the USSR, no. 62.

Nelson, L. 1990. *Ice Age mammals of the Colorado Plateau*. Flagstaff, Ariz.: Northern Arizona University.

Nemecek, S. 2000. Who were the first Americans? *Scientific America* 283(3):80-87.

Nilsson, T. 1983. *The Pleistocene*. Dordrecht, Netherlands: D. Reidel Publishing.

Niskanen, E. 1939. On the upheaval of land in fennoscandia. *Annales Academiae Scientiarum Fennicae*, series A, vol. 53.O'Connor, J. E., and V. R. Baker. 1992. Magnitudes and implications of peak discharges from glacial Lake Missoula. *Geological Society of America Bulletin* 104:267-279.Oreskes, N. 1999. *The Rejection of Continental Drift: Theory and Method in American Science*. Oxford: Oxford University Press.

Owen, R. 1846. *History of British Fossil Mammals and Birds*. London: Van Voorst.Owen, R. 1860. *Paleontology, or a Systematic Summary of Extinct Mammals and Their Geologic Relations*. London: A. and C. Black.

Owen-Smith, N. 1987. Pleistocene extinctions: The pivotal role of megaherbivores. *Paleobiology* 13:351-362.Pardee, J. T. 1910. The glacial Lake Missoula, Montana. *Journal of Geology* 18:376-386.

Pardee, J. T. 1922. Glaciation in the Cordilleran region (Spokane area, Washington). *Science* 56:686-687.

Parker, S. P., ed. 1990. *Grzimek's Encyclopedia of Mammals*, vol. 2. New York: McGraw-Hill.

Pielou, E. C. 1991. *After the Ice Age*. Chicago: University of Chicago Press.

Poinar, G., Jr. 1999. Ancient DNA. *American Scientist* 87:446–57.

Quammen, D. 1995. Up and out why big things are dead. *Outside* 20(9):41-46.

Rawn-Schatzinger, V. 1992. The scimitar cat *Homotherium serum* Cope: Osteology, functional morphology, and predatory behavior. *Illinois State Museum Report of Investigations* 47:1-118.

Raymo, M. E., W. F. Ruddiman, and P. N. Froelich. 1988. Influence of late Cenozoic mountain building on ocean geochemical cycles. *Geology* 16:649-653.

Redford, K. H., and J. F. Eisenberg. 1992. *Mammals of the Neotropics*, vol. 2. Chicago: University of Chicago Press.Reid, J. L. 1979. On the contribution of the Mediterranean Sea outflow to the Norwegian-Greenland Sea. *Deep Sea Research* 26:1199.

Rigaud, J. P. 1988. Art treasures from the Ice Age Lascaux Cave. *National Geographic* 174(4):482-499.

Roberts, R. G., T. F. Flannery, L. K. Ayliffe, H. Yoshida, J. M. Olley, G. J. Prideaux, G. M. Laslett, A. Baynes, M. A. Smith, R. Jones, and B. L. Smith. 2001. New ages for the last Australian megafauna: Continent-wide extinction about 46,000 years ago. *Science* 292:1888-1892.

Rudwick, M. J. S. 1972. *The Meaning of Fossils: Episodes in the History of Palaeontology.* New York: American Elsevier.Saussure, Horace-Benedict de. 1787. *Voyages dans les Alpes precedes d'un essai sur l'histoire naturelle des environs de Geneve,* vol. 1. Geneva: Barde, Manget.

Savage, D. E., and D. E. Russell. 1983. *Mammalian Paleofaunas of the World.* London: Addison-Wesley.

Schmidt-Nielsen, K. 1984. *Scaling: Why is Animal Size so Important?* Cambridge: Cambridge University Press.

Schultz, C. B., L. G. Tanner, L. L. Whitmore, Jr., and E. C. Crawford. 1963. Paleontologic investigations at Big Bone Lick State Park, Kentucky: A preliminary report. *Science* 142:1167-1169.

Scott, W. B. 1913. *A History of Land Mammals in the Western Hemisphere.* New York: Macmillan.Severinghaus, J. P., and E. J. Brook. 1999. Abrupt climate change at the end of the last glacial period inferred from trapped air in polar ice. *Science* 286:930-934.

Sheehan, A. 1973. *The Doubleday Nature Encyclopedia.* New York: Ottenheimer.

Shoshani, J., and P. Tassy, eds. 1996. *The Proboscidea: Evolution and Palaeoecology of Elephants and Their Relatives.* Oxford: Oxford University Press.

Skinner, B. J., and S. C. Porter. 1995. *The Dynamic Earth.* 3rd ed. New York: John Wiley.

Stanley, S. M. 1986. *Earth and Life Through Time.* New York: Freeman.

Stanley, S. M. 1995. New horizons for paleontology, with two examples: The rise and fall of the Cretaceous Supertethys and the cause of the modern ice age. *Journal of Paleontology* 69:999-1007.

Stanley, S. M. 1998. *Macroevolution, pattern and process.* Baltimore: Johns Hopkins.

Stokstad, E. 1998. A fruitful scoop for ancient DNA. *Science* 281:319-320.Stock, C. 1925. Cenozoic gravigrade Edentates of western North America with special reference to the Pleistocene Megalonychinae and Mylodontidae of Rancho La Brea. Carnegie Institute of Washington, Publication 331.

Stock, C., and J. M. Harris. 1992. *Rancho La Brea: A Record of Pleistocene Life in California.* Natural History Museum of Los Angeles County, Science Series 37.

Stone, R. 1999. Cloning the woolly mammoth. *Discover* 20:56–63.

Strahler, A. N. 1971. *The Earth Science.* New York: Harper and Row.

Taylor, K. C., P. A. Mayewski, R. B. Alley, E. J. Brook. 1997. A remains of more than one species of non-descript animal. *Transactions of the American Philosophical Society* 4:510-518.

Turner, G. 1799. Memoir on the extraneous fossils, denominated mammoth bones: Principally designed shew, that they are the remains of more than one species of non-descript animal. *Transactions of the American Philosophical Society* 4:510-518.

Ucko, P. J., and A. Rosenfeld. 1967. *Paleolithic Cave Art.* New York: McGraw-Hill Book Company.

Van Valkenburgh, B. 1991. Cats in communities: Past and present. In *Great Cats,* ed. J. Seidenslicker and S. Lumpkin, 15-23. Emmaus Road, Pa.: Rodale Press.

Voorhies, M. R. 1994. Hooves and horns. *Nebraskaland* 72(1):74-79.

Waitt, R. B. 1987. Evidence for dozens of stupendous floods from glacial Lake Missoula in eastern Washington, Idaho, and Montana. In Cordilleran Section of *The Geological Society of America Centennial Field Guide,* vol. 1, ed. M. L. Hill, 345-350. Boulder, Colo.: The Geological Society of America.

Ward, P. D. 1997. *The Call of Distant Mammoths.* New York: Copernicus.

Webb, S. D. 1978. Evolution of savanna vertebrates in the New World. Part II: South America and the great interchange. *Annual Review of Ecology and Systematics* 9:393-426.

Webb, S. D. 1985. Late Cenozoic mammal dispersals between the Americas. In *The Great American Biotic Interchange,* ed. F. G. Stehli and S. D. Webb, 357-386. New York: Plenum.

Whitaker, J. O., Jr. 1997. *National Audubon Society Field Guide to North American Animals.* New York: Alfred A. Knopf.

White, R. S., and D. P. McKenzie. 1989. Volcanism at rifts. *Scientific American* 261:62-70.

Windley, B. F. 1984. *The Evolving Continents.* New York: John Wiley.

Woodburne, M. O., and C. C. Swisher, III. 1995. Land mammal high-resolution geochronology, intercontinental overland species dispersals, sea level, climate and vicariance. In *Geochronology Time Scales and Global Stratigraphic Correlation,* ed. W. A. Berggren and others, 335-364. Society of Sedimentary Geology Special, Publication 54.

INDEX

Page references in *italics* refer to illustrations or photographs.

Acinonyx, 103, 112; extinction of, *183; studeri,* 112; *trumani,* 112
African elephant, 163, *163,* 197
African hyena, 112–113
Agassiz, Jean Louis Rodolphe, 22–25, 186
Alaskan brown bear, 6, 97, *100*
Alces: alces, 139–41, 197; appearance of, 42; *latifrons,* 140
algae, blue-green, 74
alpaca, 160
Alroy, John, 197
amber, 170
American antelope, 141
American beaver, 120, *121*
American black bear, 6
American buffalo, 82, 153–55
American cheetah, 112, *183*
American elk, 141
American hunting hyena, 113, *113*
American lion: appearance of, 44, 45; description of, 109–110, *110;* extinction of, *183;* and mummies, 151; and size, *66*
American mastodon, *68;* at Big Bone Lick (KY), 82; in Blancan Land Mammal Age, 43; in central Alaska, 44; comparison of, with Columbian mammoth, *167;* description of, 166–68; extinction of, *183;* in northeastern U.S., 45; skeleton of, *168;* skull of, *164*

Amynodontidae, 134
ancient bison, *154*
Anderson, Phil, 81
animal communities, 40–45
animals, big, 66–68
anteater, giant, 19
Antilocapra americana, 141, 141–43
Antilocapridae, 141–43
Antilopinae, 144–45
Aplodontia rufa, 117–18, *118*
appearances, determining, 125–29
Arctodus, 97–102, *183; pristinus,* 97, 98, 100–102; *simus,* 97, 98, *100,* 100–102, *101*
Aristotle, 6
armadillo(s): appearance of, 44; description of, 70–73; giant, 45; in magnorder Xenarthra, 69–70; migration of, 19; nine-banded, *69,* 72–73
art: Neolithic, 127; Paleolithic, 125–28
Artiodactyla, 137–62
Asian yak, 155
Asian elephant, 163
asphalt seeps, 170
atmosphere, composition of, 57
axis, Earth's, 52–54

Bacon, Francis, 11
Baird's tapir, 133
Baluchitherium, 66
bear(s), 20; Alaskan brown, 6, 97, *100;* American black, 6; black, 97, *100;* descriptions of, 97–102; European cave, 98; Florida cave, 43, 45, 97, 98, *99;* giant short-faced, 44, 45, 81, 97, 98, *100,* 100–102, *101;* grizzly, 6, 44, 97, *100, 101;* lesser short-faced, 97, 98, 100–102; living, 97; polar, 6, 97; short-faced, 98–102, *183;* South American spectacled, 98
beaver, giant, 120, *121, 183*
Beeb, William, 73
Beringia, 15, 16, *16*
Bernhardi, Johann, 24
Big Bone Lick (KY), 4, 81–82
bighorn sheep, 146–47, *147*
bison, 17, 27, *41,* 42, 44, 45; ancient, *154;* at Big Bone Lick (KY), 82; description of, *152,* 153–55; giant, 153, *153;* Ice Age, 149–53; at Rancho La Brea, 78; steppe, *41* 128, 149, *149,* 151, *152;* survival of, 197; woods, 154
Bison, 27; *antiquus,* 82, 153–54, *154;* appearance of, 42; *athabascae,* 154; *bison, 152,* 153–55, 197; *latifrons, 67, 152,* 153, *153; priscus, 41,* 128, 149, *149,* 151

219

black bear, 97, *100*
Blancan Land Mammal Age, 19, 25, 43
Blanco llama, 160
Blitzkrieg hypothesis, 191–92, *193*
blue-green algae, 74
Blumenbach, Johann Friedrich, 177
bobcat, 111, 112
Bootherium: bombifrons, 82;
    extinction of, *183*
Borophagus, 42
Bos grunniens, 155; *taurus*, 155
Bovidae, 17, 144–55
bovids, 144–55
Bovinae, 149–55
brachiosaurus dinosaur, 66
Bradypodidae, 73–75
Bradypus torquatus, 74; *tridactylus*,
    74; *variegatus*, 74
Brazilian tapir, 133
Breagyps clarki, 28
broad-fronted moose, 140
Brontotherium, 122
buffalo, American, 82, 153–55.
    See also bison
burial, instant, 170

Caenopus, 134
California condor, *28*
California saber-toothed cat, *28*
California sea lion, 115
California tapir, 134, *135*
Camelidae, 20, 156–60
camelids, 156–57
Camelops: description of, 158–59;
    extinction of, *183*; *hesternus*,
    67, 158; *huerfanensis*, 159;
    kansanus, 159
camel(s): appearance of, 45;
    description of, 157–58;
    dromedary one-humped, 157;
    extinction of, *183*; giant, *68*;
    giant Nebraska, 45; Huerfano,
    159; Kansas, 159; migration of,
    20; modern, *156*; Nebraska, 157;
    at Rancho La Brea, 76; spatulate-
    toothed, 157–58; Yesterday's,
    158, 158–59
Camelus dromedarius, 157
Canada lynx, 112
Canidae, 20, 94–97
Caninae, 94–97

Canis: dirus, 28, 42, 44, 45, 76, *94*,
    94–95, *95*; *familiaris*, 97; *latrans*,
    96, 96–97; *lepophagus*, 96; *lupus*,
    41, 94–95
Caprinae, 145–49
Capromeryx: extinction of, *183*;
    furcifer, 143; *mexicana*, 143;
    minor, 143
capybara(s), 19, 118–20; Pinckney's,
    119, *119*
carbon-14 age dating, 86–87
caribou, 40, *42*, 82, 139
Carnivora, 92–116
carnivores, 92–116, *93. See also*
    individual animals
Castor canadensis, 120, *121*
Castoridae, 120
Castoroides: extinction of, *183*;
    ohioensis, 120, *121*
cat(s): appearance of, 45; California
    saber-toothed, *28*; descriptions
    of, 102–13; dirk-toothed, 105;
    migration of, 20; saber-toothed,
    42, 44, 45, 78, *78*, *104*, 105, *106*,
    106–8, *107*, *183*; scimitar, *2*, 44,
    108–9; true, 109–12
cattle, domestic, 155
cave lion, 109
Ceratotherium simum, 135
Cervalces: 151; extinction of, *183*;
    scotti, 82, 140, *140*
Cervidae, 17–18, 20, 137–41
Cervinae, 141
Cervus elaphus, 141, *197*
Chasmaporthetes, 42; *ossifragus*,
    113, *113*
cheetah(s), 112; American, 112, *183*;
    New World, 112; Studer's, 112
Choloepidae, 73–75
Choloepus didactylus, 74;
    hoffmanni, 74
cirque, *50*
cladistics, 7
Clark, William, 81
classification, scientific, 6–7
CLIMAP, 45–46, 59
climate, 27–31, 45–48
Clovis culture, 188–89
Coelodonta antiquitatis,
    135–36, *136*
collared peccary, 162

Columbian mammoth: appearance
    of, 44, 45; comparisons with,
    163, *167*; description of, 172–74,
    173, *174*; at Hot Springs (SD), 81;
    at Rancho La Brea, 76; ranges
    of, *172*
complexity, structural, 67–68
complex-toothed horse, 82, 132
condor, California, *28*
Conklin's pronghorn, 143
continental drift, 13, 55–57. *See also*
    continents, movement of
continents: configuration of, 55–57;
    movement of, 9–20 (*See also*
    continental drift)
Cope, Edward Drinker, 66, 108
Cope's Rule, 66
Cope's tapir, 82, 134
cougar. *See* puma(s)
coyote(s), 76, 81, *96*, 96–97;
    Johnston's, 96
creodonts, 92, *93*
Crespi, Father Juan, 76
Cricetidae, 19
Croll, James, 51
crustal depression, 37–39
crustal rebound, 37–39
cryopreservation, 171
cud-chewers, 137–55
Cuvier, Georges, 73, 108, 184
Cyanoderma, 74
Cynognathus, 13; *crateronotus*, *12*

Dall sheep, 146, *146*
Darwin, Charles, 25, 186, 187
Dasypodidae, 19, 70–73
Dasypus, 19; *novemcinctus*, 69, 72–73
dawn horse, 122
Death Valley, 29
deer: descriptions of, 137–41; family,
    17–18, 20, 43, 82; mule, 139;
    white-tailed, 139
dehydration, 171
Deinotherium, *164*
deoxyriboneucleic acid (DNA), 90
depression, crustal, 37–39
Dicerorhinus sumatrensis, 135
Didelphidae, 19
Didelphis, 19
Dillehay, Tom, 194
diminuitive pronghorn, 143
Dinohippus, 131

Dipodomys, 42

Dipoides, 120

dire wolf, *28*; appearance of, 42, 44, 45; description of, *94*, 94–95, *95*; at Rancho La Brea (CA), 76

dirk-toothed cat, 105–6

diversity, genetic, *18*

DNA, 90

Doedicurus, *66*, *72*

dog(s), 20, 42, 97

domestic cattle, 155

domestic dog, 97

Donn, William L., 58

dromedary one-humped camel, 157

dung, 90

Dusignathinae, 114

dust, interplanetary, 55

dwarf mammoth, 5, *174*

dwarf woolly mammoth, 178–80

Earth, axis of, 52–54

Edentates, *71*. See also anteater, giant; armadillo(s); sloth(s)

electron spin resonance (ESR) method, 87

Elephantidae, 168–80

elephants and relatives, 163–80. See also individual animals

Elephas, 168; *maximus*, 163, *163*; *primigenius*, 177

elk, 44, 82, 141, 197

Eohippus, 122

epochs, 8

Equidae, 19, 20, 122–33, *130*

Equus: bones of, *131*; *caballus*, 133; *complicatus*, 82, 132; *conversidens*, 132; description of, 131–33; extinction of, *183*; *giganteus*, 132; *laurentius*, 132; *occidentalis*, *124*, 132, *132*; *przewalskii*, 133; *scotti*, 133; *tau*, 132

eras, geologic, 8

Eremotherium, 68; ground sloth, 45; *rusconii*, 19, 83–85, *84*

Erethizon, 19

Erethizontidae, 19, 118

erosion, glacial, 36–37

erratics, *23*, 25

ESR. See electron spin resonance (ESR) method

Euceratherium: appearance of, 42; *collinum*, 147–48; extinction of, *183*

Eumeryx, 139

Eumetopias jubata, 115

European cave bear, 98

Ewing, Maurice, 58

Ewing-Donn theory, 58–59

extinction: and habitat loss, 187–98; human-caused, 186–87, 187–98; introduction to, 181–84; of mammoths, *190*; of mastodons, *190*; as new idea, 184–87; by size and age, *185*; youngest dates of, *183*

Falconer, Hugh, 172

family tree(s): of Artiodactyla, *138*; of carnivores, *93*; of Edentates, *71*; of elephants and their relatives, *165*; of Equidae, *130*; of even-toed ungulates, *138*; of horses and relatives, *130*; of odd-toed ungulates, *123*; of Perissodactyls, *123*; of proboscideans, *165*

FAUNMAP, 44

Felidae, 6, 20, 102–13

Felinae, 102, 109–12

Felis, *103*; *concolor*, 110, 111, *112*; *pardalis*, 110, 111; *wiedii*, 110; *yagouaroundi*, 110, 111

fern, seed, *12*

Fisher, Daniel, 196

flat-headed peccary, 76, *161*, 161–62

Fleming, Rev. John, 186

Flint, Richard F., 2–3, 38

Florida cave bear, 43, 45, 97, 98, *99*

Folsom culture, 188–89

Forbes, Edward, 21

fossils: at Big Bone Lick (KY), 81–82; at Hot Springs (SD), *80*, 81; at Rancho La Brea (CA), 76–79

fox(es), 20, 94

Franklin, Benjamin, 4, 81

freezing, 171

fur seal(s), 114–15

gazelle-horse, 42

Geikie, Archibald, 25

genetic diversity, *18*

geologic time scale, 8, *26*

Geomyidae, 20

Geomys, 43

giant anteater, 19

giant armadillo, 45

giant beaver, 120, *121*, *183*

giant bison, 44, 153, *153*

giant camel, 68

giant ground sloth, 5, 76, 90

giant horse, 44, 132

giant Nebraska camel, 45

giant short-faced bear: appearance of, 45; description of, 97, 98, *100*, 100–102, *101*; at Hot Springs (SD), 81

Gigantocamelus fricki, 157–58

Glacial Lake Missoula, 32–33, *33*

glacial time, 25–27

glaciation, 21–25, *24*, 186

glacier(s), 1–2, 21–22, *50*; deposits of, 34–37; erratics from, *23*, 25; landforms from, 34–37; Malaspina, *3*; maximum coverage of, *47*, 182; moraines from, *24*, *34*, 34–36, *35*; Mount Hayes, *36*; in Pleistocene Epoch, 27–29; rock polished by, *24*

Glossopteris, *12*, 13

Glossotherium: extinction of, *183*; *harlani*, *67*; migration of, 19

Glyptodontidae, 19, 73

Glyptodonts, 19, 43, 45, *72*, 73

Glyptotherium: appearance of, 43; *arizonae*, *72*, 73; migration of, 19

goat(s), 145–46

Goldsmith, Oliver, 73

Gomphotheriidae, 20

Gondwana, Gondwanaland, 9, 10, *10*, 11–13, *12*, *14*

gopher(s): appearance of, 43; pocket, 20

Gould, Stephen Jay, 68

Gray, J. E., 163

Grayson, Donald, 187

gray wolf, *41*, 44, 94–95

grazing ground sloths, 88–92

Great American Animal Interchange, 17–20, *20*

grizzly bear, 6, 44, 97, *100*, *101*

ground sloth(s): appearance of, 45; in Blancan Land Mammal Age, 43; browsing, 83–88; *Eremotherium*, 45; flat-footed, 75–83; giant, 5, 76, 90; grazing, 88–92; Harlan's, 44, 45, *67*, 82, 88, 88–92, *89*; Jefferson's, 44, 45, 82–83, *83*; Megalonychid, *183*,

184; Mylodont, *183*; narrow-mouthed, *4, 75*; Rusconi's, 83–85, *84*; Shasta, 44, 45, *68*, 85, 85–88, 90, *91, 183*; and size, 19; Wheatley's, 75
guanaco, 160

Hancock, G. Allen, 76
hare, 42
Harlan, Robert, 185
Harlan's ground sloth: appearance of, 44, 45; description of, 82, *88*, 88–92, *89*; and size, *67*
Harlan's musk ox, 82
Harrington's mountain goat, 145–46, *146*
Hayoceros falkenbachi, 143
Hay's pronghorn, 143
Heinrich, Hartmut, 59
Heinrich events, 59–61
Hemiauchenia: blancoensis, 160; extinction of, *183*; *macrocephala*, 160
Heteromyidae, 20
Hippidion, 19
Hoffmann's sloth, 74
Holmesina septentrionalis, 69, 70
Holmes's capybara, 120
Homo sapiens, 7, 42, 125–28, 186–98
Homotherium, 103; crenatidens, 108; *serum, 2*, 108–9; *ultimum*, 108
horse(s): appearance of, 44, 45; comparison of bones of, *131*; complex-toothed, 82, 132; early, 122–31; extinction of, *183*; family tree of, *130*; giant, 132; Mexican, 132; migration of, 19, 20; modern, 133; in Neolithic art, *128*; Przewalskii's, 133; at Rancho La Brea, 76; Scott's, 133; true, 131–33; western, *124*, 132, *132*
Hot Springs (SD), *80*, 81
Huerfano camel, 159
humans: activities of, 61–63; appearance of, 42; first New World, 194–95; and Ice Age mammals, 1–2, 187–98; Paleolithic art of, 125–28
Hutton, James, 25
Hyaenidae, 112–13
hyaenodonts, *93*

Hydrochoeridae, 19, 118–20
hyena(s), 42, 112–13
Hypologus, 42
Hyracodontidae, 134
Hyracotherium, 122, *131*

ice ages: discovery of, 22–25; external causes of, 49–55; and the future, 63; terrestrial causes of, 55–63
icebergs, 59
ice-free Arctic Ocean theory. *See* Ewing-Donn theory
Illiger, C. D., 163
Imperial mammoth, *28. See also* Columbian mammoth
Indian elephant, *163*
interplanetary dust, 55
Irvingtonian Land Mammal Age, 25–27, 42

jaguar(s), 42, 44, 110–11, *111*
jaguarundi, 110, *111*
Jamieson, T.F., 25
javelina, 162
Jefferson, Thomas, 4–5, 81, 82, 184
Jefferson's ground sloth, 44, 82–83, *83*
Jefferson's mammoth, 44, 45, 173, 174–76
Johnson, R. G., 61
Johnston's coyote, 96

kangaroo rats, 20, 42
Kansas camel, 159
Keystone Herbivores Hypothesis, 196
Kraglievichia, 19

La Brea tar pits. *See* Rancho La Brea (CA)
Lacépède, Bernard de, 4
Lake Agassiz, *60*, 61
Lake Bonneville, 29, 30
Lake George, 32
Lake Lahontan, 30–31
lakes, 29–33
Lama: glama, 160; *guanicoe*, 160; *pacos*, 160
land bridges, 14–20
landforms, 34–37
landmasses, high-elevation, 61
large-headed llama, 160

Laurasia, *9*, 10, *10*, 14, *14*
Leporidae, 20
Lepus, 42
lesser short-faced bear, 97, 98, 100–102
Lewis, Meriweather, 4
Linnaeus, 6
Linné, Carl von, 6
lion(s): African lion, 109–10; American, 44, 45, *66*, 110, *110*, 151, *183*; appearance of, 45; cave, 109; European, *111*; Ice Age, 109–10; mountain (*See* puma(s)); primitive, 109
llama(s), 20, 45, 159–60, *183*
loess, 31
Lommel, Andreas, 197
longevity, *67*
long-nosed peccary, *161*, 162
Longueuil, Charles LeMoyne de, 81
Loxodonta, 168; *africana*, 163
Lyell, Charles, 21, 186–87
lynx, *111*; Canada, 112
Lynx: lynx, 112; *rufus*, 112
Lystrosaurus, 12, 13
Machairodontinae, 102, 104–9
Machairodus, 103
Malaspina Glacier, *3*
mammoth(s): Columbian, 44, 45, 76, 81, *163, 167, 172*, 172–74, *173, 174*; die-off ages of, *190*; diets of, 175; and DNA, 90; dwarf, 5, *174*; dwarf woolly, 178–80; extinction of, *183*; at Hot Springs (SD), *80*; imperial, *28*; Jefferson's, 44, 45, 173, 174–76; life spans of, 175; mummified remains of, *150*, 150–51; petroglyph of, *129*; pygmy woolly, *178*, 178–80; remains of, map of, *169*; southern, 25, *164*, 168–72, 172; steppe, 176; teeth of, 175; woolly, *41*, 44, *68*, 90, *164, 172, 176*, 176–78, *178*
Mammut, 43; *americanum, 68*, 82, *164*, 166–68, *167, 168*; extinction of, *183*
Mammuthus, 168, *183; africanavus*, 172; *columbi*, 42, 81, *163, 167*, 172–74; *exilis, 178*, 178–80; *imperator, 28*, 172; *jeffersonii*, 173, 174–76; *meridionalis*, 25,

164, 172; primigenius, 41, 68, 164, 176, 176–78, 178; subplanifrons, 168–72; trogontherii, 176
Mammutidae, 166–68
maned sloth, 74
margay, 110, 111
Martin, Paul, 191–92, 196, 197
mastodon(s), 5, 20, 45, 163–64, 166–68; American, 43, 44, 45, 68, 82, *164,* 166–68, *167, 168, 183;* die-off ages of, *190;* remains of, map of, *169*
Matthew's pronghorn, 143
Megalonychidae, 19, 75–83. *See also* Choloepidae
Megalonychid ground sloth, *183*
Megalonyx: extinction of, *183;* ground sloth, 184; *jeffersonii,* 82–83, *83; leptostomus, 4,* 75; *wheatleyi,* 75
Megantereon, 103; hesperus, 105–6
Megatheriidae, 83–88. *See also* Bradypodidae
Megatherium, 5, 84–85
Meizonyx, 19
Merriam's tapir, 45, 134
Merriam's teratorn, 78, *79*
Merychippus, 131
Mesosaurus, 13; brazilianensis, 12
metabolic rate, 66
Mexican horse, 132
Mexican pronghorn, 143
miacids, 92, *93*
mice, 19
migration, 15–20
Milankovitch, Milutin, 51
Milankovitch Cycles, 50–54
Miller, Gifford, 192
mineral replacement, 170
Miracinonyx, 112
Mirounga angustirostris, 115, *116*
modern camel, 156
modern horse, 133
Moeritherium, 164
Monachinae, 115–16
moose, 42, 139–41, 197; stag, 151, *183*
Mooser's pronghorn, 143
moraines, 24, *34,* 34–36, *35*
Mosimann, James, 191–92, 196
mountain goat, 42, 145; Harrington's, 144–45, *145*

mountain sheep, 146–47, *147*
mountain tapir, 133
mule deer, 139
mummies, 150–52, *150, 152*
mummification, 171
musk ox(en): appearance of, 42, 44, 45; description of, 147–49, *148;* extinction of, *183;* Harlan's, 82; and size, *66;* woodland, 147, 148–49, *183*
muskrat, 42
Mustelidae, 19
Mylodont ground sloth, *183*
Mylodontidae, 19, 88–92
Mylohyus: extinction of, *183; nasutus, 161, 162*
Myrmecophaga, 19

Nannippus, 42
narrow-mouthed ground sloth, *4,* 75
Nebraska camel, 157
Neochoerus, 19; pinckneyi, 119, *119*
Neofelis, 103
Neolithic art, 127–128, *128*
Nimravides, 103
nine-banded armadillo, *69,* 72–73
Niskanen, Erkki, 39
northern elephant seal, 115, *116,* 185
northern pampathere, *69,* 70
Nothrotheriops, 19; extinction of, *183; shastensis, 68, 85,* 85–88, *91*
ocelot, 110, 111
Odobeninae, 114
Odobenus rosmarus, 114
Odocoileinae, 139–41
Odocoileus, 43; hemionus, 139; *virginianus,* 139
offspring, vulnerability of, 67
onager, pygmy, 132
Ondatra, 42
opossum, 19
orbit, Earth's, 51
Oreamnos, 42; americanus, 145; *harringtoni,* 145–46, *146*
The Origin of Species (Darwin), 187
Ortelius, Abraham, 11
Osborn, Henry Fairfield, 163
Otariidae, 114–15
Ovibus moschatus, 147–49, *148*
Oviedo y Valdes, Gonzalo Fernandez de, 73
Ovis, 42; canadensis, 146–47, *147;*

dalli, 146, *146*
Owen, Robert, 187
Owen-Smith, Norman, 196
ox(en): musk, 42, 44, 45, *66,* 82, 147–49, *183;* shrub, 42, 44, 45, 147–48, *183;* woodland musk, 44, 147, 148–49, *148, 183*
oxyaenids, *93*

Palaeolama, 160; *mirifica,* 160
Palaeotheres, 121
Paleolithic art, 125–28
pale-throated sloth, 74
pampathere, northern, *69,* 70
Pampatherium, 19
Panamanian land bridge, 17–20
Pangaea, *9, 10, 10*–14, *12*
panther, American, 128
Panthera, 6, 42, *103;* collared, 162; extinction of, *183; gombaszoegensis, 109; leo, 151; leo atrox, 109, 110, 110, 128; leo fossilis, 109; leo spelaea, 109; onca,* 110–11; *youngi, 109*
Paramyidae, 117
Paramylodon, 43; harlani, 28, 82, 88, *88*–92, *89*
Paramys, 117
peccaries, 19, 160–62; extinction of, *183;* flat-headed, 44, 76; long-nosed, 44
periods, geologic, 8
Perissodactyla, 121–36
Perthes, Jacques Boucher de, 186
Phocidae, 115–16
phyletic size increase, 66
piglike animals, 160–62
Pinckney's capybara, 119, *119*
Pinnipedia, 113–16
plate tectonics, 13. *See also* continents, movement of
Platygonus: compressus, 161, 161–62; extinction of, *183*
Pleistocene epoch: about the, 1–5; animal communities of, 40–45; big animals of, 66–68 (*See also* individual animals); carnivores of, 92–116; climate in, 27–29, 45–48; crustal depression and rebound during, 37–39; elephants and relatives of, 163–80; even-toed ungulates of, 137–62;

extinction during, 181–98; in geologic time scale, 8; glaciers during, 25–27, 29–33, 34–37, *47*; global climate patterns during, 45–48; ice ages during, 21–25, 49–63; naming of, 21; odd-toed ungulates of, 121–36; rodents of, 117–20; sloths and armadillos of, 69–92; time scale of, *26*
Pliauchenia, 160
Pliny the Elder, 6
Pliometanastes, 19
Plionarctos, 98
Pliophenacomys, 43
pocket gophers, 20
Poebrotherium, 156
polar bear, 6, 97
porcupine(s), 19, 118
Portol, Gaspar de, 76
Pratifelis, 103
preservation, 170–71
Principles of Geology (Lyell), 21
Proailurus, 103; *lemanensis*, 102
Proboscidea, 163–80
Procastoroides, 120
Procyonidae, 19
pronghorn: appearance of, 43, 44; diminutive, 143; extinction of, *183*; Ice Age, 143; modern, *141*, 141–43; Quentin's, *142*, 143, *143*
Przewalskii's horse, 133
Pseudaelurus, 102, *103*
puma(s), 110, 111, 112
pygmy onager, 132
pygmy woolly mammoth, *178*, 178–80

Quentin's pronghorn, *142*, 143, *143*

rabbits, 20, 42
raccoons, 19
radiocarbon age dating, 86–87
Rancho La Brea (CA), 76–79, *77*
Rancholabrean Land Mammal Age, 19, 27, 42
Rangifer, 42; *tarandus*, 139
rat(s), 19
rat(s), kangaroo, 20
rebound, crustal, 37–39
rhinoceros(es), 134–36; woolly, 135–36, *136*
Rhinocerotidae, 134–36

rivers, glacial effects on, 37
Rodentia, 117–20
rodents, 117–20. *See also* individual animals
Ruminantia, 137–55
Rusconi's ground sloth, 83–85, *84*
saber-toothed cat(s), *104, 105, 106, 107*; descriptions of, 104–9; extinction of, *183*; at Rancho La Brea, 78
safety, 67
saiga(s), *144*, 144–45
Saiga tatarica, *144*, 144–45
Saussure, Horace Bénédict de, 25
Scaling: Why Is Animal Size So Important? (Schmidt-Nielsen), 68
Schmidt-Nielsen, Knut, 68
scientific names, 6–7
scimitar cat(s), *2*, 44, 108–9
Sciuridae, 20
Scott's horse, 133
sea lion(s), 114–15
seal(s), 115–16
seed fern, *12*
sewellel, 117–18
Shasta ground sloth, *68*; appearance of, 44, 45; description of, *85*, 85–88; and DNA, *91*; extinction of, *183*
sheep, 42, 146–47
short-faced bear, *183*
shrews, 20
shrub ox(en), 42, 44, 45, 147–48, *183*
Shuler's pronghorn, 143
size, of Pleistocene animals, 66–68
skunk(s), 19
sloth(s), *28*; brown-throated three-toed, 74; ground (*See* ground sloth(s)); Hoffmann's, 74; living, 73–75; in magnorder Xenarthra, 69–70; maned, 74; pale-throated, 74; and size, 66; southern, 74; three-toed, 73–75; two-toed, 73–75
sloths and armadillos, 69–92. *See also* individual animals
Smilodon, 42, *103, 183*; *californicus, 28; fatalis, 78, 104, 105, 106*, 106–8, *107*
Snider-Pellegrini, Antonio, 11
Soergelia mayfieldi, 147, 148
Soergel's ox, 147, 148

solar radiation, 49–50
Soricidae, 20
South American spectacled bear, 98
southern mammoth, 25, *164*, 168–72, *172*
southern sloth, 74
spatulate-toothed camel, 157–58
squirrels, 20
stag moose, 82, 140, *140*, 151, *183*
Stanford, Dennis, 188–89
Stanley, Steven, 67, 68
Steller's sea lion, 115
steppe bison, 128, 149, *149*, 151, *152*
steppe mammoth, 176
Stockoceros: conklingi, 143; extinction of, *183*; *onusrosagris*, *142*, 143, *143*
stout-legged llama, 160
strandlines, 29–30, *31*
Studer's cheetah, 112
Suess, Eduard, 11
Suina, 160–62
Sumatran rhinoceros, 135
Symbos, 42; *cavifrons*, 147, 148–49; extinction of, *183*

Tapiridae, 20, 133–34
tapir(s), 20; appearance of, 44; California, 134, *135*; Cope's, 82; description of, 133–34; extinction of, *183*; Merriam's, 45; at Rancho La Brea, 76; Vero, 134
Tapirus: bairdi, 133; *californicus*, 134, *135; copei*, 82, 134; extinction of, *183; haysii*, 82; *merriami*, 134; *pinchaque*, 133; *terrestris*, 133; *veroensis*, 134
Tayassuidae, 19, 160–62
Tayassu tajacu, 162
Teleoceras, 135
temperature, world, *62*
Teratornis merriami, *28*, 78, *79*
Tetrameryx, 43, 143; *mooseri*, 143; *shuleri*, 143
Thesaurus Geographicus (Ortelius), 11
Thinobadistes, 19
tiger, *104*
time scale, geologic, 8
Titanis, 17, 18, 19, *67*
Titanotheres, 121–22
Titanotylopus, 156, *157*; *nebraskensis, 68*, 157; *spatulus*, 157–58

Toxodontidae, 19
Tremarctinae, 97–102
Tremarctos, 43, 97–102; *floridanus*, 97, 98, *99*; *ornatus*, 98
Trichophilus, 74
Turner, George, 186
Tylopoda, 156–60

ungulates, even-toed, 137–62, *138*. *See also* individual animals
ungulates, odd-toed, 121–36, *123*. *See also* individual animals
uniformitarianism, 186
Ursavus elemensis, 97
Ursidae, 20, 97–102
Ursus, 97; *abstrusus*, 97; *americanus*, 6, 97, *100*; *arctos*, 6, 97, *100*; *etruscus*, 97; *maritimus*, 6, 97; *spelaeus*, 98

Vero tapir, 134
Vicugna vicugna, 160
vicuña, 160
volcanoes, 58
voles, 43

walrus(es), 114
wapiti, 141. *See also* elk
Warren, John, 167
Webb, S. David, 17
Wegener, Alfred, 11, 13
western horse, *124*, 132, *132*
whale, blue, 66
Wheatley's ground sloth, 75
white rhinoceros, 135
white-tailed deer, 139
wolf(ves), 20, 44, 45; descriptions of, 94–95; dire, *28*, 42, 44, 45, 76, *94*, 94–95, *95*; gray, *41*, 44, 94–95; at Hot Springs (SD), 81

woodland musk ox(en), 44, 147, 148–49, *183*
woods bison, 154
woolly mammoth, *41*, *68*, *164*; appearance of, 44; description of, *172*, *176*, 176–78, *178*; and DNA, 90
woolly rhinoceros, 135–36, *136*

Xenarthra, 69–92. *See also* armadillo(s); sloth(s)

yak, 44, *66*, 155
Yesterday's camel, 67 *158*, 158–59
Younger Dryas, 59

Zalophus californianus, 115

About the Author

A series of articles in *Life* magazine when **Ian M. Lange** was a kid sparked his fascination with Ice Age Animals. He saw paintings of gargantuan beasts and a photo of a baby woolly mammoth frozen in the Arctic tundra, sending him on a life-long quest to know and understand more about the Pleistocene world and its inhabitants. He is a professor of economic geology at the University of Montana in Missoula.

About the Illustrator

Dorothy S. Norton is an artist and scientific illustrator specializing in astronomy, geology, and paleontology. She illustrated *Rocks from Space* (Mountain Press, 1998), and her colorful paintings of extinct animals grace the walls of Japan's National Geological Museums. From her home in Bend, Oregon, she produces instructional science slides for use in college and university classrooms.

We encourage you to patronize your local bookstore. Most stores will be happy to order any title that they do not stock. You may also order directly from Mountain Press by mail, using the order form provided below, or by calling our toll-free number and using your credit card. We will gladly send you a catalog upon request.

Some geology titles of interest:

_____Agents of Chaos	14.00
_____Dinosaurs under the Big Sky	20.00
_____Fire Mountains of the West	18.00
_____Geology Underfoot in Central Nevada	16.00
_____Geology Underfoot in Death Valley and Owens Valley	16.00
_____Geology Underfoot in Illinois	15.00
_____Geology Underfoot in Southern California	14.00
_____Glacial Lake Missoula and Its Humongous Floods	15.00
_____Ice Age Mammals of North America	20.00
_____Northwest Exposures	24.00
_____Roadside Geology of ALASKA	18.00
_____Roadside Geology of ARIZONA	18.00
_____Roadside Geology of COLORADO, 2nd Edition	20.00
_____Roadside Geology of HAWAII	20.00
_____Roadside Geology of IDAHO	18.00
_____Roadside Geology of INDIANA	18.00
_____Roadside Geology of LOUISIANA	15.00
_____Roadside Geology of MAINE	18.00
_____Roadside Geology of MASSACHUSETTS	18.00
_____Roadside Geology of MONTANA	20.00
_____Roadside Geology of NEBRASKA	16.00
_____Roadside Geology of NEW MEXICO	16.00
_____Roadside Geology of NEW YORK	20.00
_____Roadside Geology of NORTHERN & CENTRAL CALIFORNIA	20.00
_____Roadside Geology of OREGON	16.00
_____Roadside Geology of PENNSYLVANIA	20.00
_____Roadside Geology of SOUTH DAKOTA	20.00
_____Roadside Geology of TEXAS	20.00
_____Roadside Geology of UTAH	16.00
_____Roadside Geology of VERMONT & NEW HAMPSHIRE	14.00
_____Roadside Geology of VIRGNIA	16.00
_____Roadside Geology of WASHINGTON	18.00
_____Roadside Geology of WYOMING	18.00
_____Roadside Geology of THE YELLOWSTONE COUNTRY	12.00

Please include $3.00 per order to cover postage and handling.

Please send the books marked above. I have enclosed $ _____

Name _____

Address _____

City/State/Zip _____

☐ Payment enclosed (check or money order in U.S. funds) **OR** Bill my:

☐ VISA ☐ MC ☐ AE ☐ Discover   Daytime Phone _____

Card No. & Expiration Date _____

Signature _____

MOUNTAIN PRESS PUBLISHING COMPANY
P.O. Box 2399 • Missoula, MT 59806 • Order Toll-Free 1-800-234-5308
E-mail: info@mtnpress.com • Website: www.mountain-press.com